Adlerian Psychotherapy

Adlerian Psychotherapy: An Advanced Approach to Individual Psychology gives an account of Adlerian therapy from its origins to the present day, and proposes an advanced version of the theory.

The main principles and concepts of Adler's thinking are re-examined from a contemporary perspective, placing them in the context of other approaches. The book contains:

- A comprehensive presentation of classical and contemporary Adlerian psychology and psychotherapy
- A presentation of the integrative potential of Adlerian therapy with respect to other approaches
- Proposals for future possibilities of Adlerian psychology in a postmodern world
- A range of clinical examples and case material.

Adlerian Psychotherapy will be of great interest to students, clinical practitioners and academics working with the Adlerian approach, and for psychologists and psychotherapists of other theoretical orientations.

Ursula E. Oberst is Assistant Professor for Psychological Counselling and Psychology of Personality at the Ramon Llull University in Barcelona. She also works as a psychotherapist in private practice.

Alan E. Stewart works as an Assistant Professor in the Community Counselling and Counselling Psychology programmes in the Department of Counselling and Human Development at the University of Georgia.

Advancing Theory in Therapy
Series Editor: Keith Tudor

Most books covering individual therapeutic approaches are aimed at the trainee/student market. This series, however, is concerned with *advanced* and *advancing* theory, offering the reader comparative and comparable coverage of a number of therapeutic approaches.

Aimed at professionals and postgraduates, *Advancing Theory in Therapy* will cover an impressive range of theories. With full reference to case studies throughout, each title will

- present cutting-edge research findings
- locate each theory and its application within its cultural context
- develop a critical view of theory and practice

Titles in the series

Body Psychotherapy
Edited by Tree Staunton

Transactional Analysis: A Relational Perspective
Helena Hargaden and Charlotte Sills

Adlerian Psychotherapy: An Advanced Approach to Individual Psychology
Ursula E. Oberst and Alan E. Stewart

Rational Emotive Behaviour Therapy: Theoretical Developments
Edited by Windy Dryden

Adlerian Psychotherapy

An Advanced Approach to Individual Psychology

Ursula E. Oberst and
Alan E. Stewart

Holy Family University
Newtown Campus - LRC

Brunner-Routledge
Taylor & Francis Group

HOVE AND NEW YORK

First published 2003 by Brunner-Routledge
27 Church Road, Hove, East Sussex BN3 2FA

Simultaneously published in the USA and Canada
by Brunner-Routledge
29 West 35th Street, New York, NY 10001

Brunner-Routledge is an imprint of the Taylor & Francis Group

© 2003 Ursula E. Oberst and Alan E. Stewart

Typeset in Times by RefineCatch Limited, Bungay, Suffolk
Printed and bound in Great Britain by
MPG Books, Bodmin, Cornwall
Cover design by Sandra Heath

British Library Cataloguing in Publication Data
A catalogue record for this book is available from the British Library

Library of Congress Cataloging in Publication Data
Oberst, Ursula E., 1957–
    Adlerian psychotherapy : an advanced approach to individual
psychology / Ursula E. Oberst and Alan E. Stewart.
        p. cm. – (Advancing theory in therapy)
    Includes bibliographical references and index.
        ISBN 1-58391-121-9 (hbk) – ISBN 1-58391-122-7 (pbk)
        1. Adlerian psychology. 2. Psychotherapy. I. Stewart, Alan E.,
1961– II. Title. III. Series.
        BF175.5.A33 O24 2002
        150.19′53 – dc21   2002071243

ISBN 1-58391-121-9 (hbk)
ISBN 1-58391-122-7 (pbk)

Contents

Preface

The psychology of Alfred Adler is traditionally considered to be one of the three so-called in-depth or psychoanalytic therapies, the other two being the theories of Sigmund Freud and Carl Gustav Jung. This is partly due to Adler's initial association with Sigmund Freud's Psychoanalysis and to the use of several historical expressions by contemporary Adlerian authors, such as 'analysis' or 'organ inferiority' when referring to aspects of Adlerian therapy. But quite on the contrary, Adlerian Psychology (Individual Psychology), in our view, has many more similarities with more recent therapeutic approaches, such as humanistic and cognitive therapies. There are also some striking resemblances to current constructivist theories.

On the other hand, Adlerian Psychology, though it has always had its place among other psychological and psychotherapeutic approaches, specially in Anglo-Saxon and German-speaking countries, has lived in the shadows in others, for example the Spanish-speaking countries. We can only speculate about the reasons for this phenomenon. It is certainly true that the rise of Nazism in the early 1930s did great harm to the Adlerian movement, but also to others. Furthermore, many of the formerly revolutionary Adlerian concepts have rapidly merged with other psychological theories, possibly due to the fact that Adler was a prescient observer of behaviour and relied on common sense language when explaining his ideas. Though he coined some expressions that are typical for Individual Psychology (such as Life Style, inferiority complex, etc.), they were drawn from plain German language and so, as Adlerian Psychology had no 'copyright' for them, they could easily be transferred into other theories. The founder of Psychoanalysis, Sigmund Freud, used to coin more specific expressions drawn from Greek and Latin ('libido', 'the ego'), which are still identified with Psychoanalysis and only with Psychoanalysis. Adler used to talk in common sense terms because it was important to him that his ideas were not restricted to their use in academic psychology but that they reached the general public. Apparently, it was also his wish that his theories should survive, even without associating them with his name, and the historian Ellenberger commented: 'It would not be easy to find another author from which so much has been borrowed from all sides without acknowledgment than Adler' (cited in Mosak 1989). One possible reason for the lesser influence of Adlerian Psychology with respect to the other two historical approaches could be that Adlerian psychologists may have preferred clinical practice to academia and research. Another reason may be that Adlerian scholarship traditionally has emphasised case study analyses and other qualitative approaches rather than quantitative and statistical methods.

In view of the recent developments in psychotherapy and of the increasing movement towards psychotherapy integration we think it is necessary, not only to present an overview of classical Adlerian theory and practice, but also to revise some antiquated concepts and bring them up to date. We also think it is both convenient and timely to compare the Adlerian ideas with other contemporary therapeutic approaches and to revise them in the light of therapy integration.

Thus this book aims at presenting a comprehensive exposition of Adlerian Psychology as well as the contributions of other historical and contemporary Adlerian authors, and to specify their applications in counselling and therapy. It will also reflect our own development as Adlerian psychotherapists and investigators, with respect to psychological theory and counselling practice, which is influenced by a strong integrationist and constructivist standpoint.

The first part of the book discusses traditional Adlerian theory. Chapter 1 gives an overview of the origins of Adlerian theory, its philosophical roots and the socio-political circumstances that influenced it. We present Adler's earlier ideas about psychotherapy and show the development of his own standpoint to be more and more different from that of Freud. Chapter 2 gives a critical review of classical Adlerian theory, as far as it is still in use in contemporary Adlerian Psychology and Adlerian counselling. We revise Adler's theory of personality and his view of psychological problems and mental disorder. Chapters 3, 4, and 5 are dedicated to different possibilities of Adlerian intervention. Chapter 3 elaborates the existing Adlerian assessment and therapy strategies and techniques (Life Style analysis, dream work, encouragement, etc.). Chapter 4 explores the different modalities of family and marital counselling and therapy, and Chapter 5 presents the psychoeducational approach of Rudolf Dreikurs and others, i.e. child guidance, parenting and classroom intervention. We complete these chapters with our own view and new technical developments, and also present practical examples of clinical casework.

The last part of the book goes beyond Adlerian theory and deals with the most recent developments in psychology and psychotherapy. Considering the general integrationist tendencies in counselling and psychotherapy, we discuss Individual Psychology in the context of other psychotherapeutic approaches and try to elaborate the direction Adlerian theories could (or should) take in the future (Chapter 6). In Chapter 7 we analyse the relevance of the Adlerian approach with respect to contemporary issues in psychotherapy and social psychology, such as constructivism, social constructionism, and postmodernity. We elaborate the ethical standpoint of Individual Psychology and argue that Adler's ideas can facilitate answers to present and future problems in psychotherapy and make important contributions to the pressing questions of a postmodern society.

We would like to mention that, although we consulted and present Adler's original works in German and English, we decided to quote consistently from a selected compilation of Adler's writings made by Ansbacher and Ansbacher (1956), in order to avoid translations and to make it easier for the interested reader to consult the broader context of our quotations. Ansbacher and Ansbacher's presentation is still in use and has been re-edited many times, which is not the case with all of Adler's original publications.

Chapter 1

Historical context, roots, and early developments

Alfred Adler was born on 7 February 1870, in Vienna, as the second of six children of a Jewish corn trader. Adler later developed his personality theory, which holds that second children often develop a tendency toward striving for equality and even superiority with respect to the first-born. Interestingly, the name of the family's first-born was Sigmund, like Sigmund Freud, the founder of psychoanalysis and Adler's later friend, tutor, and adversary.

Alfred was not a healthy child. As his biographers (Rattner 1972, Sperber 1983, Hoffman 1994) report, he suffered from illnesses and severe physical problems. In one of his early recollections, Adler remembers himself as a little boy wrapped in bandages because of rickets, being unable to participate in the games and play of his siblings and friends. Death was also present in the family; his younger brother died of diphtheria while sleeping, as usual, in the same bed as 4-year-old Alfred. These experiences apparently moved Adler towards the decision to study medicine in order to fight misery and diseases, but most probably also influenced him in the development of some concepts of his theory, such as organ inferiority and the human striving to overcome misfortunes.

Thus Adler became a physician. First, he inclined to ophthalmology, and later to neurology. While attending his university lectures, Adler became interested in philosophy and politics, especially Marxism and socialism. These ideas had a special attractiveness to the socially-minded young Adler. He published a booklet titled *Health book for the tailoring trade* where he not only criticises the squalid conditions the workmen and their families lived in, but also suggests corrective measures, such as improving housing, fixing the maximum working hours, etc. Manès Sperber (1983), one of his later disciples and biographers, characterises Adler's efforts as genuinely socialist and Marxist in their origins. Unlike Freud and other psychologists who described the individual without taking much account of his or her environment and relationships, Adler always considered people in a close relationship with their social context; people are socially embedded. The idea of the individual as the product of society stems from Karl Marx. But Adler, in considering the interaction of individual and society, goes further than Marxism by moving towards a humanistic point of view. We can say that Adler, though clearly influenced by early socialism, was not a socialist, but much more of a humanist. He was not so much interested in the economic and political aspects of society and citizens, but in the relationship possibilities embodied in the community of people. He emphasised the necessity of improving the living conditions for the poor, but he always insisted on the creative power of the individuals themselves to change their lives.

Adler's future wife though, Raissa Epstein, was an active Russian socialist and an early feminist, apparently much more politically radical than her husband, and it is reported by Adler's biographers that the couple's relationship waxed and waned. Adler and Raissa had four children; Kurt and Alexandra were the two to follow their father's footsteps in psychotherapy. The eldest daughter, Valentine, was politically and socially active like her mother. Valentine and her husband perished in a Russian gulag; Adler learned about this shortly before his death and this knowledge may have contributed to his demise (Hoffman 1994). Cornelia, a middle child, worked as an artist.

The concerns and challenges Adler faced in his personal and professional lives, along with the socio-political climate of his times, affected the development and expression of his theories. In this first chapter, we will analyse the origins of Adler's theory and the influences it received from other disciplines and circumstances.

Medicine and psychoanalysis

Despite the advances in medicine at that time, health conditions were still really difficult at the turn of the twentieth century. Although the existence of bacteria had just been discovered by Pasteur in 1861, germs were not yet recognised as causes of infectious diseases during Adler's childhood. It was not until 1928 that penicillin was discovered. The awareness of the influences of the living and working conditions on health also was still in its infancy, and the manifestations of psychiatric phenomena such as hysteria and psychoses were still a complete mystery to the medicine of Adler's time. Hypnosis, called 'Mesmerism' after its discoverer, Mesmer, had been used to produce spectacular and pseudo-therapeutic effects by Charcot (from 1872 on), but fell rather completely out of use after a few years and with the development of Freud's theories in the early 1900s.

The theories of Sigmund Freud marked a breakthrough in the understanding of many psychological phenomena. The founding father of Psychoanalysis was the first to postulate the existence of an unconscious mind. This gave an alternative interpretative possibility for a variety of psychopathological manifestations, which the existing medical approach had not been able to explain up to then. Though Freud continued to use a medical model, i.e. he considered neuroses and psychoses to be diseases, he argued that they are caused by an unconscious process that is psychological, and not biological, in its essence. Thus he opened the door to an explanation that sees psycho-pathology as a way of alternative psychological functioning.

When Sigmund Freud heard about the young physician Alfred Adler he invited him to attend the (later famous) Wednesday discussion meetings in his home at the Bergasse in Vienna (Hoffman 1994). By then, Adler had already a certain reputation as a hands-on doctor with good bedside manner, and he had even published his *Health book for the tailoring trade*. Adler had also publicly stood up for the controversial and ridiculed Freudian ideas in the Vienna Medical Society.

Adler is usually considered to be a follower and later dissident of Freudian psychoanalysis by some historians, but other scholars emphasise, quite accurately, that Adler never really was Freud's disciple (Hoffman 1994). Doubtless, Adler was initially interested in Freud's ideas and in his early conferences and publications, and Freud's influences in Adler's first publica-tions are noteworthy. But in spite of the mutual respect the two men had for each other, a certain rivalry between Freud and Adler existed from the incep-tion of their relationship. It seems that Adler never was wholly convinced of all of Freud's ideas, especially the concept of sexuality being the primary motivator of most behaviour. Nonetheless, Adler stayed in the group for nearly a decade and was even president of the Vienna Psychoanalytic Associ-ation for some time until the final breaking-off in 1911 when he published an article criticising Freud's theory of human sexuality and subsequently founded the Society for Free Psychoanalytic Study.

Psychology at the beginning of the twentieth century was a very young academic discipline. It was founded in 1879, when Wilhelm Wundt opened the first experimental psychology laboratory in Leipzig, Germany, where he could investigate human memory and reaction time processes. Wundt and his successors created the 'Psychology of the elements of consciousness' and used systematic self-observation as their empirical method. As a positivistic countermovement, Behaviourism (Pavlov from 1904 on and Watson from 1913 on) refused self-observation as scientific methodology and argued that only objectively observable and quantifiable events (stimulus and reactions) could be the subject of scientific investigation. This is also contrary to Freud's Psychoanalysis. Initially a method of treating neuroses, Psycho-analysis expanded into a general theory of human psychological functioning; it emphasised unconscious processes, which cannot be observed and meas-ured. Psychoanalysis and other psychodynamic theories have developed in a way that is quite different from, and often contradictory to experimental psychology.

In the years before 1911, Adler tried to think in medical and also in Freudian terms. Adler's *Study on organ inferiority*, for example, published in 1907, is probably the one where most Freudian influences can be found. It can be considered an attempt to think, at least formally, in psychoanalytical terms and it is one of Adler's first attempts to explain the psychological aetiology of medical diseases (in this case urological disorders), hitherto thought to have exclusively organic causes. But traditionally psychoanalytic terms such as 'psychic instances' (Ego, Id, Superego) or 'Oedipal complex' were absent from this study. We can summarise the *Study on organ inferiority* in the following way. Taking the functional disorders of the kidney and the bladder (especially enuresis) as an example and then generalising to the rest of the organs and body members, Adler hypothesised the existence of a hereditary morphological or functional 'organ inferiority'. This **organ inferiority** was expressed as incomplete development or functional insufficiency; the inferiority can affect a specific organ, a member of the body, or a whole group of organs. 'Inferiority' (*Minderwertigkeit*) was a widely used medical expression in Adler's times and did not have the pejorative connotations it has nowadays, when we would probably talk of 'handicap', 'deficit' or 'dysfunction'. The term 'organ inferiority' at that point of Adler's development still refers to exclusively somatic aspects, but already traces the way of Adler's later concept of 'inferiority feelings'.

In his *Study on organ inferiority* Adler also introduces the concept of **compensation** as a general tendency of life. In his view the insufficient functions of an organ can be compensated either by using the symmetrical organ (e.g. the healthy kidney), or by using another part of the affected organ or other organs that can assume similar functions. But it can also be compensated – and this is the beginning of genuine Adlerian thinking – by giving special attention and special training to the affected organ and thus making the most of it. Finally, compensation for the reduced functions of the 'inferior' organ can be achieved by compensatory changes of the superordinate structures, the neuronal pathways and other parts of the central nervous system. These neuronal structures can be reinforced or new ones can be developed. As we can see, Adler apparently tried to translate his ideas from physiological terms, via neurology, to psychological terms.

This leads us to the psychological aspects of the disorder, which form the basis of neuroses. In Adler's view, the compensatory efforts of the organism can lead to an *over*compensation of the functions. This means that the individual is giving a high degree of special attention to the affected organ and its dysfunctions. On one hand, this kind of attention could be followed by a major training of the organ and a subsequent 'superiority' of this part of the body. In a later publication, *Heilen und Bilden* (*Healing and education*, 1914) Adler uses anecdotal examples of famous artists whose physical and sensorial deficits led to superior artistic performances because they (over) compensated for those dysfunctions by constant and massive training (e.g. the composer Smetana, who had poor hearing). On the other hand, an incomplete or imperfect compensation was, for Adler, the breeding ground for neurosis. Adler's explanations of this aspect at that point in the development of his psychology were not very clear. Basically, he argued that the demands of the cultural environment cause a certain tension in the affected organism. When this tension becomes stronger and stronger, the individual finally is unable to cope with those demands. Eventually, the inferior organ gives up and then functions on a more primitive and infantile level, exclusively to achieve pleasure. Disease is the result of organ inferiority and external demands.

The *Study on organ inferiority* itself is of mere historical interest. But the terms 'organ inferiority' and 'compensation' or 'overcompensation' are still basic notions in contemporary Adlerian Psychology, although the existence of an 'organ inferiority' (physical, mental, or sensorial deficits, or any other chronic health problem) is now seen only as one possible additional factor in the aetiology of psychological problems. It can never be considered to be a determining cause of neurosis, neither is it indispensable for the development of a neurotic disturbance.

As we can see, Adler's reasoning as reflected in the *Study on organ inferiority* is couched primarily in anatomical and physiological terms, with few psychological concepts. His point of view is still characterised by natural science, and psychological manifestations are ultimately reduced to physiological processes.

Yet, some of Adler's observations on organ inferiority and compensation have been confirmed in modern psychosomatic medicine. In 1936, Selye (see Kaplan and Saddock 1995) wrote about 'stress' as a non-specific reaction of the organism to any external demand that functions as a stressing stimulus (general adaptation syndrome) and described how the presence of coping mechanisms can neutralise this stimulus. Modern psychoneuroimmunology and psychoneuroendocrinology study the interaction between the behavioural, neural, endocrine and immunological responses that allow the organism to cope with physical or psychological stress factors and try to explain how unsuccessful adaptation can lead to psychosomatic disorders, such as some coronary diseases or gastrointestinal dysfunctions. The compensating capacity of most of the organs and even of the central nervous system (by functional adaptation of healthy parts when one functional unit fails) is now commonly accepted and empirically validated (e.g. Oddy and Humphrey 1980). The dysfunctional organ is seen as the *locus minoris resistentiae* (place of least resistance; the Latin term was already used by Adler) where the organic expression of a basically psychological problem can be located (e.g. stomach ulcer, migraine, cardiovascular disorders, etc.). Sperry's (1991, 1999, 2001) biopsychosocial approach in Adlerian therapy is based on the initial Adlerian assumption that biological functioning is related to psychological and social functioning, as well as the notions of organ inferiority and organ dialect. Sperry describes how the Adlerian approach can contribute to a better understanding of the brain–mind interactions and outlines an integrative therapy that takes into account all levels of biopsychosocial functioning. Dreikurs, in his 'Holistic medicine' (1997) also sets the basis for an

Adlerian psychosomatic medicine that is specifically designed to be applied by the general practitioner.

Adler himself was troubled by 'organ inferiorities' and apparently had to exert considerable effort to compensate for them. None of Adler's biographers can resist – nor can we – the temptation of pointing out his early experiences and relating them to the development of Individual Psychology. As we have mentioned above, Adler's earliest childhood recollections deal with illness and death. During his episode of rickets he observed his elder brother Sigmund moving around effortlessly, while he, Alfred, had to struggle to move at all. When 5 years old, a bout of pneumonia nearly killed him. The doctors had already given him up, and Adler remembered hearing the doctor say that he was probably going to die. Terribly scared of dying, and with some good fortune in overcoming his infection, young Alfred made a quick recovery.

It is Freud's great merit to have 'discovered' the unconscious and to explain certain pathological manifestations in the individual as having psychological foundations. His classical model of the unconscious as part of the personality hypothesised that repressed infantile wishes are hidden from the person's awareness and pop up from time to time – when defences are low – and bother the individual with neurotic ailments. Freud's model has been described as a physicalist (hydraulic) model: tensions (also called 'drives') accumulate in the organism as a result of intra-psychic energies and external demands and have to be relieved from time to time and in some way – like steam under pressure through a valve – either in a mature, culturally accepted way (known as sublimation) or in an immature, pathological way that results in conflicts, the need to repress, and ultimately in neurosis.

Adler, in his study on organ inferiority, tries to find a balance between the scientific medicine of his time and the newly developed Freudian thinking, using explanatory models like the Freudian 'tension', 'drive', or '*Lust*'. Following Freud's thinking, the body–mind dynamic is still seen as an intra-organismic process. Only a few years later, Adler abandoned this solipsistic viewpoint – the individual stands alone with his or her intra-psychic conflicts – in favour of a social model: instead of organs among organs there will be persons among persons.

In his article 'Der Agressionstrieb im Leben und in der Neurose' ('The aggression drive in life and in neuroses', 1908a), Adler postulates – still in the Freudian tradition – the existence of an innate aggression drive as a unifying dynamic principle in the human being (probably similar or in opposition to Freud's notion of libido). A few years later, he withdraws from this concept by denying the existence of any 'drives' in the human being. In his early publications, Adler used the expression 'aggression drive' in an ambiguous way. On one hand, he refers to the normal activity impulse of a healthy organ and, in the psychological field, to the active coping with difficulties. On the other hand, he regards this aggression as a pathological manifestation in the neuroses: in hysteria, paranoia, hypochondria, neurasthenic and hysterical pain, self-mutilation and suicide, but also in epilepsy (not yet recognised as a neurological disorder) and in temper tantrums.

Whereas Freud, from 1920 on, also started to postulate an aggression drive – later called 'destructive drive' or 'death instinct' (*thanatos*), Adler, in his later publications, took a detached view of the aggression drive and generally abandoned the Freudian idea of the individual being dominated by drives. The aggression drive was renamed and became the famous 'striving for power', with aggression only its pathological expression.

Published in the same year as the 'Aggression drive', another of Adler's early publications deals with Freud's concept of libido ('Das Zärtlichkeits-bedürfnis des Kindes', 'The child's need for affection', 1908b). But while libido, in Freud's view, is autoerotic and narcissist and directed towards one's own person, the child's need for affection is, according to Adler, related to other people (especially primary caregivers). It is also the key to socialisation, education and culture: the child's needs for love and care have to be met, and Adler warns against the negative consequences of lack of care and love in early childhood. But these needs have not to be satisfied in just any way. Children should not be spoiled or pampered, but instead must be affection-ately guided to become adapted and useful members of the human com-munity. This aspect of human psychology will later be called **Social Interest** by Adler. Thus, in that article, we can find a first turn from the psychoanalyt-ical inner-psychic viewpoint to the future Adlerian stance of the human being as a social being who cannot be understood outside the context of other people; again, the theme of social embeddedness appears.

The split with Freud came in 1911 with the publication of 'Zur Kritik der Freudschen Sexualtheorie des Seelenlebens' ('Criticism of Freud's sexual the-ory') where Adler refutes Freud's ideas of human sexuality and the sexual aetiology of neuroses. He tries to break down the pillars of psychoanalysis by declaring the stages of psychosexual development (oral stage, anal stage, and genital stage) mere artefacts of education and not an innate and autonomous natural development. And the famous Oedipus complex, instead of being related to sexuality, has more to do with power and authority in the family. The sexual disorders, often found in neurotic individuals, might also be the consequences or metaphoric expressions of neurosis and not its causes. Fur-thermore, Adler refutes the existence of 'repression' (of infantile sexual wishes) and accuses Freud of applying a circular conclusion: on one hand, Freud postulates that human civilisation is the result of repression and sub-limation, but on the other hand maintains that culture and civilisation promote repression.

With these arguments, Adler hit at the core of Freud's system and could no longer be a member of the Vienna Psychoanalytical Society. This made him free to found his own discussion group, the Society for Free Psychoanalytic Study, which marked the onset of his own theory-building.

Society and politics

Being an Austrian citizen was something very special at the turn of the nineteenth to the twentieth century. Emperor Franz Josef had ascended to the throne at the age of 18 and had now been reigning for half a century. Vienna was a city of arts, music, and sciences. As Manès Sperber (1983) notes, this *belle époque* constituted the very last years of the clear conscience of the ruling classes in Europe. These years were also a time of social contrasts, of political conflicts, of rising anti-Semitism, of Marxism. Some of Adler's later disciples considered themselves Marxists or socialists. Sperber always emphasised the dialectical character of Individual Psychology and drew parallels between the worker's emancipation movement and the Adlerian idea of the relationship between man and society.

Adler, as well as Freud, was a Jew, but as a young man he converted to Protestantism. The reasons for this decision are not clear. Sperber holds that Adler was actually an atheist and interprets his conversion as an escape from being Jewish, from being different – and of course from suffering anti-Semitism. Adler never took a clear public standpoint on religion. Together with a German protestant minister he published a small book (Adler and Jahn 1933) in which they discuss the similarities and differences of psychotherapy and pastoral care. Both authors express their mutual respect for each other, but Adler keeps a neutral stance with respect to the spiritual aspects of life.

In extension of his theory of the aggression drive, in 1910 Adler published a short article, 'Der Hermaphroditismus im Leben und in der Neurose' ('Psychic hermaphrodism in life and in neuroses'), on what he called the '**masculine protest**' and what he considered then to be the most important dynamic force in the human being. The expression 'masculine protest' is very unfortunate and misleading. But since it is a milestone in the development of Adlerian theory and is still in use in a slightly different form in contemporary Adlerian Psychology, we will discuss it in some detail.

Several well-known authors of Adler's time (Fliess, Krafft-Ebing, and Freud) commented in their publications that many neurotic people show physical and psychological traits of the opposite sex. Adler regards these traits as a form of organ inferiority (e.g. underdeveloped genitals), which can give rise to a subjective feeling of inferiority in children with respect to normally developed peers. And children who are affected by organic problems can end up feeling inferior with respect to completely healthy people, especially when their weaker physical conditions make them more dependent on other people and they therefore have increased affective needs. These situations can make male children feel less manly because, as Adler pointed out, society generally identifies strength, power, aggression, and even health, as being manly, whereas weakness, illness, powerlessness, or inhibition of aggression are considered as typically female traits. Thus a young boy with a physical weakness or illness might come to the conclusion that he is less masculine. This problem can lead to tendencies of submission to parents and educators on one hand – because of his greater dependency – and/or to fantasies of grandiosity and striving for superiority as compensation on the other. Thus the boy moves sometimes in the feminine and sometimes in the masculine direction. In general, the striving for superiority of a boy who feels inferior, his hypertrophied masculine wishes and efforts, are seen as compensation for his negatively evaluated condition and therefore as an overcompensation that makes him neurotically disposed.

In women, the masculine protest is a similar phenomenon. According to Adler, the masculine protest in women as compensation for inferiority feelings is covered up and transformed; the girl tends to strive for power and triumph with more soft and 'feminine' means, such as crying or asking for pity or admiration, behaviours that are usually more accepted in women than in men. Adler argued that these attitudes could result in neurotic problems such as vaginismus, sexual anaesthesia or hysteria, the typical observed female neuroses in Freud's and Adler's times.

Adler always pointed out the metaphorical character of the masculine protest. The term 'masculine protest' was later replaced by the more appropriate term '**striving for superiority**'. Only with respect to females is masculine protest still used in Adlerian Psychology, to describe women who have difficulties in accepting their 'womanliness' or who protest against their role as females in society. This protest can have a neurotic character, giving rise to nervous disorders that are often related to the menses, pregnancy, childbirth, and the menopause, and it can also lead to a late marriage and to relationship problems. But it can also result in positive adjustment, providing greater energy and encouragement to the girl. A healthy form of masculine protest is considered necessary to struggle against certain aspects of social discrimination. Adler always criticised the undervaluation of women in family and society and was well aware that this could be an additional source of inferiority feelings for females. The masculine protest, in its culturally 'useful' expression, can help to eradicate social injustice, as when women democratically struggle for their rights.

The culturally 'useless' expression is seen as the woman's individual and egocentric striving for superiority by means of psychopathological symptoms, in order to compensate for the inferiority feelings with increased attention-getting behaviour. It is interesting to read Sperber's (1983) explanation of the phenomenon of hysteria, so common in Freud's and Adler's times. Sperber argued that the hysterical woman tried to conceal from herself the psychological and often also physical dissatisfaction that marriage and family produced in her. Instead, she staged a drama in several acts with herself as the protagonist, but not in order to provoke a change of her situation, for which she had no courage. With her spectacular hysterical symptoms she revelled in an intensity that life had denied her; at the same time she received compassion and a position of superiority in the family. So, for the Adlerian Sperber, hysteria was not an expression of repressed sexual wishes as it was for Freud, but a way of getting attention and power for a woman who feels disregarded and powerless.

Sperber also pointed out the different viewpoint in Freud and Adler with respect to society: what Freud supposed to be an Oedipal conflict inherent in normal psychosexual development, for Adler is only the reflection of the power structures in an authoritarian society. What is of influence in the psychology of people is not sexuality; it is the authoritarian structures that force their way into every human aspect, sexuality being only one of them.

As we can see, Adler adopts, in contrast to Freud with his more misogynous concepts of penis envy etc., a more 'feminist' standpoint. While Freud proclaimed the existence of invariable biological tendencies, these were for Adler only metaphors of social discrimination. He called the exaggerated preference for males in society the 'carcinoma of our culture' (Adler 1911: 210) and declared himself in favour of the women's liberation movement. He considered disdain for women to be the striving for superiority of a male who fears to lose his privileged position in society. But this same male chauvinism, as we would call it nowadays, makes men suffer too, since it hinders them from having satisfactory emotional relationships with women. This position in favour of the female sex brought Adler the approval of many female Adlerian and non-Adlerian authors.

Philosophy

Apart from Freudian psychoanalysis and Marxism, we also find in Adler's publications the influence of several German philosophers, such as Kant, Hegel, Dilthey, Nietzsche, Bergson, and Vaihinger, and of several ancient thinkers, like Aristotle and Seneca. A detailed analysis of these influences is beyond the scope of this chapter. We will only discuss the most important influences, especially those that stem from Aristotle, Seneca, and Vaihinger.

Several Aristotelian principles have found their way into Adler's works: the idea of the human being a *zoon politicon*, a social being, but also the holistic principle (the whole is more than the sum of its parts), and the teleological principle. The teleological principle refers to the consideration of the physical and psychological world under a final viewpoint. Aristotle distinguished the causal principle (the cause of things happening) from the final principle (the purpose of things happening), which became the basic idea of Adler's goal-oriented view of human behaviour. Adler also incorporated Aristotle's concept of *poiesis*, or the creative force of the human being. This is significant in that it bears on people's tendencies to create a workable whole from the different influences and variables that exist in their lives.

From the Roman philosopher Seneca, Adler adopted the idea that everything depends on the opinion people have of it. It is not so much the facts or givens that are decisive for what we feel, think and do, but the opinion we have of them, the attitude or the standpoint we take. Adler also talks of our 'private opinions' or 'fictions'. This is one of Adler's most essential contributions to psychology: what actually happens to us is of lesser importance than what we make out of it.

Adler adopted this idea of fictions from the German philosopher Vaihinger who published the German original of his *The philosophy of 'As-if'* in 1911 (the year of Adler's split with Freud). Vaihinger (1925) defines fictions as ideas – mental creations of the individual that may have little or no correspondence with the real world, but are extremely useful for co-operation between individuals and for dealing with reality. For instance, measurement units such as inches, pounds and hours, concepts like the meridians and the latitudes, notions of mathematical infinity and proof by induction, do not exist in the real world. Instead they are conceptual artifices that are of practical (pragmatic) importance for daily life, for orientation, co-operation, understanding and prediction. Psychological, ethical, aesthetic and scientific ideas and systems (e.g. 'all men and women are equal') can also be considered fictions. It is important to point out that a fiction can become the basis of our acts and behaviour, even when their 'truth' is doubtful. We only must agree on using a particular fiction in a specific way. In language, we use the expression 'as if' to describe this phenomenon: we act as if these creations were true. For Vaihinger, this non-real world of fictions is as important as the real world of things. He argues that what we normally call 'truth' is only the most useful fiction, or better: truth is the most pragmatic or most expedient error. Thus an important aspect of fiction is its usefulness to predict the course of events and to help people to find their bearings in a changing world. 'Fiction' is also different from 'hypothesis': a hypothesis is a prediction that can be empirically tested against reality and proved to be true or false. A fiction is only an auxiliary mental construction, which can be removed when it is not useful anymore. According to Vaihinger, a hypothesis that has proven to be false still can be a good fiction. A fiction does not need to be true; it only needs to serve well. Adler was the first to adapt the philosophical concept of fictions to psychology. For him, fictions are the individual's creative and subjective constructions and cannot be reduced to objective causes; most of them emerge unconsciously.

In the next chapter, we will discuss the importance these philosophical concepts of holism, fictionalism, and finality have acquired in Individual Psychology in greater detail.

Chapter 2

Classical Adlerian Psychology

Sigmund Freud's idea of explaining present psychological phenomena by searching for objective causes in the individual's past (childhood) was a revolutionary new vision of certain problems and illnesses that could not be understood in purely medical terms, but it also has its limitations. Though Adler does not deny the influence of childhood experiences, he refuses to accept an exclusively causal explanation for the person's present problems. Instead of being a victim of past experiences, the human being is seen as having a free will and an innate creative force, and as guided by fictions and final goals. Thus Adler refuses to accept historical experiences as an exclusively causal explanation for the person's present problems. Adler also assumes an innate disposition for social life and community. The child is born with the innate possibility of what Adler will later call 'community feeling' (*Gemeinschaftsgefühl*), usually translated as 'Social Interest'. This feeling or interest in living in a community and in sharing experiences, emotions and ideas must be developed and defined by means of the child's interaction with primary caregivers. An insufficient degree of Social Interest is expressed in a psychopathological striving for power.

In this chapter, we will provide an overview of the historical and contemporary notions of Individual Psychology.

Theory of personality

Holism and the creative self

Adler supposes that there is a creative force inborn to the child, which increases with activity; it enables people to make their own decisions and to develop their opinions on what happens to them. In this sense, individuals are not just the product of their circumstances – as assumed in classical Behaviourism (behaviour as a result of specific stimuli) or as in classical Psychoanalysis (psychological problems as result of traumatic childhood experiences) – but are also the creators of their circumstances and of themselves. This creative force works throughout the whole personality. In the classical Freudian view, personality is seen as divided. In contrast, Adler proposes a holistic view of the personality: the individual acts as a whole, his or her feelings, beliefs and behaviours are guided by the same organising principle: the fictionate goal. This unifying principle can be seen as the individual's unique way of responding to situations. It is not only the essential part of the personality; it also distinguishes him or her from other people and makes the individual unique and personal.

The capacity of the human being and other living organisms for self-generation is called *auto-poiesis* by the biologists Maturana and Varela (1980). We have already mentioned Aristotle's concept of *poiesis*, the individual's creative force. *Auto-poiesis*, self-generation, is a recursive process and implies that the processes of production regenerate the set of production that had produced them. Thus a process A does not only generate B, but also reproduces itself. By influencing somebody else, I make a change not only in his or her opinions/feelings/behaviours, but also in myself and in the relationship that defines both of us. In this sense, product and producer are the same, or at least cannot be told apart. In Adler's more simple and at the same time more poetic words, 'the individual is thus both the picture and the artist' (Ansbacher and Ansbacher 1956: 177).

Fictionalism

We mentioned in Chapter 1 the philosophical roots of Adler's concept of *fictions* as conscious and non-conscious ideas that have not necessarily a correspondence with reality, but that serve the purpose to guide us to cope better with reality. I act 'as if' my fictions were true, as if the hours of my watch really existed although they are a mere convenience, as if I had a free will although I react to external influences, as if I would live eternally, as if I were the most important person in the world, etc. In Vaihinger's (1925) notion, a fiction is only an auxiliary construct that has to be abandoned when it is no longer useful; this implies that a fiction has to be put through constant critical revision, because the use of an outmoded fiction is not only a waste of time but can also lead to considerable problems. To make this concept more understandable, Vaihinger compares 'fiction' to 'hypothesis': a hypothesis has to be submitted to empirical reality testing (its truth and correspondence with reality must be proven), but a fiction is a mere auxiliary scaffolding that is removed when it is no longer necessary. According to Vaihinger, a hypothesis that has proven to be false can still serve as a good fiction, if it is useful for some purpose. A fiction does not need to be true.

Adler incorporated this perspective on fictions in the development of his theory. Vaihinger's notion of truth being only the most expedient error was especially appealing to Adler and later acknowledged by another prominent psychologist, George Kelly. Adler holds that human beings create fictions as idiosyncratic ways of perceiving themselves, others and their environment, in order to guide their feelings, thoughts and acts according to them. For instance, somebody who is convinced of God's existence will feel, think, and behave in a different way than an atheist does.

In Vaihinger's view, all subjective aspects are fictions; Adler goes further than that and considers most fictions to be not only subjective, but also unconscious, i.e. the individual is unaware of maintaining them. The idea of 'I need to be someone important' can be a conscious aim or an unconscious desire. In any case, this individual will behave in a way that is congruent to this fiction (pursue a career, become a politician, become an authoritarian father, collect rare butterflies, or whatever this particular person considers to be 'important').

One purpose of fictions can be to reduce the complexity of psychological aspects to something simpler and easier to cope with: some people may thus reduce the complexity of gender conflicts to 'men are emotionally immature' or 'women have a special sensibility'. Reduction can be helpful in some situations, but may be an obstacle in others. It may be useful – though not necessarily true – to believe that 'men have problems in controlling their sexual instincts, so I'd better not stay alone with an unknown man', but not so useful to think, 'men have problems controlling their sexual instincts, so I'd better avoid all of them'. Psychologically 'healthy' individuals should be able to revise their fictions constantly and to change and adapt them if necessary. We emphasise the point that it is not the degree of correspondence with reality, i.e. the degree of truth, which decides whether a fiction is 'good' or 'bad'; it is only its degree of usefulness with respect to its purpose. It can be tremendously useful for a woman to avoid empty streets at night; but inferring that all men will take advantage of her whenever they can, might be not useful when she wants to find a boyfriend.

The usefulness of fictions is determined by their predictive capacity. If they allow us to prepare for future events and make adequate predictions, they may even contradict reality. Thus, in Vaihinger's terms, what we use to call 'truth' (the correspondence of reality and our mental representation of reality) is only the most expedient error, whereas an error is an inexpedient (useless) fiction. It is unimportant whether our ideas about reality, our scientific or personal theories, are 'right' or 'wrong' in terms of truth; it is only of importance if they work, if they help us to lead the life that we want, to have relationships in a way we want them to be, to develop technologies that help us to make our work easier to do, to find a medical cure for a former incurable illness. A superficial reading of Adler's works may lead to the impression that Adler defines the neurotic individual as somebody who sustains 'fictions' whereas the healthy one does not. But having fictions is not only a common but also a necessary condition for human beings. Without fictions we would not be able to find our bearings in the world and to make sense of our experiences. It is only the sticking to useless (inexpedient) fictions that leads to psychological problems. As we have said, a psychologically healthy person also has fictions (and needs them), but is able to submit them to constant revision.

In the cases of 'neurotic' (we will define 'psychologically healthy' and 'neurotic' later) individuals, or healthy people in moments of insecurity and distress, when going through a difficult personal situation, suffering a loss, etc., the contrary is the case: in these situations, people tend to cling to their fictions, because this is what they know and what has helped them before, so they try and try again to apply the same concepts to a changed situation, but where they no longer work in the same efficient way. Thus these fictions are no longer useful constructions that can be built up and torn down at convenience, but they have a life of their own. Instead of serving the individual's purposes, the individual now becomes their slave. The formerly useful fiction has become a dogma. A dogma is something we have to believe in, and where we do not act 'as if' our fictions were the truth. They are the truth and cannot be questioned nor revised, even when they are apparently contradictory to the individual's perception.

But why do people sometimes refuse to revise their fictions that have become useless in a new situation? Why is a woman who was her father's little princess so reluctant to change her idea of 'men do everything to please a woman' when confronted with a slightly more demanding husband? As we will see this is because the neurotic fiction has an additional function: it is a compensation for feelings of inferiority and serves to produce positive feelings in a situation that is perceived as negative.

Finality

With another concept, 'finality', Adler abandons Freud's more deterministic world-view completely. Humans set their own fictionate goals, which serve as guidelines for their acts. The concepts of fictions and finality also explain the apparent divergence between conscious and unconscious behaviour, which Freud had explained as a conflict among intra-psychic instances. The more instinct-driven Id has wishes that the moral-guided Superego refuses. By mediation of the Ego, the resulting conscious behaviour is a compromise between these unconscious conflicts. From Adler's holistic viewpoint there is only one organizing force: the **fictionate final goal**. This goal usually has been established in early childhood (e.g. by the age of 5 years) and is always present, though mostly unconscious, and influences the totality of behaviour. For instance, a kleptomaniac steals, although consciously he knows that it is forbidden; he does so because he obeys an inner unconscious and fictionate goal that guides his acts. An agoraphobic may be unable to leave her house and go to her workplace, because unconsciously she wants to avoid facing the conflicts she is having at her job.

Thus, with respect to human psychology and psychopathology, Adler does not ask 'why' (why does this man steal compulsively, why is that woman agoraphobic) or 'where from' (at which life stage), but 'what for' and 'where to'; he gives preference to the question of goal and purpose as an explanation for our behaviour, because this **teleological** (final) view provides a better explanation for behaviour than the classical causal attribution. Instead of restricting his efforts to finding the 'cause' of behaviour, Adler gives more emphasis to the 'final cause'. In order to understand a person, it is not (only) necessary to know why certain circumstances have occurred and what were the individual's reactions to them, but also where his or her life's pathway is leading. The voluntary starving of an anorexic adolescent could be causally explained by traumatic childhood experiences, genetic predispositions, personality factors, her parent's excessively demanding educational style; but it is more precisely defined by the young girl's desire to be as slim and perfect as the fashion models she sees every day in the advertisements. If you have traumatic childhood experiences and demanding parents you might become anorexic; but you may also develop different problems or even become a completely healthy person. But if you want to be slim you must go on a diet, and if you want to be extremely thin, you must stop eating.

Adler writes: 'Causality, removed from all philosophy, was a hurdle to Individual Psychology, and one which was taken. We regard man as if nothing in his life were causally determined and as if every phenomenon could have been different' (Ansbacher and Ansbacher 1956: 91). Interestingly, in the statement above Adler uses the formula 'as if'. This is, as we have shown, the way a fiction is linguistically expressed. This means that Adler's view of the human being is, naturally, a fiction, too. The usefulness of this fiction is that it allows us to understand individuals and to understand neurotic symptoms.

Knowing a person's fictions also allows us to predict approximately his or her next steps. Adler makes a sideswipe at the rising experimental psychology of his time when he states that when we know causes, reflexes, reaction times and memory capacity we do not know anything about what really happens in the person's mind. The only way to understand a person really is to know his or her goals. This goal-directedness is what is essentially human:

> A person would not know what to do with himself were he not oriented toward some goal. We cannot think, feel, will, or act without the perception of some goal. All the causalities in the world do not enable the living organism to conquer the chaos of the future and the planlessness of which we should be the victims. All activity would persist in the stage of an indiscriminate groping, and the economy in our psychological life would remain unattained. Without any self-consistency, physiognomy, and personal note we would rank with the amoeba. Inanimate nature obeys a perceptible causality, but life is (subjectively) a demand.
>
> Ansbacher and Ansbacher 1956: 96

Adler does not deny the influence of genetics and education, of experience and 'organ inferiorities'. All these factors contribute to the formation of individual fictions. But the most important aspect is the individual's creative force, his or her standpoint or opinion with respect to these factors. Ansbacher and Ansbacher have called this 'soft determinism'. This means that genetics and environment have an influence but are not decisive.

But why does the anorexic girl does not revise her fictionate goal (I must lose weight, because then I will be desirable and may become famous) when her weight is so low that she becomes too underweight to be attractive and even at risk of severe illness or death? Could it be that behind this apparent and conscious goal of losing weight and thus being attractive, there is another, more important fictionate goal she pursues with her illness, by maintaining some semblance of control or esteem in her life?

Social Interest

What Adler called 'Social Interest' refers to the notion of the individual as a social being. The way he or she interacts with other people is of extreme importance for psychological health. As we have said before, Social Interest is an inborn capacity of the human being, but it must be fostered during childhood. Having Social Interest means feeling like part of a family, a group, a couple, and the human community. Some Adlerian authors have argued that it means even feeling part of the universe. It means to participate, to contribute, to share; to feel accepted, appreciated, and loved, as well as to accept, appreciate and love other people. But this social embeddedness also means being able to cope with the obstacles and misfortunes of life in a socially adaptive way; not by seeking one's self-interest and personal advancement, but by pursuing, at the same time, the benefit of – theoretically – the whole of humankind. In this sense, Social Interest is a humanistic concept that stems from the idea of a progressive improvement of the human condition. One's own improvement – physically, mentally, and psychologically – should go along with the improvement of mankind. In searching for a cure for my illness I may invent a cure for all people who are affected by it. In a more global sense, people who pursue their life tasks well will develop a heightened sense of Social Interest.

Thus Adler refused to consider just the individual as such, but always in context with other people, the relationship. In this sense, the expression 'Individual' Psychology is misleading; it was coined by Adler in opposition to Freud's division of the psyche into Id, Ego and Superego and meant to express Adler's view of an indivisible personality (*in-dividuus*). But it does not mean 'psychology of the individual', as some translators into other languages understood. On the contrary, Individual Psychology deals with the whole person in context, the individual in relationship and in their living together. One particular individual can only be understood sufficiently within a wider set of people. Thus Adler indicated that Individual Psychology 'is probably the most consistent theory of the position of the individual towards the questions of social living, and in the same sense therefore, social psychology' (Ansbacher and Ansbacher 1956: 126).

Since the human community is of such importance for the individual, 'character' (Adler's expression for what we nowadays prefer to call 'personality') is also a social concept. We can only talk about a character trait with respect to the individual's relationship with his or her social environment. Character is social positioning, the way a person faces his or her environment. If we accept this psychosocial view of the human being, we must also accept the influence human community has on the individual; community is the ethical framework for the individual's acts. It establishes standards and rules and it makes demands on people which serve as guidelines for them but, on the other hand, as community is a set of individuals, it is the individuals who fix and revise these standards continuously. It cannot be told from an absolute viewpoint if a person is good or bad, sick or healthy, but only from the standpoint of the community the person is part of.

For Adler, all problems stem from the tasks and necessities of living together. The satisfaction of all conceivable human needs depends on a sense of community and collaboration to fulfil the tasks of work, love, and friendship (or community life). Dreikurs and Mosak (Dreikurs and Mosak 1977a, b) later added two more tasks: the task of spirituality and the task of coping with oneself. Every individual has to face these life tasks and to resolve them successfully.

It is difficult to give an exact definition of what Social Interest means. Its relationship to conceptions of empathy is highlighted clearly by Adler's words 'to see with the eyes of another, to hear with the ears of another, to feel with the heart of another' (Ansbacher and Ansbacher 1956: 135). It should not be confused with simple altruism and living completely for others, although an altruistic attitude may comprise the predominant feature of Social Interest in some people. The basis for Social Interest is a feeling of equality, not necessarily in the sense of social equality, though this may be a consequence of it, but of equivalence and being 'equally good' as a human being, despite all the possible social, sexual, physical, etc. differences. Thus an altruistic attitude that implies a disdain of one's own worthiness is not an expression of Social Interest.

On the other hand, an altruism that emanates from a superior attitude, looking down on others ('I'm so good, so rich, so superior, that I can do good to others') is not Social Interest either. Social Interest, or community feeling, does not mean to simply 'be good'. As the expression 'community *feeling*' suggests, it has to be something felt, not only done. The act is a consequence of the feeling. Doing a good deed without the 'right' attitude has the opposite finality: not to contribute to the community, but to care exclusively for one's own self ('Am I not a really good fellow?').

On the subjective field, Social Interest is a feeling of belonging to others and not being 'outside'. People's capacity for co-operation can serve as a measure of the degree of Social Interest: to what degree do they take into account the needs of other people when dealing with their own problems? To what degree are they able to act in a 'task-oriented' (*sachlich*) way? To solve their problems adequately, but without worrying about their personal prestige?

Adler also pointed out that the concept of Social Interest, though difficult to grasp and subject to changes through the development of human community and from culture to culture, is universal and nobody can ignore it. It is the 'iron logic of communal life' (Ansbacher and Ansbacher 1956: 127). Ignoring this principle can lead, as we will show, to psychological problems.

Life Style

To understand somebody means to understand their emotional and cognitive organisation, their personality, their **Life Style** (*Lebensstil*). This expression does not refer to a particular way of life, but to how different aspects of the personality function together. Adler introduced the notion of Life Style (sometimes also translated as style of life) around the 1920s in his publications – a notion that progressively substituted other expressions of similar meaning, such as 'private logic', 'private world', 'life plan', and others. In many cases, Adler uses Life Style as synonymous to character and personality, or simply the 'I', expressing the wholeness of personality, the set of conscious and unconscious fictions and goals. Life Style develops in early childhood by the interaction of the child's experiences and the child's creative answer to these experiences. As we have already pointed out, we do not deny the influence of genetics and childhood experiences on the development of personality; but in an Adlerian view, the child's attitude to these factors is of greater importance. Thus, in the 'nature or nurture' debate of academic psychology in the first part of the 20th century, Adler had already introduced a third element, the 'opinion' (*Meinung*). This concept was not completely new; Adler himself cites the ancient philosopher Seneca's words: 'Omnia opinione suspensa sunt' (everything depends on the opinion). Adler adapts this philosophical statement to psychology and suggests that the opinions people have about things come to characterise their personalities. Of course, a boy with severely negative childhood experiences, raised in poverty by drug-dependent and neglecting or abusive parents, has a certain probability of becoming an adult with psychological problems; but he may also 'stand up and fight', overcome his obstacles, cope with his disturbing recollections and even develop a high degree of Social Interest, struggling against social injustice.

Nevertheless, the degree of 'free will' we possess to take our stance has to be discussed. Every experience and every answer to it restrict the next possible experience that can be made and the next possible opinion to it. If a girl has her first experience with her mother running to her help every time she cries, she may try the 'water power' (Adler's words) the next time, too. And the more her mother reacts promptly, the more she may believe that this is how life works. Experiences never determine our reaction to them and opinion of them, but they may limit the possible answers we can have.

In the same sense, in the Adlerian holistic view, it is not a person's cognitions that influence his or her emotions and behaviour, as assumed in Cognitive Psychotherapy, but cognitions, emotions and behaviour are all derived from the individual's Life Style. Conscious and unconscious aspects also make up Life Style. But the conscious and the unconscious are not seen as two opposite parts that influence each other. The unconscious is simply what we have not (yet) completely understood.

The child's Life Style is created at an early age. Traditionally, Adlerians talk about the first 5 to 8 years (e.g. Dinkmeyer, Jr and Sperry 2000), but we prefer to be slightly more flexible, as we suppose that Life Style is ever changing throughout the whole life. But we assume that most of the individual's guiding fictions about others and the world are formed at an age when children have not yet developed a sufficient degree of language or adequate cognitive concepts to put their experiences into words. Experiences and the opinions of them are felt rather than understood, because rational understanding requires words to exemplify lived experiences. The young girl does not think, 'Every time I cry, my mother comes running, so I always must express my needs strongly, and I'll be served and comforted.' But she learns her lesson well even without verbal awareness or verbal symbolisation. And once a specific fiction has become part of the individual's Life Style, a process of selective attention to further experiences takes place: the **tendentious apperception**. By this process people – unconsciously but systematically – direct their attention to what they want to perceive, and neglect aspects they want to ignore. Experiences are perceived in a way that makes them fit more seamlessly into the individual's Life Style. If I think that immigrants are unwilling to work and come to my country in order to have an easy life at my expense, I may selectively attend to these aspects and ignore others, such as the difficulties they have to get a work permit. Or ignore that there are also people of my country who behave in the same way. Tendentious apperception is also reflected in the fact that pregnant women may report seeing many more pregnant women in the neighbourhood or community than they did before. And seeing what one's Life Style wants to see and hearing what it wants to hear is a psychological mechanism that tends to reinforce Life Style in the line already traced out. Again, this restricts the next possible experiences I have, and my next possible answer. Thus, in the Adlerian view, the unconscious is not made up by 'repressed contents', as in the classical Freudian view, and which have to be kept there safely – the tendentious apperception provides that undesirable contents do not even enter the mind.

We can also say that Adler conceptualised the unconscious as made up of 'tacit' knowledge. Tacit knowledge is difficult to challenge: something for which there are no words to directly characterise, something that cannot really be understood and is unassailable to criticism. A logical debate is done in words, and when there are no words left to speak about a situation or experience, one cannot question it. That is why these early tacit fictions are so resistant to change, even by psychotherapy. In order to change them, people must make a conscious effort to give words and meaning to these unconscious aspects of their personality.

It is precisely their early creation, their tacit nature and their resistance to change that makes these guiding fictions important for the Life Style, especially because they tend to be super-ordinate to other fictions, which are created later and possibly represented consciously. Thus we might have a conscious aim that we believe we are following ('I want to be slim and attractive'), but behind (or 'above') there is another aim that rules it ('I want to get the maximum amount of attention from my parents and other people to feel in control of my life'). It is the task of psychotherapy to find out these tacit guiding fictions (for example with the technique of Life Style analysis), to challenge and to change them.

As we have seen, Adler's conceptualisation of what motivates people changed as his theory developed over time. The following list summarises the evolution of Adlerian thinking about what fundamentally motivates behaviour.

- **Organ inferiority** (1907) The least-developed or weakest body part can be affected negatively by the demands of living and can constrain the individual. We all have some organismically-based weakness for which we strive to compensate.
- **Aggression drive** (1908) A person may act against the environment when thwarted in meeting his or her needs and in obtaining satisfactions. These drives may be transformed into opposites, displaced, or related to another drive. Here the person is seen as acting outwardly and beyond oneself.
- **Masculine protest** (1910) Striving of the young and somewhat helpless child to be in control, to be competent, and to become the master of his or her own life. This reaction has as its goal the elimination of feelings of inertness and inferiority.
- **Striving for superiority** (1920s) There is an inherent tendency for individuals to grow and to master the challenges of life. There is a trend towards growth and accomplishment.
- **Striving for perfection** (from 1930s on) Exerting effort to realise idealised conceptions of oneself. The desire to fulfil dreams and chosen goals. This is based on fictional and subjective knowing.
- **Striving for completion and belonging** (1950s to present, contemporary

Adlerian authors) Here the goal is to contribute and to belong. Individuals try to find a place among people. They try to answer the question: 'How can I fit in and also be all that I can be?'

Theory of mental health and psychological disorder

The past two decades have witnessed increased interest in psychotherapy integration. Although we will discuss the many similarities between Adlerian Psychology and Psychotherapy and other theoretical orientations (see Chapter 6), what distinguishes Adler's model of psychopathology from other theoretical positions is the conceptualisation of the symptom as an excuse or pretext for not complying with the life tasks and with the requirements of a community existence. Alternatively, Social Interest emerges from meeting the tasks of life effectively and is both a cause and an effect of mental health. We have also discussed that this Social Interest, though inborn to the child, must be developed in relationship with primary caregivers. The child must feel loved and cared for. It is the parents' and other family members' task to foster Social Interest and to help the child to extend it progressively to larger communities. But what happens if these ideal conditions are not given? If the child is neglected, abandoned, battered, or abused? If the child is pampered, spoiled or overprotected? If the child's opinion differs from that of common sense? What happens to an adult who has developed fictionate goals that do not allow him or her to meaningfully engage others in important romantic or social relationships?

Feelings of inferiority

The observation of 'organ inferiorities', such as those postulated in his study of the bladder, and their compensation made Adler maintain that any psychological trouble is a consequence of 'inferiority'.

It was probably not Adler who coined the famous expression 'inferiority complex' associated with him, as Ansbacher and Ansbacher (1956) state, but later he also used to talk about an inferiority complex where he had formerly spoken of inferiority 'feelings'. Striving for superiority is Adler's expression for the attempt of the individual to overcome these feelings. Many contemporary psychologists, when asked what they know about Adler, refer to these two expressions and think that Adler suggested that this drive for power should be the natural human striving – that the human being is possessed by an innate striving for power. This would certainly be quite a negative view of the human being. But we have seen that the concept of Social Interest reveals a much more positive and humanistic view of humankind. Striving for power (superiority for its own sake) is precisely the pathological aspect of human behaviour.

When Adler investigated the organ inferiorities, he argued that an incomplete or unsuccessful compensation for this inferiority leads to neurosis, because the demands of the cultural environment cause an increased level of tension in an organism affected by such inferiorities. In his later publications, the idea of organ inferiorities loses importance in Adler's theory. The existence of a structural or functional organic problem is now seen as only one possible factor in the aetiology of neurosis, one that can never be the only determining cause. Nor is organ inferiority an indispensable factor. But the notions of compensation and overcompensation become more and more important in Adler's mature theory, not in the sense of physiological, organic compensation, but in the sense of psychological restoration.

Inferiority feelings arise when a child is 'discouraged'. A child can be discouraged when he or she is not loved, not adequately cared for, pampered or neglected, or, of course, affected by a health problem. Inferiority feelings arise when I compare myself with other people whom I perceive to be more skilled, accomplished, or better off than I am. If other children are healthier, prettier or more intelligent, run faster, achieve higher grades, have richer parents, etc. and I feel less healthy, pretty, rich, etc. then I may feel inferior to them. It is not only the feeling of envy; it is a feeling of personal worthlessness, which challenges the whole concept of myself. And this is hard to endure. As we will show later, not only 'organ inferiorities' and social conditions, but also the parents' erroneous educational style can make a child feel insecure and inferior. A pampered child can develop inferiority feelings, although initially, she may become accustomed to the idea of having power over her parents who are always prepared to remove all obstacles from her way. But she never learns to struggle by herself or to delay her wants and needs. It is not love and care she receives, but only the advantages of a parasitic existence. She rarely experiences the encouraging effects of coping with difficulties by herself, and so she will be a discouraged adult. Similarly, a boy whose parents are extremely severe and rigid, who take advantage of their physical or psychological superiority, neglecting or maltreating him, will not achieve a positive self-esteem either, because he has few possibilities to experience his value as a person.

But of course, 'anything can also be different', as Adler used to say. We have mentioned the 'opinion', the personal standpoint everybody, every child and every adult, adopts with respect to experiences. A child with a handicap may want to be healthy but may feel as loved and as much a part of the family as his sister. A pampered child may be able to work out a positive self-image and overcome her difficulties and learn how to make it by herself. Alternatively, a person with Social Interest may also want to be as rich as his neighbour or as pretty as her best friend and will probably make certain efforts to improve in the desired direction. And someone ill-treated in childhood may always have to bear the effects of such overburdening situations. But they will not question their worthiness and value as a human being.

Compensation and overcompensation

Let us study the case of a child who does not receive enough caring or is treated with extreme severity. Any expression of healthy self-esteem is repressed; most of his wishes are denied, maybe he is also neglected. Or his mother simply is single, has to work a lot and is too busy to attend to his needs adequately, although she does her best. But sometimes she is over-strained or anxious and unable to react positively to her son when he tries to get her attention. As a consequence, the boy has few possibilities to develop a strong, active, and assertive self-image that enables him to express his needs and achieve the adequate quantity of attention and caring. The direct way 'up' is forbidden and the boy becomes discouraged. As a consequence, he will probably try out more indirect ways to get what he wants, more strange and complicated manoeuvres. If mother does not react when he simply wants to play with her, she might come when he cries. He may also try out temper tantrums or aggressiveness. By means of trial and error he will find out how to get his mother's attention and he will learn to re-finalise his initial weakness into indirect power. Children can use active ways (temper tantrums, hitting, kicking, insulting) or more passive ways (crying, shyness, etc.) to make the adult be at their command.

Adler stated:

> Whether the neurotic dominates by bullying or by whining will depend on his training: he will choose the device which he has tested best and found most effective for his purposes. Sometimes, if he is dissatisfied with one method, he will try the other. In either case the goal is the same – to gain a feeling of superiority without working to improve the situation. The discouraged child who finds that he can tyrannise best by tears will be a cry-baby; and a direct line of development leads from the cry-baby to the adult depressed patient. Tears and complaints – the means which I have called 'water power' – can be an extremely useful weapon for disturbing co-operation and reducing others to a condition of slavery.
>
> Ansbacher and Ansbacher 1956: 288

Of course we would not deny that the babies' crying is useful and necessary for their physical and emotional survival and development. But if children learn that any time they cry, even when they do not need anything, their parents come immediately, they may begin to feel a wondrous power over them.

Adler explained Freud's concept of 'oedipal complex' in the following way. A boy with oedipal complex is, in his view, only a boy who is extremely pampered by his mother. This boy has developed the conviction that all his whims have to be satisfied immediately, and so, he will never learn to get acknowledgement, appreciation, and love by giving the same to others. As an adult, this boy is at risk of staying his mummy's darling. And for his wife he may try to choose a girl with the disposition to serve him as well as his mother did. Adler called this the 'pampered Life Style'. Later in life, these individuals show extreme discouragement, continuous hesitation, impatience, over-sensitivity, exaggerated need for support, etc.

Although these pampered children apparently achieve a certain power over their parents, deep down in their hearts – i.e. unconsciously – they know how weak they are. If mummy dies or refuses to put me in the centre of her life, how can I go on by myself? They are extremely afraid of things changing. And so, the fictionate goal of these discouraged children and adults is to banish a possible failure. On one hand, they know they are weak and feel inferior; on the other, overcoming this weakness and inferiority would mean starting to struggle, to try to make it on their own, to give up their pampered Life Style. Since this is difficult and since they have little experience of over-coming obstacles, they prefer to stay where they are, because this is more comfortable and less risky. So these discouraged people develop fictions that allow them to escape from their inferiority feelings; at the same time, these fictions provide them with excuses for not giving up their comfortable, pam-pered Life Style. The process of tendentious apperception is a good means to perceive the world in a way that puts both opposites together. What is con-sidered useful for the individual's purposes is perceived and processed, and what is not, is neglected or distorted in the functioning of the fictionate goal.

More than only tendentious apperceptions, these people develop what Adler called 'a **private logic**'. We all more or less have a private logic – hidden or unconscious reasons for feeling, thinking, and behaving as we do. But with the neurotic, these reasons may be more hidden, harder to find, and function in a more self-defeating way. Adler's concept of private logic (or 'private sense') also refers to a way of interpreting reality as quite different from the way most people do. The perception of neurotic people is different from 'common sense', where common sense is the most current beliefs, percep-tions, interpretations in a specific society. Adler (1931) gives us the example of the leader of a religious sect who proclaimed that the end of the world was due on Wednesday. Wednesday came, but not the end of the world. Instead of revising her beliefs and assuming her error, she felt that she had to maintain her infallible authority in order not to lose her position as a leader. So when she was accused of having made a false prediction, she proclaimed that 'my Wednesday is not your Wednesday'. This private meaning cannot be shared with others who are not members of the sect. It is not 'common sense'. But since none of the possible outcomes can disconfirm the prediction, it has the advantage of being unassailable.

Striving for superiority and safeguarding behaviour

An adequate compensation for inferiority feelings like those we have described would represent an active coping with the situation that requires both courage and effort. The kind of efforts that lead to an adequate compensation are those which respect Social Interest and which were called 'useful efforts' by Adler, because they are not only useful for the individual but also for other people (the community). We can call efforts that are consistent with Social Interest '**striving for perfection**', though 'perfection' may not be a good expression, because it has the connotation of something absolutely that exists and can be achieved. Perfection means that there is an ideal of personal and social perfection that can serve us as a guiding line to fix the direction we are pursuing, but we must be aware that this absolute ideal can never be attained. Striving for perfection would be the positive side of compensation and implies achieving a feeling of equality, of equal worth, self-esteem and esteem of others.

But in the case of discouraged individuals, the overcoming of inferiority feelings goes along with a striving for power. For these people, it is not enough to be equally as good as others. They want to be better. In order to stop feeling inferior they need to feel superior and have – real or imaginary – power over others. We call this 'overcompensation', because its purpose is not to match others, but to be more than they are. To overcome inferiority, these people apply 'useless' means. '**Useless**' does not mean 'in vain', since discouraged individuals usually really manage to feel superior, at least for some time. But in the Adlerian view, these people's efforts are useless for the community and ultimately for themselves, because they gravitate to the '**wasting side of life**'.

For example, our pampered young boy turns into an adult who believes that all women, especially the woman he wants to marry, must please him and do his will, just as his mother did; consequently, he will probably marry a girl whom he considers to be compliant and submissive. He will probably exert power over her and she will do his will, at least in the first years of the marriage, and so he manages to keep his inferiority feelings under control. But he contributes nothing to her and nothing to society, so his efforts are, in the Adlerian sense, 'useless'. More than that, his striving for power may turn against him. Few modern women accept male superiority without questioning, and so partnership problems may arise. Or other things may happen which put his weak inner harmony into doubt. This is the beginning of neurosis.

Any symptom or any psychological problem is, in the Adlerian view, a particular manifestation of (over)compensating for inferiority feeling with striving for power. Even when the individual suffers from his problems (which is usually the case, as in anxiety, depression, etc.), neurosis is an attempt to reduce inferiority feelings; in this sense, the neurosis is an excuse, a pretext, for not complying with one's human duty: that of Social Interest. We insist on the point, that these 'neurotic manoeuvres' with which the individual evades his or her responsibility are not a conscious act – if they were, it would be simulation and would not be credible for other people in most cases. They are aspects of human psychology that develop tacitly and out of the person's understanding. It is usually in therapy when these aspects come to light. What is conscious for the patient is the function of the symptom as an **excuse** ('I want, but I can't'); the unconscious or hidden aspect of the symptom is called **safeguarding**. The neurotic symptom has the function of safeguarding the patient from the experience of his or her inferiority feelings, similar to what in Psychoanalysis is called 'neurotic defence'. Adler distinguishes a variety of safeguarding behaviours, mainly aggression and distance. Clark (1999, 2000) describes four categories of safeguarding behaviour: distancing complex, hesitating attitude, detouring around, and narrowed path of approach. Another frequently used way of avoiding inferiority feelings is to depreciate others. Just like in the fable of the fox and the sour grapes, the neurotic depreciates (i.e. has **depreciation tendencies** towards) what he cannot get or those with whom he cannot compete. Making fun of the spouse's weak points is a common means of safeguarding oneself against feeling inferior to him or her. Another common trick is the overt or veiled accusation of others. An overt accusation would be to blame others (usually a family member) for one's misfortunes. In the case of psychopathology, the accusation is done by means of the neurotic symptom, and the victim of this kind of aggression usually is the family member who suffers most from the patient's problems. There are many unhappy marriages where couples refuse to get divorced and that are maintained by the partners' continued accusations against each other. Depression, in Adler's view, is often a veiled accusation and revenge against the spouse or the family.

Self-accusation and feelings of guilt can also be effective safeguarding devices (cursing oneself, self-torture, suicide, etc.). This may seem strange, because it is more difficult to detect the aggression behind these behaviours. Juan, a patient of one of us (UO), had developed a severe clinical depression and continuously tortured his wife with his feelings of guilt and unworthiness because he had been going with prostitutes repeatedly during the first years of their marriage. His wife had long forgiven him his 'sins'; she was not even terribly concerned about this fact. Furthermore, she herself never was much interested in sex, and the couple slept in different rooms. With his depression, the patient was now taking his revenge for all those years with only sporadic intercourse.

Safeguarding behaviour is also expressed through what Adler called the **'hesitating attitude'**, a movement back and forth, a standstill, or even a moving backwards. These individuals waste their time with useless activities, they find obstacles and difficulties in everything, they are full of doubts and scruples, they have difficulties making decisions and coming to terms with life situations. It is the typical 'if' attitude: 'If I didn't suffer from insomnia, I would be able to . . .'. The net effect of the hesitating attitude is to preclude people's useful engagements in meeting the tasks of work, relationship, and community. The psychological movement required by pursuing these tasks is substantially blunted as a way of preserving a fragile sense of competency and mastery, fleeting though it may be.

This conceptualisation of psychological problems as safeguarding and as excuse-making is unique in Adlerian therapy. No other psychotherapeutic school shares this idea, at least not to this degree. We find this notion in concepts like 'secondary benefit of the illness', which talks about the advantages that psychologically disturbed people can take of their situation: the agoraphobic does not need to go to work, the depressive enjoys the preoccupation and caring of her family members, the stressed manager with heart problems is treated with delicacy by his wife and is excused from his duties in the family household, etc. But in an Adlerian view, this secondary benefit is a self-perpetuating 'cause', or more exactly: the main purpose of the problem. If the individual resolves the problem he wants to avoid, the symptom disappears or should at least improve.

This is intuitively understandable in the case of psychosomatic problems. We can imagine a case of a woman with migraine headaches. She may have a genetic predisposition for suffering from migraines or she may have some hormonal dysfunctions that make her prone to have migraines during menstruation. Or perhaps there is no physical basis at all. For a few years she has been having severe headaches every now and then, but now they are getting worse. In psychotherapy we find out that the headaches have coincided with her husband's frequent travelling for business reasons. On some occasions her husband had to cancel his trips because she needed attention during her headache episodes. When we investigate further, we may find that both have been having marital problems for some years, due to an affair he once had during a business trip. So we can put forward the hypothesis that the fictionate (unconscious) goal of the woman's migraine is to make her husband stay, thus reducing the possibility of another infidelity. The headaches are an excuse for making her husband stay at her side. The safeguarding is to avoid feelings of inferiority, loneliness, and helplessness.

Of course, she is not aware of her purposes, she is only aware of her terrible headaches. If she were feigning, her purpose would be too obvious – unless she was a really good actor – and her husband would not believe her, nor would the doctors. Her 'trick' would not work. It works only because she pays the price of suffering. And suffering is always the price – the 'costs of the war' in Adler's words – people have to pay for their lack of Social Interest. If this woman had more Social Interest and felt more encouraged, she would probably try to solve her marital problems directly: by talking with her husband or, if he is not prepared to solve the problems together with her, by getting divorced. But this would be much more complicated, would require different and stronger efforts and the ordeal of going through uncomfortable and troubling situations. In a way, it is easier to have headaches, though the price is higher in the long run. Adler used to say that these people, instead of struggling to resolve their real problems, fight a battle in a sideline theatre of war. Just like in the anecdote of the man who has lost a coin at night in a dark street; instead of searching for the coin where he lost it, he steps several feet away because there is a street lamp that sheds light so that he can see. Our woman with headaches fights a battle on a sideline, because in her (unconscious!) view, it is easier to win here than on the real battlefield. If she enters into overt arguments with her husband it might be difficult for her to obtain what she wants. She may even be compelled to recognise her own faults. Or her husband may insist on travelling and maybe also on having affairs. Being confronted with his infidelity, he may argue that it is preferable to get divorced, etc. But with her symptoms she can simply make him stay at her side. She has power over him. And this is the function of the neurotic symptom: to avoid feelings of inferiority, to achieve superiority and to maintain a false sense of security.

When people suffer from inferiority feelings they tend to be especially sensitive to the manifestations of others; their distorted perception makes them interpret comments of others as if they were real or imaginary denigrations. A person with neurotic disposition is less able to interact with other people in a natural, spontaneous way. Quite on the contrary, in order to avoid more inferiority feelings, they try to attain triumph over others. Adler described characters (personality traits) such as cruelty, stinginess, envy, vindictiveness, spitefulness, etc. as the typical traits of a person with a 'ruling type' of neurotic disposition. These people may not have clinical psychopathological symptoms, but are prone to develop them under certain circumstances. And even when they do not, they are individuals with very low Social Interest, and in the strictest Adlerian sense not mentally healthy. These personality traits are safeguarding devices against impinging feelings of inferiority. To raise one's emotional status, the individual has to despise others, as the only possible measure to maintain one's self-esteem. We see clearly the differences from the classical Freudian view: neurosis is not a fight between intra-psychic instances, but the striving for superiority of an individual who, at the bottom of his heart, feels inferior. 'Neurosis', i.e. any psychological problem or disorder – depression, anxiety, psychosomatic problems, adaptation problems, even delinquency – is, in Adlerian terms, a security measure against the unbearable fear of being less than others.

Thus the striving for personal power is not the universal vital drive in human beings; it is its pathological expression, it is the neurotic reaction of an individual who feels humiliated and unable to maintain an adequate level of self-esteem and equal worth with others under the usual circumstances of human life. Therefore, he or she has to aspire, in imagination, to an idea of infinite superiority, or godlike nature, as Adler once said. Striving for power, therefore, is not the expression of a real existing power in the context of the individual's group, family or society. On the contrary, it is an expression of felt powerlessness, of personal insecurity, of incapacity for coping with the tasks of life. An individual who is psychologically healthy may feel 'powerful', but not with respect to other people, rather with respect to the demands of human existence.

The neurotic's attitude is that of 'yes–but'. The 'yes' expresses the individual's awareness of the social demands ('I should . . .'), while the 'but' is the alibi, which prevents him from complying with them ('. . . but I can't because . . .'). This excuse is different from individual to individual, depending on their particular fictions (the 'because' is what is different). The weaker the 'yes' and the stronger the 'but', the more difficult it is to change these attitudes. We have commented several times that this 'but', the excuse, is an unconscious attitude. We have to bear that in mind, because a superficial understanding of Individual Psychology may give the impression that Adlerians consider neurosis to be a vice or a lack of morality, and this is not the case.

To safeguard their self-esteem and self-image as a 'person with good will' and with the best intentions, the 'but' is disguised as a trick, a self-deceiving arrangement in the twilight of consciousness: 'Yes, I want to be a great professional, but I always have this anxiety, so I can't take the exams.' Or: 'If I hadn't these panic attacks before an exam, I would be an excellent pupil.' Instead of struggling in the area of academic success and risking possible failure, this individual, for fear of failure, fights on a sideline battlefield. This allows him not only to avoid confrontation with hard work and possible disappointment, but also to enjoy the compassion or even care of others because he feels so bad. If the individual had more successfully engaged the tasks of work and community, perhaps he would stop struggling for self-elevation and searching for easy acknowledgement. In the case of the aforementioned patient, he would dedicate his efforts to his studies. Or, if he lacked intellectual capacity, to another satisfactory occupation.

Suffering is the patient's justification for his lack of engagement in life tasks and which disguises his striving for superiority. These individuals, obviously, cannot allow themselves to enjoy their desire for power and their looking down on others, because this would mean that they have to stop considering themselves to be 'a good person'. That is why they prefer to suffer. We must again emphasise that we are talking about unconscious or 'semi-conscious' processes; these people are not crooks, but 'guilty–innocent' at the same time. Psychotherapy has to help them see what they did not want to see before, what they do not know yet, because they had their eyes shut in face of the consequences. Obviously, we do not simply 'tell' them their 'faults' and exhort them to 'care a bit more for others' or to 'face their real problems'. Before all, there is encouragement: the therapist has to encourage the patient to develop a healthy degree of self-esteem.

We have seen that behind the patient's sufferings, there is a striving for superiority. In some cases, like the case of the woman with headaches, this seems obvious even to psychologists who are not trained in the Adlerian method. It can at least be understood as a secondary benefit, i.e. the patient suffers, but obtains certain advantages that maintain the symptomatology. But what happens with cases of severe depression, where the suffering is so strong that not even the slightest advantage can be detected, and where there is even a risk of suicide? Students often ask us this question and think that it is impossible that such a person should be striving for superiority. But we maintain that even in most cases of severe depression, a striving for superiority can be found: the depressive patient is unable to think of anyone other than himself. Many depressive patients are unable to do their work, to care for their children, etc., and their family members or others must do it for them. They do not have to care for anything that is not them.

As we have said before, the idea of the symptom as excuse is unique to Adlerian Psychology and can only be found in an embryonic form in other therapy orientations. Although there is an increasing tendency in other psychotherapies (e.g. in constructivist psychotherapy) for emphasising the patient's own responsibility for his or her symptoms, in general, they tend to exonerate the patient and to blame the conditions under which he or she was raised (parents, environment, education style, society, etc.). Understanding symptoms as something that are my parents' or the society's fault allow me to think that I am not responsible for my problems ('I am anxiety-ridden, because my father battered me'), nor for my failures ('I could not attend university because my father . . .'), and not even for my criminal acts ('I steal because I have always been poor and society has to give me now what should be mine'). The patient, instead of being responsible for what happens, ultimately is seen as a victim of circumstances.

The apparent divergence of conscious acts and unconscious attitudes is explained by the concept of finality. Humans do what they – unconsciously – aspire to and act according to their 'secret' fictional goals and life plans. One of us (UO) treated a young woman who was about to marry. A severe attack of colitis the day before forced her to postpone the wedding. She married later anyway, but developed repeated gastroenterological problems. In psychotherapy she began to see a connection between her symptoms and the relationship with her husband with whom she was unhappy. Later she argued that the colitis attack might have been an attempt by 'her unconscious' at not getting married, because she should have known that her boyfriend was not an adequate husband for her.

In summary, neurotic disposition and fully developed neuroses are born of inferiority feelings, overcompensated by strivings for superiority, and psychopathological symptoms are safeguarding devices that impede the patients from realising these inferiority feelings and from acting according to Social Interest, because this would imply a greater effort than they think they are capable of. Suffering is the price they pay. Of course, the patients suffer and want to be cured or at least symptom-free; therefore they see a doctor or undergo psychotherapy. But what they do not realise consciously at that moment is that their symptoms disguise another, apparently more severe pain: the pain of feeling inferior, the pain of feeling worthless, the pain of being a failure, the pain of being unloved or unlovable.

The neurotic fiction is a psychological, self-deceiving trick to compensate for inferiority feelings, and at the same time, it provides pleasant feelings (of transcendence and mastery) for the individual who is in an unfavourable situation. The stronger the inferiority feeling ('inferiority complex'), the more necessary is this safeguarding guiding line. Psychologically healthy people also have fictions which guide them and help them to cope with obstacles; but on one hand, these fictions are more or less guided by Social Interest and, on the other, they are only useful constructions that can be created and revised according to the person's needs. But in times of problems or personal insecurity, and in life transitions, such as puberty, people tend to revert more to their fictional guiding lines, because in all these situations, they have fewer resources to cope effectively with the problems; in new situations, new fictions have to be created, and this is a process that requires adaptation. After that, a healthy person has revised his or her fictions, has eventually construed new, more useful fictionate goals, and regained his or her psychological equilibrium. But the neurotic cling to their fictions like drowning people; they confer on them a reality that does not correspond to them (dogmatically maintaining them rather than changing them). Or they even try to make them real, which would, in an Adlerian view, correspond to psychosis. We have now come to the point to explain the concepts of neurosis and psychosis in greater detail.

The Adlerian model of psychopathology

Adler, in his publications before World War I, applied the general medical model to his theory of psychopathology and divided mental disorders, like other authors did, into neuroses and psychoses, according to their symptomatology. The term psychosis was used then in a way that is similar to its contemporary usage, mainly to describe schizophrenia and paranoia (today: delusional disorder). The 'neurotic disposition', as we have seen, is used for personality disorders or 'character flaws'. 'Neurosis' is used for everything else and thus represents a more loose categorisation of distress.

Today, the terms 'neurosis', and also to a certain degree that of 'psychosis', are used less frequently in discussion of psychopathology because psychologists and psychiatrists have refined and developed the taxonomy of mental disorders since the inception of Individual Psychology. Instead of neurosis, we would probably talk of 'psychological disorders' or simply 'psychological problems'. The current classification systems, such as the *Diagnostic and statistical manual of mental disorders* (DSM-IV) developed by the American

Psychiatric Association (1994), have elaborated more precise diagnoses based on the patient's symptoms.

The purpose of Adlerian therapy is to increase the likelihood that people will successfully engage in the tasks of life. This has been called the dynamic unity of mental disorders. Instead of addressing the psychological intervention to the syndrome, as in medicine, where treatment varies according to the specific symptoms and diseases, psychotherapy in Individual Psychology treats the patient as a whole. Basically it is not the specificity of the disorder that is particularly interesting to the Adlerian therapist, but the individuality of the patient. Nonetheless, the individual manifestation of the disturbance (the symptoms, such as anxiety, depression, drug abuse, psychosomatic disorders, etc.) should not to be ignored and must be addressed specifically in many cases; an increase in self-esteem does not necessarily lead to less smoking, for example.

In Adler's view, mental health and psychopathology are not dichotomous concepts; there is a continuous line from 'neurotic disposition' (sometimes also called 'the nervous character') to psychosis; from high Social Interest to high striving for superiority. A 'nervous individual' (e.g. an anxious individual) may have experienced a pampered family life as a child and, under adverse circumstances, may develop a manifest neurosis (anxiety disorder). If things get worse for this person the neurosis may transform into a persecutory ideation (psychosis). A person with neurotic disposition would be a basically healthy person with more or less pronounced psychological problems (mainly problems in relating with other people), but who leads a more or less normal life, and who may not seek psychotherapeutic help. Neurosis, in its strict sense, begins when the individual cannot stand the strain any more – the tension between his or her unsatisfactory state and the ideal self he or she dreams of.

Adler goes very far in his concept of neurosis and includes any socially deviant behaviour; criminals, alcoholics, homosexuals, prostitutes, and paedophiles, among others, are seen as neurotics. Some of Adler's concepts sound old-fashioned in the light of today's diagnostic terminology. We must take into account that although he can be seen as a precursor of a great deal of contemporary psychological thought, he was a child of his times. The conceptualisation of neurosis is only one aspect. Another aspect is his view of some manifestations of human behaviour. Congruent with the interpretation prevailing at the beginning of the 20th century, Adler considered homosexuality to be a mental disorder and prostitution to be a vice or a character flaw. Contemporary psychologists, however, do not view homosexuality as a mental disorder or as a cause for psychotherapy unless people present for therapy with specific problems related to their sexual preferences (e.g. ego dystonic homosexuality). The phenomenon of prostitution is studied under its social and political aspects; psychological help for both groups does not intend to 'cure' a supposed underlying neurosis, but to give support to these groups, to enable them to deal with the problems that secondarily arise from their condition.

On the other hand, psychological disorders are also subject to fashion. In Adler's and Freud's times, hysteria was the 'disorder of choice' for women of the bourgeoisie. Conversion symptoms were so frequent that they constituted the paradigm of neurosis and one of the basic objects of study in Psychoanalysis. Today, the classical hysterical symptoms can hardly be seen in psychiatry, whereas anorexia, depression and drug abuse seem to be more 'fashionable' now. There are external factors of the environment that promote certain behaviours. For instance, in former times women were supposed to be weak and less able to stand certain physical or psychological strain, whereas presently they have to possess slim and supple bodies, while at the same time they have to be tough and pursue a career. If weakness is what you are supposed to have, fainting is an admissible behaviour under certain circumstances, and when you are supposed to be slim, anorexia is, to a certain point, a condition tolerated by some people. These external factors underline the 'guilty–innocent' or 'semi-conscious' aspect of psychological disorder in the Adlerian view. Of course, neither the hysterical nor the anorexic woman is guilty, nor is she aware of her low Social Interest. But 'consciously–unconsciously' she chooses her symptoms according to what brings her the most benefit. And, probably, starving to near death gives her more serious attention and caring from her worried parents than would falling to the ground stiffly with her pelvis lifted up (the classical symptom of the 'hysterical arc'), a behaviour which would probably be dismissed as completely ridiculous.

Neurotic symptoms are also subject to the personal, social, and socioeconomic situation. We dare say that it is probably 'easier' for a man to develop agoraphobic symptoms and therefore stay away from work when his income is assured in spite of his illness, than it is for a man who must make his family's living by appearing daily at his workplace. Neurotics may have tried several possibilities before they make a decision (again: an **unconscious** decision) and settle for what works best for their purposes. The woman with headaches may have found out that an apparent medical illness is what makes her husband stay and care for her, more than her pleas would do.

But we cannot take this as a general aetiological rule. Although we may have a tendency to 'select' our particular symptomatology out of a variety of possibilities in a way that allows us to receive the maximum benefit at the same time as it guarantees us a minimum of functioning and responsibility in some area, the symptom choice follows more than one criterion and depends on possible 'organ inferiorities', learning experiences, milieu and environment, relationships with others, and – why not – chance.

In Chapter 1, we mentioned and explained another old-fashioned and unfortunate expression in Adlerian Psychology, the term of 'masculine protest', coined by Adler in his publication on 'Hermaphroditism in life and in neurosis'. The authors of the present book recommend de-emphasising this concept as a contemporary explanatory mechanism. Although masculine protest has heuristic value in illustrating the evolution of Adler's theory and can describe the feelings of inertness experienced by the oppressed, as a modern construct for describing distress it is probably unnecessary and somewhat misleading. We think that the other concepts of Adlerian Psychology are sufficient to explain neurotic behaviour in both males and females.

Nevertheless, differences in neurotic manifestations between men and women can still be observed. Due to the differences in sex roles, aggressive behaviour and striving for power are still more tolerated in men than in women. Parents tend to tolerate manifestations of aggressiveness and violence in boys more than they do in girls. On the other hand, crying and sulking, anxiousness, shyness, and vanity, are usually more accepted female behaviours. This means that, in order to strive for power, girls tend to use more indirect, more 'soft' means, such as crying, demonstrative weakness, shyness, etc. or being a 'princess'. For a boy, it is easier to get power by direct means, such as aggressiveness, dominance, etc., whereas a girl often obtains attention using what are stereotypically viewed as 'female tricks', such as coquettishness, sulking, demonstrative weakness, incapacity, or ignorance, fishing for compliments, asking for pity and compassion, etc. These behaviours are of course not inherent to the female sex, but the loophole of a girl who has learned that 'male' behaviour does not lead to the desired outcome. A boy who detects that willpower makes his parents succumb to his wishes will develop in the line of dominance, and a girl whose parents give her attention when she is weak will tend to use 'a woman's arms' when dealing with difficult situations. These circumstances can lead to two different manifestations of striving of superiority: the striving for power per se, and the striving for prestige or significance. The striving for power is represented by direct dominant behaviour, while the striving for significance is its softer, more traditionally 'female' variation: getting attention, commiseration, etc. As we have said before, obtaining someone else's pity is a way of exerting power over them.

To summarise the differences between neurotic disposition, neurosis and psychosis, Adler relies on the concept of fictions. Normal individuals are more or less aware that their fictionate goals are what they are: fictions. Their validity has to be contrasted with reality. They are able to give up a non-adaptive fiction and create more useful ones. The neurotics, in comparison, cling to their fictions, convert them into hypotheses, and confer on them an arbitrary reality value: fictions are taken not as metaphors, but literally. The psychotics go even further: they raise them to dogma and try to put them into practice. Adler gives an example of these three possibilities: the normal person acts 'as if' he could lose his money and takes preventive measure so that this will not happen (precaution); the neurotic acts as if he was losing his money (anxiety), and the psychotic individual thinks that he has actually lost his money (psychotic depression or delusion). In this sense, for Adler, psychosis is only an exaggerated degree of private logic that has been concretised into 'reality' and not something qualitatively different from normality.

Thus, for Adler, neurotic disposition, neurosis, and psychosis all have a common aetiology: underdeveloped, unsuccessful attempts to meet the three tasks of life and decreased Social Interest as an indicator of this. He has been severely criticised for this apparent oversimplification by Freud and other authors. Freud wrote:

> Whether a person is a homosexual, or a necrophilist, or an anxiety-ridden hysteric, or a shut-in obsessional, or a raving madman – in every case the Individual Psychologist of the Adlerian persuasion will assign as the motive force of his condition the fact that he wants to assert himself, to overcompensate for his inferiority, to be on top, to move over from the feminine to the masculine line.
>
> Freud, quoted in Ansbacher and Ansbacher 1956: 301

Adlerian explanations of selected mental disorders

As we have repeatedly mentioned, in the Adlerian view of psychopathology all neuroses have a common aetiology. This is precisely what distinguishes psychotherapy from the medical model: in medicine, the ætiological diagnosis is more important in determining the treatment procedure. In many contemporary psychotherapeutic orientations no diagnoses are made (e.g. in Rogerian therapy, in constructivist approaches, etc.) or only in order to guarantee fluent communication between professionals (e.g. psychotherapists and psychiatrists). The prevailing medical model is seen as irrelevant in psychotherapy, as it is the person as a whole who has to be treated and not a 'disease'. There are other contemporary models to explain mental illness, usually summarised under the 'biopsychosocial' model. They represent an interesting attempt at conceptualising mental disorders in their biological, psychological, and social dimensions (for its application in Adlerian therapy, see Sperry 1999). Sperry and other authors have also argued that the DSM-IV classification system with its multiaxial assessment can effectively be used in Adlerian therapy (Sperry 1999, Sperry and Carlson 1996). In this sense, axis I of the DSM-IV ('clinical disorder') would represent the patient's presenting problems, while axis II ('personality disorder') has to do with the patient's Life Style. Axis III ('general medical conditions') can give information about organ inferiorities, axis IV 'psychosocial and environmental problems') about the individual's specific overburdening situations, and axis V ('global assessment of functioning – GAF') would represent the individual's functioning with respect to the life tasks (Dinkmeyer, Jr and Sperry 2000). As individual psychologists, we have to keep all these dimensions in mind. We also have to take the neurophysiological factors into account and not restrict ourselves to reducing the patient's inferiority feelings. A timely psychophar-macological intervention can be of great help in many neurotic (e.g. depressed) patients.

But traditionally, Adlerians do not insist on psychiatric diagnostic classifi-cations with their patients, since Adlerian theory is not based on a medical or disease model but on a growth model, which tends to view the dysfunctional individual as discouraged rather than mentally ill (Mosak 1989). For Adler-ians, it usually is of higher importance to assess the individual's Life Style than to make a clinical diagnosis of the disorder. Mosak (1971a) presented a typology of fourteen basic Life Styles or personality types and related them to DSM diagnostic categories, but usually, only four are commonly described: getters, pleasers, rulers, and controllers. Other authors prefer to talk of 'personality priorities' (Kefir 1971), and the Langenfeld Inventory of Personality Priorities (LIPP) by Langenfeld (Langenfeld and Main 1983) has been designed to identify five priority themes: pleasing, achieving, outdoing, detaching, and avoiding. Kutchins, Curlette and Kern (1997) have made an attempt to evaluate the relationship between Life Style themes and personal-ity priorities. There are also tendencies to conceptualise Life Style not as something people "possess" (typological view of personality), but as a per-sonal narrative, the characteristic way of the individual to handle life. In this sense, Life Style can be viewed as the individual's "dominant story" (Disque and Bitter 1998).

Despite his idea of the dynamic unity of mental disorders, Adler did give attention to some specific disorders and discussed their aetiology from the perspective of Individual Psychology. Although the taxonomy of disorders has been much further refined since the development of Individual Psychology, and more modern theories of intervention have emerged, Adler's conceptualisations of different life problems still possess heuristic value. In the following we will critically analyse some of the most frequent mental disorders in the light of contemporary Adlerian Psychology.

Psychosomatic disorders

Psychosomatic disorders are normally expressed as physical symptoms (e.g. aches, pains, tingling, numbness, etc.) without a clear organic cause. Instead, psychological distress is canalised and expressed through bodily symptoms. Classical psychosomatic distress can manifest through symptoms expressed by the heart, the stomach and the bowels, the urinary tract, the muscles (pain caused by tension, especially headache), respiration and sleep (insomnia). Because it is very difficult, even unlikely in some cases, to identify an organic factor that explains the patient's problems sufficiently, physicians often tend to diagnose a 'psychosomatic disorder', but we should be careful, because many of these problems probably do have a medical origin, although it has not been detected with standard and current diagnostic methods. For example, some stomach ulcers that a few years ago were classified as 'psycho-somatic' and seen as due to the patient's stressful life situation, workload, or family problems have now proved to be an infectious disease caused by a bacterium. That does not mean, of course, that environmental factors, stress and existing medical problems cannot aggravate these troubles. In many cases, we can suppose an 'organ inferiority' (genetic disposition, functional disorder, minor anatomic peculiarities, etc.) as the place of least resistance, where psychological problems find their easiest way to express themselves in the body. In situations of increased subjective inferiority, people experience highly unpleasant feelings together with a general arousal of the nervous systems. If the unpleasant situation continues or is experienced repeatedly, the 'inferior' organ, which is affected the most by this psychophysiological arousal, may cease to operate normally and begin to show signs of disease or disorder. It refuses to go on with its normal activity and reacts with a func-tional disorder; if the stress continues, even a permanent anatomical or physiological change can occur. This constitutes the specific psychosomatic disorder for that patient.

These assumptions are not inconsistent with most contemporary theories of psychosomatic disorder. But Adler went even further and talked about a specific 'organ dialect'. He supposed that every organ is capable of expressing the patient's emotions and feelings, and, on the other hand, the patient expresses his or her psychological troubles by certain organs that are most likely to represent his or her particular problem. People 'choose' their organ in a certain way. A child who is obedient during the day but wets her bed at night may manifest her desire for rebellion against her parents by 'choosing' her bladder to express her feelings.

For Adler, psychosomatic pain was an expression of jealousy and desire; insomnia, of ambition; gynaecological troubles, of the woman's masculine protest. It may be common sense to interpret frigidity or vaginal spasm as related to a woman's partnership problems. But interpreting abdominal pain or thoracic oppression as defences against pregnancy would mean, in our view, going much too far without additional specific indicators in a psycho-therapy case to warrant such a conclusion. Overall, the authors of this book advise therapists to be very careful in relying on pat, ready-made explanations for what appear to be psychosomatic problems.

For the general practitioner and even the medical specialist it is sometimes quite difficult to determine whether the patient's complaints are due to a medical disorder difficult to diagnose or whether they are of psychological origin. Or to what degree organic dysfunction and psychological reactions are overlapped. Traditionally, Adlerians use 'the Question' (Dreikurs 1997) to differentiate between both factors. They ask the patient: 'What would you do or what would be different if you hadn't these symptoms (headache, insomnia, etc.)?' If the patient replies that nothing in his or her life would change in particular, but he or she would just feel better, then the problems are more likely to stem from medical origins. If the patients replies with something like: 'Then I would be able to pass my exams/get married/do better at my job/etc.', then the symptom would be seen as the excuse for what the discouraged patient wants to avoid (work for the exams/find a spouse/work for professional promotion) and the symptom is seen as psychosomatic. But here again, the medical doctor or psychotherapist must be very careful. Even if the symptom is an excuse for something that the patient does not want to face, the avoided situation or dilemma may be so disguised that no particular explanation can be given. On the other hand, medical diseases can also provoke all those impediments the patient mentions as a reply to the Question: if you have a headache caused by a brain tumour, you will most probably be unable to pass your exams, get married, or do better at your job. Furthermore, even psychosomatic disorders may require intense medical attention (stomach ulcer, tachycardia, etc.). And finally, some organic disturbances due to psychosomatic problems tend to become autonomous, i.e. they persist even when the psychological problems that initiated them have been resolved. Clinical symptoms, after some time of 'training', continue even in the absence of the factor that provoked them initially. For instance, headaches due to a permanent muscular tension can persist even when the psychological tension is relieved and when the woman has resolved her marital problems, because the neck muscles have acquired chronic contractions and, thus, an organic lesion. Similarly, the phobic reaction takes place even when the phobic stimulus is absent; the stomach ulcer, once present, does not disappear when the patient is less overworked. That is why in therapy we must not only rely on fostering Social Interest and personal growth; medical and pharmacological intervention together with cognitive-behavioural or other techniques to reduce symptoms may be helpful and necessary in many cases.

Thus what for Adler was the paradigm of neurotic disorder and on which he founded his whole theory of compensation and overcompensation is actually what we nowadays call psychosomatic problems. The role of the autonomic nervous system in the aetiology of psychosomatic disorders is now well documented and can be regarded as evidence for at least a part of Adler's theory.

A case example:
Gloria, a woman of 34, came to psychotherapy because of intestinal problems. She presented recurring diarrhoea and felt an urge to go to the bathroom in situations where it was difficult to go (on the bus, in work meetings, in social situations). She was shy and did not make any special effort to present herself in an attractive way. She commented that she would like to have a relationship with a male but except for one

failed attempt, she never had sexual relationships and had never fallen in love. Her symptomatology was related to her fears of sexual contact, but her looking for a male friend or husband was apparently more due to the perceived pressure of society than to her own wish. Psychotherapy focused on her problems with relationships (male and female) rather than on her bowels, and her symptoms diminished steadily while her social skills improved. After 15 months of therapy she decided that she was a person with no sexual desire and that she wanted to stay single. Rather, she would intensify her friendships (mainly female) as a means of not feeling lonely. At the end of the therapy process, she was symptom-free. Here, one could argue that having no sexual desire does not mean being symptom-free, as the lack of sexual desire could be considered as a pathology. In an Adlerian sense, the abstention from partnership and sex could also be interpreted as not complying with one of the three life tasks. But in the view of the American Psychiatric Association, a symptom is considered to be clinically important only if it causes suffering or impairment in the individual (or harm to other people). This seemed not the case with Gloria. She did fine with her work, friends, and family of origin, and she enjoyed taking care of her nephews and nieces as often as possible.

Anxiety disorders

Anxiety disorder is the common denominator of a variety of problems: panic attacks, agoraphobia, phobias, post-traumatic stress disorder, and also obsessive-compulsive disorder in the cases where anxiety is the predominant feature and the compulsions are directed to reducing this anxiety. In the Adlerian view, anxiety arises when feelings of inferiority become predominant. According to Adler, anxiety is used to put psychological distance between the individual and his or her life task, in order to maintain self-esteem when the person is at risk of defeat. It is the classical motivator of the hesitating attitude.

Adler viewed agoraphobia, for example, as an attempt to get help from other people (usually family members), to make them stay at home, and to make them accompany the patient anywhere he or she goes. Adler observed that agoraphobics lose their fear when they are at home or when other people accompany them. When a person is no longer able to leave his room, everything must be subordinated to his anxiety; everybody must come and see him, while he is excused from having to go anywhere.

Two case examples:

Maria suffers from severe, long-term agoraphobia, together with dizziness. She is now in her late fifties and had not been able to leave her house by herself for years, but in the little Spanish village where she lives she always finds a friendly neighbour to walk her to the market place and back home. While walking and shopping she has lively conversations with the accompanying neighbour and other villagers. She is known to nearly everybody in the village and, despite her peculiar character, apparently everybody likes her. The therapeutic interview revealed that she is unhappy with her uncaring and unloving husband who had always despised her. Her adult son still lives with them but adopts his father's position with respect to his mother. Maria comments in therapy that she grew up in this village as the daughter of 'red' parents (former combatants of the Spanish communist government, defeated by the general and later Spanish dictator Franco). She is intelligent, but never received an adequate education. She went to a school run by Catholic pro-Franco nuns who not only used to express their overt hatred against the daughter of 'rojos', but also denied her learning material and the school milk. Nobody ever took her side. These recollections explain her opinion of herself as an underprivileged person with no rights. Although she always felt inclined to the female sex, she married a man from the village, because this is what she was supposed to do, and worked in a local textile factory. For many years she has been wanting to get divorced, but her precarious economic situation prevented her from carrying out her plans. So there is an apparent contradiction between her wishing to leave her husband and her illness that forces her to stay at home. We can interpret her agoraphobia as a (not incomprehensible) excuse for not putting into effect her desire for living alone, since this would mean having to face and to resolve many known and unknown problems. It would also mean facing what has been very difficult to do for Spanish women of her generation: getting divorced. On the other hand, her symptoms provide her with a great deal of contact and affection from other people who help her. While she is being accompanied, she has the possibility of getting attention and power over the accompanying people who patiently adapt their paces to hers and gently listen to her sorrows. In therapy, which is still ongoing, we are working on self-esteem, assertiveness with respect to her husband and son, and personally satisfying activities (diary writing, attending the needlework group of the village, etc.) rather than revealing to her the unconscious purpose of her symptoms, because she is probably not prepared to accept it for the time being. Additionally, a trained family helper from the village participates in a systematic exposition programme. Maria is constantly improving and is now able to walk alone to the local market place and to the general practitioner.

Manuel is a 49-year-old accountant with a variety of phobic symptoms and panic attacks. Though he is intellectually gifted, he restricts himself to working in a little company, because a better job would mean using the subway to go to work. He was raised by his father, because his mother had left the family one day, without explanation; he remembers watching her leaving the house with her baggage. His father never showed any sign of love and caring, and the environment was not very stimulating either. In therapy, we could elaborate the meaning of his being a 'poor abandoned child' for his symptoms and see how he used them to exert a certain power over his wife (who had to drive the car, who had to take care of things he could not do because he was afraid, etc.). But a long-term, exposure-based training was necessary to enable him to use the public transport system and to alleviate his panic attacks.

Obsessive-compulsive disorder

Compulsion neurosis (today: obsessive-compulsive disorder) is usually characterised by obsessive thoughts and/or by compulsive acts, which cannot be stopped voluntarily by the patient, e.g. to wash one's hands incessantly, to count numbers or signs or objects over and over again, to pray hundreds of times a day, to control again and again, etc. Obsessive-compulsive patients feel compelled to do these obviously absurd acts, which they themselves recognise as strange, but they must perform them in order to avoid anxiety. For Adler, this is again a

> secondary field of action, where [the patient] expends all his energies instead of devoting them to solving his primary problem. Like a veritable Don Quixote he fights windmills, concerning himself with matters, which have no proper place in our social world, and only serve to dally away time.

> Ansbacher and Ansbacher 1956: 306

A case example:
Elena is a 36-year-old homemaker with a 4-year-old son. She was expecting another baby when she came to therapy, urged and accompanied by her husband who complained that she spent all the day cleaning the house. According to her, she had to spend so much time in cleaning, washing, airing, and tidying up the house, because 'it smells strange'. She was so convinced of the bad smell that family members who came to visit her could not convince her to the contrary. Her husband, who took a shower twice a day, also 'smelled'. Her compulsive cleaning had made her give up nearly every other activity. While she had been taking neuroleptics previously her symptoms were better, but her pregnancy now forbade pharmacotherapy. Unfortunately, she had very little insight into her symptoms; her compulsive disorder was of the delusional kind, which meant that she was not motivated to undergo therapy because the bad odour was real for her (though to nobody else). Eventually, she agreed to do a few sessions together with her husband. At the same time, we developed behavioural strategies to fight the compulsion to clean (mainly engaging in other activities incompatible with cleaning). This was difficult because she hardly had any interests apart from keeping the house. We found that she felt disappointed by her husband who, according to her, did not live up to the expectations she had put in him (professional success and income). So the compulsive symptoms can be seen as expressing the disdain she felt for her husband and as an excuse for not being the wife he had wanted her to be (or for not getting divorced, if she really had the impression that her husband was not adequate for her). Over time she improved, but then stopped coming to therapy, complaining that the sessions had not made the house stop smelling. In such a case, pharmacotherapy prior to or simultaneous with psychotherapy is recommended.

Depression

In the DSM-IV, the main symptoms of clinical depression are depressed mood during the whole (or nearly the whole) day, and decreases in the level of interest in daily activities and in the capacity to feel pleasure. These symptoms must have persisted for several weeks and represent a change with respect to the patient's former behaviour. Milder forms of depressive disorders comprise dysthymia (i.e. low-grade depressive symptoms for at least 2 years) and cyclothymia (mood fluctuations less intense and severe than in bipolar disorders). Adler, who used the then current expression 'melancholia' to describe this kind of affective disorder, seems to place particular responsibility on patients for the development and maintenance of the disorder. In his own words:

> Melancholia develops in individuals whose method of living has from early childhood on been dependent upon the achievements and the support of others. Such individuals will always try to lean on others and will not scorn the use of exaggerated hints at their own inadequacy to force the support, adjustment, and submissiveness of others. When a difficulty arises, they will evade the main issue, the continuation of their development, or even the adherence to their own sphere of action. According to the melancholic perspective, life resembles a difficult and enormous hazard, the preponderant majority of men are hostile, and the world consists of uncomfortable obstacles. By concretising their subjective inferiority feeling, melancholiacs openly or implicitly raise the claim to a higher 'disability compensation'.
>
> Ansbacher and Ansbacher 1956: 319

In depression, inferiority feelings are overt and apparently the predominant feature of the disorder, while the striving for superiority cannot be detected so easily. Feelings of culpability and delusional ideas are, in fact, often present in severe clinical depression. The fact that depressive patients often claim their worthlessness and guiltiness makes it sometimes difficult for psychotherapists to see the aggression that lies behind their dramatically pessimistic views. But if we observe patients who are so deeply depressed that they even have problems getting out of bed in the morning, we can often identify a particular relationship with their relatives who are committed to take care of them and do their tasks for them. Depressive patients have difficulties doing things by themselves, they rely on others, and their thoughts only revolve around themselves and how bad they feel, how guilty they are, how much bad luck they have always had, and how unlucky they have been in all their life, while their family members constantly try to convince them of the contrary. Suicidal ideas are often menaces used to reinforce the family's efforts, or fantasies of grandiosity and revenge. The patients often imagine the reactions of their family to their death: the family member would blame themselves for not having done more for them, and this fantasy about the others being full of pain and remorse increases the patient's neurotic fiction of importance (striving for significance, which is, as we have said before, a form of striving for superiority). And committing suicide is the utmost expression of discouragement. Of course, we do not want to give the impression that Adlerians consider depressive patients to be revengeful lazybones fishing for compliments; but we should always be aware that their overtly expressed feeling of being worthless is only the surface manifestation of their difficulties.

A case example:
Juan is a 54-year-old unemployed computer specialist. We know him already from an example before; he is the one who tortures his wife with his 'guilt complex' for having gone with prostitutes. Juan had lost his job a few years ago because of a reduction in manpower of the enterprise he had worked for, and now he is unable to find employment. In appearance, this was the cause of his severe depression. His wife is a successful university teacher and apparently she had been the leader in this marriage, while Juan had always felt a little 'less' with respect to her. Before his depression, Juan was able to maintain his self-esteem by being a great do-it-yourselfer and thus creating a wonderful home for the family. The loss of his job was a severe blow for his self-esteem; while he was useful to the family with his income and his doing things with his hands he was able to maintain his psychological balance, but now his safeguarding had broken down and his inferiority feelings with respect to his wife had come fully afloat. So he needed another 'trick' to avoid his intense inferiority feelings. Making his wife suffer with his feelings of guilt, his depression, and his suicidal tendencies was a successful attempt at regaining power over her. It was she who asked for psychotherapy for herself. She had become so despairing of her husband and so anxious about his potential suicide that she finally gave up her job at the university and became a teacher at the nearby high school.

In this example we can appreciate the aggressive potential of depression. We do not deny Juan's suffering. He is potentially suicidal and his depression needs pharmacological and psychological treatment while he must be prevented from killing himself. But we can also see the destructive effects on his wife: not only does he make her take care of him all day. He has also managed to make her give up her promising university career for his sake and thus unconsciously to reduce her 'superiority'.

Schizophrenia and paranoia

For Adler, schizophrenia is an extreme form of striving for superiority: striving to be godlike. In some of the symptoms – delusions and hallucinations – the goal of superiority is expressed in an undisguised form (the classical 'I am Napoleon'). On the other hand, the predominant symptoms of schizophrenia – thought disturbances, incoherent language, and the schism between the content of thought and the emotions that are displayed – express a complete isolation from others. No Social Interest is possible, because this would require effective and affective communication, and schizophrenics are impaired in both of these areas. While the delusions in schizophrenia are strange and weird (i.e. the delusions can easily be identified as such, because it is not possible that the patient is, for example, a messenger of God), paranoia (today: delusional disorder) is characterised by less strange (non-strange) delusions (the idea of being persecuted by spies, of being loved at a distance, of being cheated by others, etc.), usually organised in a whole paranoid system, coherent in itself. Except for the ideas that revolve around the paranoid system, the patient usually functions correctly in daily life. A non-strange delusion is a delusion, but what the patient says can – at least theoretically – represent real facts (for example, spies do exist). Adler defined paranoid patients as people engaged in mock battles against self-created difficulties and who fight in a secondary theatre of operations (*Nebenkriegsschauplatz*). Psychotic patients have extremely high feelings of inferiority and thus, in their fantasies, strive for extremely high and unattainable goals, for absolute perfection and security. Of course, these attempts are doomed to failure, and thus these patients have to use more and more sophisticated strategies to eclipse reality, because all their tendentious apperception and erroneous beliefs are not strong enough to deny the facts of experience and rational thinking. This is the onset of psychosis. The function of the psychotic symptoms, hallucinations and delusions, is to allow the patients to move in their chosen directions (to pursue their goals of absolute superiority) without feeling responsible for them.

The paranoid system is, in Adler's view, safeguarded against the greatest objections from reality, therefore it is more difficult to change. The coherence of the paranoid ideas allows the patient to retain the fiction of superiority and importance without submitting such ideas to reality testing, and makes them so resistant against all evidence from reality and rational thinking. Thus psychosis would be a kind of intellectual suicide of an individual who feels unable to live up to the demands of society or the attainment of his or her own goal. The outbreak of psychosis occurs when the patient comes to the conviction that the place in life he or she seeks is definitively lost. In most westernised cultures this realisation may occur as people make the transition from the teenage years to adulthood in their early 20s. Adler's son Kurt Adler (1959) and Shulman (1980) have elaborated comprehensive theories of the psychotic process.

Although the authors of this book accept inferiority feelings and compensatory striving for superiority to be the basis of psychological problems and disorders, we do not necessarily agree completely with Adler's understanding of psychosis. In the last decades, a great deal of neurophysiological research has been done on psychotic disorders, especially on schizophrenia, which reveals that there are certain neurochemical dysfunctions underlying these disorders. There are several biopsychosocial models that aim at explaining the different aspects of psychotic disorders and the concatenation of psychological factors and neurological predisposition. For these reasons we recommend treating psychosis with certain precautions. It would probably be too haphazard to declare that all psychotic people lack Social Interest, and to maintain that schizophrenia is the expression of the patients' uncontrolled striving for superiority is perhaps too daring. Their illness may be of a kind that does not allow them to show Social Interest, or perhaps deficient Social Interest is but one symptom among many that stem from a common cause. In schizophrenia and related disorders, pharmacological treatment with neuroleptics is of outstanding importance. Nonetheless, fostering the psychotic individual's interest in other people, encouraging him or her in engaging with others, etc. may help them to overcome certain aspects of their disorder (insecurity, few social skills, etc.) and for relapse prevention. This kind of intervention, together with adequate anti-psychotic medication, has proved to be of great effectiveness in the therapy of psychosis.

Conclusions for counselling and psychotherapy

In Chapter 3, we will discuss Adlerian counselling and psychotherapy techniques in further detail. For the moment, we want to record that, as we have seen, inferiority feelings and a relative lack of Social Interest appear to underlie, at least in part, many psychological problems. Consequently, the goal of Adlerian psychotherapy is to help the patients decrease their inferiority feelings and to increase their Social Interest. The patients' basic fictionate goals must be identified and those that are 'useless' and self-defeating must be changed into more 'useful' (= adaptive) ones. Most of the Adlerian strategies and techniques, some of which will be explained in the next chapter, are meant to increase the patient's Social Interest.

This does not mean that the patient's particular symptoms are not addressed; although in many cases the symptoms are not treated as such, because it was the erroneous fictions that made the patient 'choose' this particular symptom for his or her purposes. We think that it is often useful to apply techniques derived from other therapeutic orientations in order to help the patient to develop new behaviours and attitudes. So we may decide to use a progressive desensitisation when a patient is afraid of heights or large places (make him expose himself to higher and higher buildings), relaxation training, or other techniques that stem from behaviour modification or other psychotherapies, in addition to the classical Adlerian techniques.

Neither does identifying the patient's fictionate goal mean that his or her past experiences are of no interest. On the contrary, in order to understand the patient, the Adlerian therapist first makes a careful analysis of the patient's Life Style, i.e. his or her view of himself or herself, of others, of life and what are his or her fictionate goals. Life Style analysis also allows us to understand the factors that have contributed to the development of the patient's fictions, by analysing his or her early recollections along with other indicators of the client's cognitive and emotional processes. Although we do not assume a causal attribution to these factors, they play a role in the aetiology of the symptoms, and it is useful for the patient to understand how his or her early experiences have contributed to the present problems. It is true that some phenomena may appear to us as being causal of others; for instance, we can think of an unhappy childhood as the cause of depression, but this causal attribution is arbitrary. A childhood 'trauma' does not necessarily provoke neurosis, but a neurotic patient can attribute later misfortunes and psychological troubles to such experiences; even more, the trauma can be used as an excuse for not complying with her duties as an adult, e.g. for being depressive, anorexic, delinquent, etc. She can say: 'I am not a good mother, because I was maltreated when I was a child', or: 'I am depressed and cannot go to work because my parents didn't give me enough love and caring'. Of course, when you are maltreated or abused as a child, your parents did not serve as a good example to learn how to be a good father or mother. Lack of love and caring do also contribute to low self-esteem and a depressive attitude. But how can one understand the following statement of a middle-aged female patient of one of us (UO): 'I am afraid of grasshoppers because my uncle once molested me when I was a little girl'?

In Adlerian therapy we do not only explore the past experiences, we put emphasis on the detection of the patient's future goals, because, as we have shown, all the patient's manifestations, thoughts, feelings, symptoms, are under the control of the (unconscious) goal. Just like in a good drama, the characters' actions and the plot are determined by the last act. The individual's experiences cannot be changed; what can be changed is the individual's opinion of them. The past is unalterable, but the future is open.

Chapter 3

Adlerian counselling and psychotherapy today

Our objectives in this chapter are to convey the basic principles and procedures for conducting Adlerian counselling and psychotherapy. Beyond discussing the foundational aspects of Adler's approach (Adler 1927, 1929, 1931, Ansbacher and Ansbacher 1956), we also will attempt to present a contemporary perspective on the ways that individual psychologists work with their clients. Because a wide spectrum of psychotherapeutic approaches now exist (Snyder and Ingram 2000), we will illustrate, where appropriate and informative, how other therapeutic perspectives might be integrated with Adlerian counselling and psychotherapy. The chapter begins with a discussion of two issues that frame the context of Adlerian interventions, the first of which involves the differences between counselling and psychotherapy and what these mean for the nature of the intervention. Second, we briefly review Adler's conceptualisations of three categories of client problems (i.e. neurosis, psychosis, and criminal/antisocial behaviour) and discuss the objectives of Adlerian therapy. Beyond these introductory considerations the remaining sections of this chapter draw on Dreikurs' (1967) framework to discuss the issues of: (1) establishing a therapeutic relationship with the client, (2) assessing the Life Style and clients' mistaken goals, (3) promotion of clients' insight and understanding of their mistakes, their life plan, and private logic, and (4) reorientation of clients toward fulfilling, meaningful, and co-operative life goals and roles. We also will discuss both recent and classical contributions to the Individual Psychology literature that relate to these intervention phases.

Adlerian counselling and psychotherapy

Individual Psychology's approach to intervention is particularly broad and encompasses a very wide range of client problems. At least two dimensions meaningfully characterise the ways that individual psychologists work with their clients, the first of which is bounded by the domains of counselling and psychotherapy (Dreikurs 1967). Interventions that help clients to deal with life problems stemming from developmental causes (i.e. choosing an academic major, finding a career or vocational path, managing a romantic relationship) or existential causes (children leaving home, divorce, or death of family members), among many others, typically have fallen under the rubric of *counselling* (Lynn and Garske 1985). Alternatively, *psychotherapy* involves helping clients to manage or overcome problems such as major depression, bipolar disorders, schizophrenia, and various personality disorders. Adlerian interventions span this counselling–psychotherapy dimension by addressing a wide variety of client problems with a number of different conceptualisations and technical approaches. In this regard, counselling and psychotherapy are used somewhat interchangeably in Adlerian circles insofar as they are useful to convey the general nature of clients' problems and the interventions that are being attempted.

A second dimension refers to the timelines and objectives of the intervention with brief, solution-focused, and problem-solving interventions at one end of the continuum and long-term, comprehensive, and personality-reconstructive work at the other. The inventions of individual psychologists also span this continuum. Adlerian practitioners are as likely to work with people who are searching for solutions to specific life problems (e.g. career changes, parenting, relationships, ageing) as with clients who wish or need to examine their problems in a more comprehensive, and thereby lengthy, course of therapy. Depending on the nature and duration of the problem along with the resources and resolve of the client, a reorientation towards socially useful goals and co-operation may require a very brief course of treatment (Bitter and Nicoll 2000, Kopp and Lasky 1999, Schaumberg 1959). In fact, to convey a client's capabilities and responsibilities to change, Adler made the somewhat tongue-in-cheek statement that: 'You can be cured in fourteen days if you follow this prescription. Try to think every day how you can please someone' (Ansbacher and Ansbacher 1956: 347). With this recommendation, Adler is not encouraging over-adaptation to socially desirable behaviour. He rather is trying to change the patients' persistent and pointless thinking of themselves by fostering their interest in other people's life and concerns.

The psychotherapy community has not always recognised Individual Psychology's versatility in informing both brief and long-term interventions, however. In fact, some practitioners may believe Individual Psychology provides a largely outdated and outmoded approach in the current era of managed care and brief therapies because it emerged during a time in the evolution of psychotherapy where lengthy, reconstructive therapies were in vogue (Freedheim 1992). This impression is unjustified because, true to its name, Individual Psychology is attuned and responsive to the unique needs that people bring to practitioners and the range of short- or long-term solutions that may be required to alleviate their distress (Watts 2000). As will be elaborated further, practitioners of Individual Psychology do not assimilate clients into a single model or modality of treatment. Instead, Adlerian therapy is as adaptable and applicable as the range of most presenting problems that modern practitioners encounter.

Individual Psychology's perspective on emotional problems and objectives for treatment

As we discussed in Chapter 2, individual psychologists see the primary symptoms of emotional problems as stemming from failed attempts to achieve a sense of competence, self-esteem, and significance that emerges from successfully meeting the life tasks of work, love, and community (Social Interest). In addition, people use various methods of safeguarding themselves to preserve some semblance of worth and to avoid public performances, comparisons, and evaluations. These manoeuvres underlie distortions in the perception of reality and consequently lead to an estrangement from useful relationships with others. As Adler suggested, there is a dynamic unity to most forms of distress that involves abortive efforts to achieve feelings of significance amid challenges or obstacles that seem insurmountable: 'All mistaken answers [to the tasks of life] are degrees of an infinite series of failures or abnormalities, or of the attempts of more or less discouraged people to solve their life-problems without the use of cooperation or Social Interest' (Ansbacher and Ansbacher 1956: 299).

The major categories of pathology that Adler discussed, along with their modern variants and exemplars, all stem from differences in the degree to which people have attempted to meet life tasks while erecting safeguards against their feelings of inferiority and insignificance. In this regard, people with neurotic types of problems (e.g. generalised anxiety disorder, obsessive-compulsive disorder, phobias) distort or deny aspects of reality so that some sense of efficacy and self-esteem is maintained while evaluations that would reveal actual or perceived weaknesses are avoided or deprecated. People experiencing neuroses live by the same rules as healthy people do, perhaps even more so; however, they perceive themselves to be insufficient in some way and maladaptively struggle to compensate.

Psychoses (schizophrenia, bipolar disorders, delusion disorders) involve a more extreme compromise whereby life's challenges are perceived as so overwhelming and insurmountable that the only way to thwart inferiority feelings and to salvage some vestige of significance and self-esteem is to create an inner fantasy world of dreams and aspirations. The world is perceived as an especially dangerous place that promises to humiliate people and to render them inert and insignificant. In seeking a rewarding life through such protective fantasies, psychotic people become cut off, sometimes irrevocably so, from the world of things and people.

In contrast to neurotic and psychotic disorders, antisocial and criminal behaviour emerge from a choice not to engage the tasks of life rather than an inability to do so. Such people view co-operation and Social Interest as pointless or disadvantageous and seek power over others by manipulating, conning, or dominating them, among other ploys. In short, antisocial people believe the rules for communal living do not apply to them or that they are above such rules and thus are not overwhelmed by life's challenges, especially if they can make an end-run around them through dishonest or illegal means (Dreikurs 1989).

Adlerian counselling and psychotherapy for the aforementioned disorders, as well as other life problems, have three overarching objectives. The first goal is to restore people so that they can more easily and effectively meet the tasks of work, love, and friendship. Success in this area may have different effects ranging from better job performance and career security, to an enhanced, deeper relationship with one's partner. Helping people get back into the 'community' may have myriad effects that include a restored sense of integrity for the major/principal roles that are portrayed, increased social support in times of stress, knowledge of having contributed to the welfare or enhancement of others, and overall participation in the forward-moving process of life. Successfully re-engaging people to meet their tasks represents a kind of externally observable end-result of the therapy that can be achieved in many different ways, depending on the nature of the client and his or her Life Style challenges and resources.

A second objective that is not entirely exclusive or unrelated to the first is to build within people a sense of encouragement, worth, efficacy, and significance. Such feelings of courage come from a heightened **degree of** engagement and **activity** along with an increased level of Social Interest (Ansbacher and Ansbacher 1956). Regardless of the diagnostic category, people experiencing problems in living typically present for counselling or therapy feeling demoralised, inert or helpless, and discouraged by the way they have framed the real or perceived dilemmas in their lives. Further, people's strategies for dealing with problems may have created even further difficulties in work, relationship or friendship circles, leaving them feeling stuck and doomed to repeat previously unsuccessful patterns of responding. Accepting clients on their own terms and attempting to collaborate with them to unravel and change the apparent 'mysteries' presented in their problems will begin to build a renewed sense of courage.

A third objective of treatment involves the reduction of maladaptive, self-defeating, and compensatory behaviours that, while promising the short-term maintenance or safeguarding of self-esteem, have negative long-term effects that perpetuate rather than resolve life problems. The emphasis here is on the behaviours that people use (i.e. retiring, avoiding, demurring, manipulating, cajoling, aggressing, berating, dominating, etc.) that effectively limit or pre-ordain the kinds of interpersonal transactions that will occur with other people. Such patterns may persist even as changes occur at other levels of the personality, simply because they are so deeply ingrained or habitual. Therapeutic work to change these habits directly, along with the discovery of new sources of encouragement and feelings of significance, may produce beneficial growth of the Life Style. Other specific or circumscribed life problems may have separate behaviourally based objectives in addition to the three described here.

General considerations about the nature and course of therapy

Adlerian therapists will become more potent agents of change in their clients' lives to the extent that they creatively use the methods for assessment and intervention described here. Therapists will benefit in this regard by keeping several considerations about their work in mind, the first of which is that the progression from initial consultation to termination does not advance linearly from the beginning to the end. Establishing the therapeutic relationship is particularly important because we believe that the client–therapist dyad is the primary vehicle for change. Working on the relationship with a client will be necessary throughout therapy, especially during the insight and reorientation phases (discussed below) when the client is most truly himself or herself as basic mistakes and faulty relational patterns are instantiated with the therapist. A solid relationship needs to be in place at this point and, as a result of successful work in the latter phases of therapy, the relationship may very well deepen and become more intense.

Second, although clients may present with a particular issue or dilemma, the intervention is almost always broader in scope and will target the wider maladaptive Life Style as the primary cause of the client's difficulties. This implies that as the presenting problem is being addressed, other difficulties may arise and require therapeutic attention. A consequence of this is that different problems will be at different levels of awareness and resolution as therapy proceeds. It is the therapist's task to identify these common themes in life problems and help the client to integrate this awareness. This approach does not preclude a problem-oriented or solution-focused therapy, but just involves different therapeutic goals. That is, it is perfectly acceptable to address a single problem the client identifies and then to prepare the client for subsequent therapeutic work at a later time that could comprehensively address the underlying Life Style issues. Overall, therapy will progress in a non-linear, cyclical manner through both time and client-generated issues.

Finally, therapists should work both to assimilate Adlerian treatment methods into their own personal therapeutic styles and to accommodate themselves to the central and common tenets of Individual Psychology (e.g. the necessity of addressing life tasks, social embeddedness, etc.). Clients will benefit from the creative and spontaneous use of the therapist's self along with the application of Adlerian methods. Adlerian therapeutic style is very much like the individual Life Style in that many productive and helpful variations exist so long as the overall professional goals of being responsive, flexible, and helpful to others are given priority over other commitments.

Phases of Adlerian counselling and therapy

Phase I: Establishing the therapeutic relationship

The first phase of an Adlerian intervention, and for almost all other approaches as well, is the establishment of a meaningful therapeutic relationship with the client. In fact, this relationship becomes the vehicle through which the significant attitudinal and behavioural changes occur (Rogers 1961, Teyber 1997) Advances in telehealth notwithstanding, this relationship optimally is established in person so that both the client and therapist can communicate effectively across all available verbal and nonverbal channels.

The therapeutic relationship does not develop and evolve in a completely freestyle manner, however, if for no other reason than that clients will attempt to instantiate previously dysfunctional interpersonal patterns with therapists to maintain the status quo of their problems and relationships. Instead, Adlerian practitioners attend to several issues that frame the ground rules of treatment and that orient them and their clients to the work that lies ahead (Adler 1998, Langs 1992). Three components create the frame for Adlerian interventions: (1) parameters of the therapeutic contact, (2) relationship with the client, and (3) agreement on goals for treatment.

Parameters of the therapeutic contact

The parameters for therapy essentially define how treatment will occur for a particular client and include considerations about the length of the treatment, frequency of sessions, contacting the therapist between sessions, therapist reimbursement, and so forth. Individual psychologists, like other practitioners, remain flexible regarding the number and duration of therapy sessions that may be required. This aspect of the treatment is typically determined once the client and therapist have agreed on the treatment goals to pursue. We offer several recommendations for setting these parameters, which optimally will occur during the initial meeting with a new client.

Individual psychologists believe that clients should be responsible for participating in their treatment. Consequently, it may be optimal, if allowed by the practitioner's or the clinic's calendar, to schedule standing therapy appointments for a client on the same day of each week and at the same time during the day. This will acclimatise both the therapist and the client to regular meetings for 'their own time together'. In addition such standing appointments may preclude clients from rationalising their hesitating ways and other forms of resistance on the basis of shifting week-to-week appointments. Once the day, time, and duration of the sessions (e.g. 30, 50, or 60 minutes) is set, these time limits should be observed as much as possible to minimise the development of positive or negative transferences associated with either regularly extending or cutting short the client's time with the therapist.

Individual psychologists also recognise that inter-session contacts with their clients will occur either as a result of emergencies or of the need to reschedule appointments, among other possible reasons. As part of establishing an effective therapeutic frame, therapists should convey what kind of extra-session contact is allowed as well as the form of communication (phone, voice-mail, email, etc.). To maintain the client's responsibility and commitment to working within the sessions, most individual psychologists do not agree to perform phone or electronic forms of treatment between sessions unless it is necessitated by what they can determine is a genuine client emergency. These rules or policies, again, are best conveyed at the beginning of treatment so that when situations are encountered that involve extra-session communications clients are not left feeling either cut off or especially privileged by their therapist's behaviour.

Clients' payment of their therapy fees creates another opportunity for them to be engaged and responsible for their treatment (Adler 1998). Individual psychologists, like practitioners from other orientations, should make their fee schedule clear at the outset of treatment and discuss policies regarding payment for cancelled or missed sessions. Agreement for any specialised payment plans also should be established at this time. The fee should be a reasonable one, based on considerations such as the going rate for given professions (psychiatry, psychology, social work, etc.) in particular locations. Care also should be exercised in determining an appropriate charge if a sliding fee scale is used. Further, Adler (1998) cautions against the acceptance of gifts or bartering for therapy services since these may introduce unknown power dynamics into the sessions that the client later may use to depreciate the therapist. Although managing issues of fees may seem commonsensical, clients can and do create therapeutic issues in this domain that can be challenging to resolve (Herron and Welt 1992)

As an illustration of these issues, one of us (AES) was providing counselling for a middle-aged man who presented with complaints of self-doubt, low self-esteem, and difficulties arranging his finances. The client was in the midst of a career change and was attempting to start a restaurant consulting business that promised to be quite successful if he could manage his growing workload and make sound business decisions. The client's Life Style analysis revealed a history of failed attempts to achieve a level of success that the other members of his family of origin enjoyed. In almost every case the client seemed to sabotage his chances for achievement at the last minute and then set his former goals aside, vanquished and discouraged. As these repetitive Life Style patterns became clearer during counselling, the client began either to come late to his sessions or to not show up at all. In the latter case, the client received a charge for each missed appointment.

After several weeks and an ever-increasing unpaid balance, it was clear that the client was enlisting the therapist to fulfil his unconscious goal to avoid the challenges of moving forward in his life. Not only was this client not receiving the counselling he began, but he also was further jeopardising his business opportunities by letting his fees accumulate out of control. The therapist confronted the client about his behaviour and contextualised it in terms of his past hesitating tendencies to avoid real tests of his skills and abilities. The therapist also refused to continue letting him accumulate unpaid fees: he must either attend his counselling and pay his fees or discontinue his treatment altogether. After the therapist identified his game of sabotage as a way to solidify his failure, and even predicting specifically how it might occur in this instance, the client paid his balance and recommitted himself to the treatment.

Relationship with the client

The second component of the individual psychologist's therapeutic frame pertains to the establishment and maintenance of the relationship with the client. More than other components of the frame, the therapeutic relationship occupies a central role in fostering both encouragement and a renewed sense of co-operation in clients (Adler 1931). In this regard, clients will experience the relationship as soothing, comforting, and restorative while also experiencing feelings of threat to their continued use of dysfunctional, but familiar, Life Style patterns. For this reason, therapists should be attuned to the relationship because of its dynamic, changing nature through the course of therapy. Practitioners should consider several issues in this regard.

First, Adler (Ansbacher and Ansbacher 1956) has aptly noted that most clients will experience the therapist as a threat to their tenuous senses of significance because of the possibilities of change and the risk of having to face their real or perceived shortcomings during treatment. Clients may therefore attempt to safeguard their feelings of superiority and maintain the status quo by depreciating either the therapist or possibilities of change through therapy. This depreciation may occur in many ways, one of the most beguiling of which is to prize, idealise or worship the therapist. This behaviour may subtly feed the therapist's need to be perceived as effectual, potent, and so forth. Adler (Adler 1998, Ansbacher and Ansbacher 1956) has cautioned therapists against becoming more than casually invested in the therapeutic success with their clients. The danger here is that the therapist is being set up for a fall – the only possible movement in terms of credibility and stature is down. At the cusp of a significant Life Style insight or before committing to a major change, the client may, almost arbitrarily, find something that the therapist did that was crushing, disappointing, or otherwise worthy as a rationalisation to avoid insight or action. This ploy has the effect of minimising the client's responsibility for failure and maximising the therapist's 'perceived' contribution to the therapy failure or impasse. Consequently, it is helpful for practitioners to remember that clients are not purchasing a 'cure', but instead are paying for the therapist's time and attention in helping to solve life problems.

Alternatively, some clients will more directly disparage the clinician personally or professionally. Sometimes clients threaten behaviour (e.g. suicide, self-mutilation, law suits) that promises to make the clinician look bad to his or her peers or to other clients. The message behind these behaviours is usually: 'If you push me, I'm going to push you back!' The temptation to the therapist here is to become occupied with defending himself or herself and being drawn into the diversionary content of the client's problems or accusations. The therapist is colluding with the client to avoid change to the extent that both persons become embroiled in these issues. Adler's (Ansbacher and Ansbacher 1956) guidance for managing the relationship was to strive to be as neutral and even-handed as possible while finding ways to thwart the client's usual lines of movement in the session:

> For successful treatment it is absolutely necessary that the physician [and psychologist] have a great deal of tact, renounce superior authority, be equally friendly at all times, be alertly interested, and have the cool-headed feeling that he is facing a sick person with whom he must not fight, but who is always ready to start a fight. Take the wind right out of the patient's sails!
>
> Ansbacher and Ansbacher 1956: 338

Although active effort is required to maintain this position of balance throughout the treatment, clients will benefit at the beginning of their therapy from a discussion about the nature and scope of the therapist–client relationship. In this regard we recommend that the therapist portray himself or herself as a sympathetic but disinterested collaborator in helping the client to change (Ansbacher and Ansbacher 1956). Although the relationship is an emotionally intimate one, it differs from friendships and romantic relationships because time and attention are not divided equally, but focused instead exclusively on the client. Making these issues clear, along with other ones such as how the therapist and client will behave if they happen to see each other outside the clinic, will assist greatly in managing the relationship. Further, it is important that the relational parameters be discussed at the inception of the treatment rather than later when a therapeutic issue arises. At these later points, clients may experience the imposition of a relational frame as arbitrary or contrived and attempt to test or breach relationship boundaries. It also is important not to let relationship discussions take on an excessively moral, legal, or ethical tone regarding what kinds of behaviours are pre- or proscribed, lest clients perceive their therapists as scared, unavailable, or conveniently hiding behind standards for professional behaviour. Therapy under such conditions may feel contrived and inauthentic.

A successfully framed and managed therapeutic relationship will have several benefits for the client. First, experiencing the therapist as stable, reliable, and steadfast despite the client's attempts to test or depreciate him or her will cultivate Social Interest (Ansbacher and Ansbacher 1956). Clients may attempt to emulate the relational style of their therapists in their other relationships and experience some initial successes in these realms that further spur the person's useful reinvestment in friendships and community. Second, the therapist's good-natured acceptance and understanding of the client's Life Style and attempts to thwart therapy will build courage and confidence (Weiss 1993). The therapist's acceptance and valuing in this way will further enable the client to adopt a similar attitude towards himself or herself. As clients feel more inherent worth then the need to distort reality, to safeguard, and to depreciate others will decrease.

Agreement on goals for treatment

The client and therapist must come to some agreement about the goals of the treatment so that the therapeutic relationship can be put to its best use. Although some tentative agreements about the purposes of the therapy may become apparent during the first meeting, two or sometimes three sessions are customary for clear and attainable goals to emerge. There are several reasons necessitating this interval of time, the first of which is that some clients may articulate an 'entry issue' that they later lay aside once they feel comfortable and trusting. In addition, although therapists may clearly see dysfunctional Life Style contours, the client may need to talk about his or her experiences for several hours before being able to articulate some initial goals.

The Adlerian therapist can move this process along by directly enquiring about the events or experiences that occasioned the scheduling of the first appointment (i.e. 'What brings you in to see me today?'). Further enquiries along the lines of 'What kind of person would you like to be six months from now? How about a year from now?' will also reveal something about the client's expectations for personal transformation through the therapy.

Adler cautions that therapists should not promise or even strongly hint that complete recovery or the client's image of an ideal self will be realised by the therapy (Adler 1968, Ansbacher and Ansbacher 1956, Dreikurs 1989). Providing such assurances effectively gives the balance of power to clients who, in moments of safeguarding and depreciation, may frustrate the therapist's desire to produce a 'success'. Leaving open the possibility that the client may feel worse before feeling better or that another therapist may provide more rapid results, and so forth, will disarm some of the high expectations that clients and therapists may unwittingly develop. In addition, retaining the option for evaluating progress and renegotiating therapy goals periodically also keeps therapists from over-committing.

Consistent with Adler's emphasis on shouldering progressively more responsibility for oneself, clients that have not previously been in therapy will benefit from an introduction to what is required of them during the counselling (Adler 1968, Murphy 1984). That is, clients should be told what the process of therapy may be like for them, what they might feel, and also what their tasks and responsibilities are. Some clients may view going to the therapist the same way they do their dentist – a little bit of pain, but the doctor does most of the work. Unlike other forms of health care, therapy requires clients to work in the traditional sense of the word (i.e. being willing to explore and sit with painful emotions, realising one's limitations, etc.). This orientation, too, will help to prevent clients from heaping the bulk of the responsibility for change on to the therapist.

Finally, as part of goal alignment and agreement, the counsellor and client should agree on the criteria for the termination of counselling (i.e. what has to happen to signal that the work is nearing completion?). Although the exact moment and criteria for terminating work may change as the treatment proceeds and as clients' goals evolve, the current era of managed care requires that therapists attune themselves to opportunities to punctuate their work. Adler (1998) indicated that a significant proportion of the therapeutic work, if not all of it, could be completed within approximately three months. The criteria for termination may be the achievement of tangible, external goals or, alternatively, may emerge through a felt sense that the time is near for completing the treatment. Rosenthal (1959) described the role of dreams and the positive changes in dream imagery from the beginning of therapy to later stages as a particularly valuable tool to evaluate the timing of termination.

Phase II: Assessing and understanding the Life Style

Once the therapeutic frame is established within the first few sessions, the focus of the meetings shifts to assessing and understanding the client's Life Style. The purpose of this assessment is to build the client's awareness of the various contemporary and historical forces that have shaped his or her personality and eventuated in life problems. Rather than merely generating factual information for the therapist or insurance company, Life Style assessments represent active, process-oriented interventions that can lead to change (Sperry 1992). In this regard the distinction between assessment and insight phases of treatment often blurs because the goal of assessment is to build self-awareness and to heighten clients' abilities to understand their own reactions (i.e. to build psychological acuity).

Life Style assessments also provide useful information for the counsellor, although Adler (Ansbacher and Ansbacher 1956) noted that experienced clinicians can discern the major guiding lines in a client's life within the first hour. From the therapist's perspective, the goal is to develop a functional diagnosis (versus a descriptive, categorical, or nomothetic one) of how clients uniquely have experienced challenges in striving for significance and completion and subsequently begun to safeguard and to strive perniciously for personal superiority. Formalised Life Style assessment also provides useful information for research and clinical evaluation (e.g. therapy outcome) purposes.

Life Style assessment (traditionally also called Life Style analysis) typically employs several procedures that reveal the client's attitudes, behaviours, and ways of coping in different domains. Although individual Life Style assessment tools and techniques should be used in ways that best suit particular clients, the general approach involves assessing the client's family constellation and atmosphere (of both the contemporary and original families), birth order, early recollections, and an analysis of client dreams. Dinkmeyer, Sr, Dinkmeyer, Jr and Sperry (1987) provide a very useful template for organising observations in these areas. Life Style assessment techniques vary in format from interviews with little structure to the completion of paper-and-pencil measures. We discuss many of the existing techniques as well as some new approaches below.

Interview methods

Some of the most effective and informative ways of understanding clients come from informal or semi-structured interviews that are designed to elicit their perspectives of the presenting problems. These methods typically allow the assessment to assume a disarming and conversational tone that offers opportunities for follow-up questioning and clarification. Adler (Ansbacher and Ansbacher 1956: 404–409) provides a useful set of questions to guide interviews with child and adult clients. A similar template can be found in Dinkmeyer, Sr, Dinkmeyer, Jr and Sperry (1987).

If clinicians choose not to use one of these guides, they should remember to make enquiries in several areas, the first of which has to do with the client's subjective perception of his or her current life difficulties. Second, questions should be included that enquire about the client's orientation and success in facing the challenges of the three life tasks. As a part of this line of enquiry, the therapist should attempt to assess the client's sense of Social Interest and co-operativeness. Third, enquiries about the client's earliest recollections may reveal more about his or her current concerns and wishes as well as possible lines of movement. The imagery in clients' dreams conveys similar information. Fourth, it is important to assess clients' experiences in their contemporary and original families. Attention to the roles and responsibilities clients portray in these two areas will reveal their specific goals for achieving completion and belongingness. Mosak's (1972) classic paper provides a very helpful illustration of how interview methods can elucidate features of the family constellation.

In addition to enquiring about clients' medical histories, we have found it useful to ask about their relationships to prescription and recreational drugs (e.g. alcohol, marijuana, caffeine, tobacco). This is a profitable line of enquiry because it reveals how they may be using substances to cope with or, alternatively, to perpetuate situations that relieve them of taking responsibility and co-operating with others. Taking medications, especially in front of others, is an ostensible sign that people are sick, disabled, or otherwise limited in what they are able to do and the responsibilities for which they should be held accountable. We also enquire about clients' relationships to food, exercise, and vitamin supplements. Especially for women, maladaptive eating or exercise behaviours may reveal ways that they have attempted to seek both significance or perfection (i.e. through working towards physical beauty or thinness) and a sense of control in their lives (i.e. deciding not to eat or choosing when and how long to exercise, etc.).

Therapists may also pose 'the Question' to their clients during the initial interview. This question involves asking clients how their lives would be different or what they would be able to do if they were not experiencing the chief complaint that they presented to the therapist. The significance of this question, as Adler noted, is that the client's response usually indicates the very activity or challenge that threatens to reveal his or her perceived limitations, inadequacies, or shortcomings. If the client's response to the question is that some kind of physical relief would be experienced or that a legitimately unpleasant, noxious, or dangerous situation or condition would be averted, then the therapist may need to keep searching to find the impasse that the client is avoiding through maintaining his or her symptoms.

For instance, suppose that a client is referred to an individual psychologist and complains of lower back pain that has no known physical causes. The question to be asked is: 'If you didn't experience this back pain, what would you be able to do that you can't do now?' If the client responds with something of the form: 'Well, I would be able to sit in front of the computer and to complete some important projects for work', then it is likely that the client is threatened by the challenges of work and is clinging to the back pain symptom as a face-saving way to avert the feared 'moment of truth'. Alternatively, if the client responds, 'I just wouldn't have to deal with this pain and could sleep better at night' then the back pain may be just that – an annoyance that keeps the client physically uncomfortable. As we have already pointed out in Chapter 2, the therapist should probe answers to 'the Question' carefully, especially those given by clients with above-average intelligence, because such clients can 'use' symptoms in more complex and elaborate ways to support their lines of movement.

Beyond the factual content that is gathered, therapists should note the nonverbal and emotional responses that accompany their answers in the interview. That is, therapists should listen with their 'third ear' on an intuitive level to what clients convey (Reik 1948). Does the content of clients' responses match the affect that they display? What additional emotional content is being conveyed or withheld? What are clients not revealing by the answers that they provide? Do clients describe themselves or only the forces that impinge on them? The language that clients use to describe their family of origin experiences can reveal how they experienced themselves in that arena as well as the active or passive status of their current orientations (Stewart 2001). That is, the use of passive voice in characterising family experiences is related to negative, unhealthy family environments in which people are understood in terms of unidimensional traits and labels instead of how they behave or what they do. Overall, the narratives that clients construct to communicate their experiences in interviews are quite revealing and, consistent with the process nature of Adlerian assessment, represent meaning-making opportunities.

Techniques for understanding the family constellation and family atmosphere

The **family constellation** and **family atmosphere** are included in the Life Style assessment because of their foundational role in affecting how the person becomes oriented to fulfilling the **tasks of life** and to finding a way to achieve completion and belonging. The family of origin represents the first social arena that most children experience. Consequently, the number and type of family members, the quality of relationships that exist between them, and the ensuing emotional climate that is created will affect the extent to which children choose to co-operate and strive towards the useful and productive sides of life. Several methods exist for assessing the various components of the family constellation and atmosphere.

The family constellation represents the family's structural organisation and 'cast of characters'. The objective of assessing the constellation is to understand who lived with the client's family of origin during most of the childhood years and to understand the myriad patterns of relationships that exist between family members. A survey of the effects of birth order also may be included in the family constellation assessment; discussion of this topic, however, is provided in more detail below.

Although it is possible to elicit and discuss family constellation information through questionnaire or interview methods (e.g. Shulman 1962), a very effective way of making this exploration is through the use of **genograms** (McGoldrick and Gerson 1985). Genograms are diagrammatic representations of several generations of the family of origin; they are typically completed on an easel or board so that both the therapist and client can survey the information and Life Style themes that emerge. Although genograms have not been considered as a uniquely Adlerian technique, the process- and intervention-oriented nature of completing a genogram fits quite well with other Life Style assessment methods.

Without describing the technique in extensive detail (see McGoldrick and Gerson 1985), a single family member (i.e. the client or perhaps identified patient in family therapy) is asked to name and briefly describe the people in his or her immediate family of origin. Family members' ages and significant dates (marriages, divorces, births, deaths) are also recorded on the chart. Next, the client describes how each of the family members relates to the others. This includes enquiries about problematic relationships between siblings, and parents, as well as information about who is particularly favoured or disparaged in the family. Other information, using guides such a Shulman's (1962), can be solicited about the family of origin during this time as well. After the client's immediate generation is discussed in this way, information about the preceding generation of families from which the client's mother and father originated is solicited. This process continues until three or perhaps four generations of family members and their relationships have been discussed.

Completing a genogram can produce several therapeutic effects, the first of which is that the activity allows clients to generate narratives that convey heretofore private meanings of family relationships. As clients describe their families and answer questions, they may hear themselves describing relationships, problems, and concerns aloud for the first time. Second, the visual aspects of a genogram facilitate the processing of reflexive and circular questions about family relationships (e.g. 'So, your older brother did well in sports and the family was proud of him. How did this affect you? What did you do to stand out? How did your brother react to this?'). Third, a relatively complete genogram depicting three or more generations allows the client and therapist to observe the extent to which family problems, styles of coping, conflicts, and so forth have been passed down to younger generations. A case example will illustrate some of these effects.

One of us (AES) completed a genogram with a young woman who complained of problems in maintaining steady relationships with men. The client described a history of desperately trying to please a succession of men so that she could salvage a relationship with them. The client would engage in a variety of largely ingratiating behaviours that did not reflect her true self, wishes, or values. As a last-ditch effort in this regard she would have sex with her boyfriends to keep them in the relationship. Although sex kept her boyfriends physically close until the novelty of the encounter wore off, she reported never feeling emotionally close to her boyfriends during sex. The client typically felt manipulated and used after her partners broke up with her. To re-establish some sense of control, the client reported a series of affairs with married men. Knowing that she could disclose the affair to the men's wives put her into a position of power that she did not enjoy with single men.

Because she still lived with her parents and indicated that her mother attempted to dictate the type of men that she should date and how she should relate to them, family of origin issues were very salient for the client and were explored by completing a genogram early in her therapy. The client was an only child, although she did not convey that she was pampered or overly indulged. If anything, her parents were somewhat protective and more involved in her life than she wanted. Her mother was also an only child and her father was the second of two boys. The client indicated that her maternal grandparents were old-fashioned and wanted always to keep tabs on her mother. The client described her father as pushing her to accomplish and achieve more than she felt capable of. She saw her father as analytical, somewhat cold and always competing with his older brother. She described her parents' relationship as hit-and-miss in that the two never seemed close or affectionate with each other. Although her mother seemed to control the relationship, there were times when her father asserted his independence within the family. This usually produced big, emotionally toxic arguments that resulted in her mother temporarily giving in to her husband's ways of doing things.

The genogram was useful because in the process of describing her mother's relationship with her parents, the client realised that she and her mother had had very similar childhoods (i.e. scrutinised, over-protected, enmeshed). The client liked when her maternal grandparents came to visit because her mother suddenly became preoccupied with her own parents. In fact, the client felt that she enjoyed a more 'normal' relationship with her mother during her grandparents' visits. Further, in describing her mother's dating relationships, the client revealed that her mother also felt unattractive to other men and resorted to the use of sex to hold on to them. Further, the mother's cynicism about men coloured the client's views about relationships and made it difficult for her to trust men. The client also revealed that when her parents fought, she suspected that her mother would retaliate by withholding sex. In many respects the client was a younger version of her mother – a realisation that startled the client and motivated her to find an alternative life course. Mapping these relationships visually and enquiring about the inter-generational relationships helped the client to understand that her current choices in dealing with men were not arbitrary but instead were affected in part by how her mother portrayed the role of women to her.

Family atmosphere pertains to the emotional climate of the family and what it feels like to spend time in a family as it deals with the challenges, successes, and failures of life (Griffith and Powers 1987). Family atmosphere is an emergent quality of the different members that comprise the family and the overall tenor of their relationships. Family atmosphere also is coloured by the ways that members attach importance to things, people, or situations and pursue goals together (i.e. collective family values). A wide variety of possible family atmospheres exist – about as many as there are adjectives to character-ise them. The family atmosphere possesses significance in the Life Style analysis because it affects the assumptions that people make about situations and people outside the family and, consequently, can affect how they choose to fit in and to pursue the life tasks.

Several methods exist for assessing the family atmosphere, beginning with the genogram. As clients progress through their genograms it is possible to see, at least in general form, what it must have been like to be a member of the family. Specific questions about the overall emotional tone of the family also will reveal the family atmosphere. Another method involves providing clients with an adequate and representative list of adjectives and asking them to circle terms that especially describe their family and to draw a square around terms that are the opposite of what it was like to be in the family.

Clinicians who desire a quantitative assessment of the family atmosphere should consider administering the 90-item Family Environment Scale (FES; Moos and Moos 1986). The FES consists of ten sub-scales (cohesion, expres-siveness, conflict, independence, achievement orientation, intellectual and cultural orientation, active/recreational orientation, moral and religious orientation, organisation, and control) that broadly assess family relation-ship, maintenance, and growth dimensions. Taken together, these scales pro-vide a varied assessment of some important family atmosphere dimensions. Because the FES is completed by family members working alone with their question and answer sheets, this assessment is necessarily more content-oriented and offers less of an intervention opportunity than the genogram or an interview.

Assessing actual and psychological birth order

Although the contributions of birth order to the Life Style may be assessed through discussions about the family constellation or the completion of a genogram, we discuss it separately here because it is probably the most mis-understood variable of all those that influence the Life Style. Birth order is an important consideration in the Life Style assessment because it can power-fully affect the ways children seek to fit in, find significance, and attempt to belong within their families. Because the family comprises the first real social group that children encounter, finding a place among one's siblings can affect how people attempt to assume roles in extra-familial contexts.

The problem with the birth order construct is that some practitioners may make inferences about clients' Life Styles or personalities by relying on stereotypical descriptions of the first, middle, youngest, and only child that have developed over time and have been publicised in works such as Leman's (1985) *Birth order book* or through the rote and uncritical application of the Individual Psychology literature. Given Adler's emphasis on how people use creative and constructive processes to find a way to belong, the perceived or psychological birth position in the family is more clinically significant than the exclusive consideration of actual position. In this regard Adler states:

> There has been some misunderstanding of my custom of classification according to position in the family. It is not, of course, the child's number in the order of successive births which influences his character, but the situation into which he is born and the way in which he interprets it.
> Ansbacher and Ansbacher 1956: 377

A client's **actual birth order** represents a starting point in determining the perceived or psychological role that he or she occupied in the family of origin. Adlerian therapists with experience in this area may be able to observe the client's behaviour in sessions and put this together with the actual birth order and reports of the client's roles and responsibilities in the family of origin to ascertain the perceived position (Jordan, Whiteside and Manaster 1982). Alternatively, clients can be asked to indicate the position they felt they occupied in their families or to choose a birth position name (first, middle, youngest, only, second, etc.) or a family experience that describes the essence of their role (Lohman, Lohman and Christensen 1985, Pulakos 1987). These methods for assessing birth order effects and roles rely largely on clinical experience and judgement.

A quantitative measure of **psychological birth order** exists in the White–Campbell Psychological Birth Order Inventory (PBOI; Stewart, Stewart and Campbell 2001, Stewart and Campbell 1998, Campbell, White and Stewart 1991, White, Campbell and Stewart 1995, White et al. 1997). The PBOI contains forty-six yes-or-no items that describe the ways that people may experience themselves (i.e. behaviours, attitudes, feelings) in their families of origin. The items generate four scales that correspond to first, middle, youngest, and only child. The psychological 'first' scale measures the experiences of leading, directing, and achieving among siblings as well as pleasing adults. The 'middle' scale taps themes of feeling rejected, neglected, or otherwise not fitting into one's family. The 'youngest' scale assesses experiences of being an initiator, charmer, or manipulator as well as being popular and outgoing. Finally, the 'only' scale assesses perceptions of being scrutinised, controlled, or intruded on by the family, especially by parents. The PBOI items and directions for its administration and scoring appear in Appendix 1.

The items for the PBOI were developed on the basis of Adlerian theory concerning the prototypical experiences of persons within each of the four birth positions (first, middle, youngest, and only child). The initial content of the scales was reviewed and agreed on by a panel of experienced Adlerian therapists. The PBOI also has been validated empirically through studies that related psychological position to actual position (Campbell, White and Stewart 1991), to Life Style themes (White, Campbell and Stewart 1995), and to career interests (White et al. 1997). Stewart and Campbell (1998) demonstrated the PBOI's construct validity as well as the stability of its four constituent factors. The PBOI's 3-week test–retest reliabilities ranged from 0.84 to 0.94 and 8-week reliabilities ranged from 0.81 to 0.95 (Stewart and Campbell 1998). Because men and women responded differently to the PBOI items, perhaps due to the interaction of gender role with one's family role, the PBOI scales are scored separately for each gender (Stewart 1994).

A newer and more process-oriented method for assessing perceived family or sibling position is the Birth Role Repertory Grid (BRRG; Cavalleri 2001, Stewart 1994). The BRRG represents an adaptation of George Kelly's (1955) repertory grid technique. In this exercise the client applies selected and salient items from the PBOI not just to himself or herself, but to all people in the family of origin; each person is rated on the extent to which the birth-role construct applies. Although most of the role constructs relating to family position are drawn from the PBOI, the client is required to produce five of his or her own unique constructs for describing family relationships.

The BRRG exercise requires about 30–45 minutes to complete and requires clients to think actively of their family relationships. In many cases clients will articulate meanings and reactions that were only implicit or even out of awareness beforehand. It is not unusual for people to comment, 'Wow – I never thought of people in this way before.' Consequently, just like the genogram, early recollections, and dream analysis techniques, the completion process of the BRRG can yield more useful experiences for therapy than the content conveyed by numerical construct ratings or scores, although these may be valuable for research purposes (Cavalleri 2001).

Early recollections

An analysis of **early recollections** is probably the most direct and useful method of understanding clients' fictional life goals and the laws of movement that govern their attitudes and responses (Adler 1929, Ansbacher and Ansbacher 1956). This technique represents the classical Adlerian Life Style analysis. The content of the memories is typically generated by asking clients to remember the very earliest events that occurred in their lives. Then they are asked to report and briefly describe each memory, beginning with the first one that comes to mind. If the therapist desires, questions can be asked about the people that appear in the memories, their relationships, the overall feeling quality of the recollection, and so forth.

Early recollections, like dreams, function as projective stimuli in that clinicians are not interested so much in the historical accuracy or repressed content contained in the memory (Mosak 1958). Instead, such memories represent the concerns, goals, and ways of coping that exemplify the present Life Style as they are projected on to events of the past. In other words, early recollection exercises involve a reconstruction of past events in terms of present Life Style concerns. As Adler stated:

> We do not believe that all early recollections are correct records of actual facts. Many are even fancied, and most perhaps are changed or distorted at a time later than that in which the events are supposed to have occurred; . . . old remembrances are not reasons, they are hints. They indicate the movement toward a goal and what obstacles had to be overcome.
>
> Ansbacher and Ansbacher 1956: 352–353

Once the client produces several (usually around five) early recollections, the therapist's task is to make inferences and interpretations about their meaning, together with the client's associations and comments. Because clients' Life Style patterns will be evident in other modalities as well (e.g. dreams, perceived family roles, etc.) these may offer an initial starting point for evaluating the significance of the recollections. In addition, the presence of particular people, events, or outcomes in the memories may reveal outlines of the Life Style and the goals the client is pursuing. It is important to attend to the emotional tone of the recollections because this will provide some indication of the extent to which the person feels either happy and affirmed or unhappy and set apart, for example. To consider an example, pleasant recollections of a parent followed by memories of negative or frustrating events with a sibling could suggest themes of dethronement (Ansbacher and Ansbacher 1956). As another example, memories of being sick and out of school could suggest a number of themes such as concern about maintaining health and comfort, feeling unprepared for work or community tasks, or a desire to overcome physical limitations and to excel. Although the therapist may have some idea of what the recollections mean, the emerging hypotheses are best evaluated by presenting tentative interpretations of the memories to clients and observing how they respond. In this regard a knowing smile (i.e. recognition reflex) could be a sign that at least some part of it may be significant for the client.

Lingg and Kottman (1991) have developed an interesting use for early recollections that goes beyond the elicitation and interpretation of the memories. After clients produce their memories they are asked to visualise them in a relaxed state and to experience the images, feelings, and meanings of the memories. Once clients experience their memories in this way, the adult self of the client is introduced into the visualisation as a figure to comfort, protect, or otherwise assist the child self safely through the scenario. The goal of this variation on the early recollection technique is to bring the clients' contemporary emotional resources to bear on problems or issues that confronted them at earlier points in their lives when they were overwhelmed by their experiences.

Finally, Eckstein (1999) describes an intriguing workshop that is designed to help groups or classes of mental health trainees or professionals to build their skill in understanding and interpreting the meaning of early recollections. This exercise makes use of early recollections from the lives of Adler, Jung and Freud and teaches some of the principles of interpretations. Attendees work with one-half of a theorist's memories and then, based on their knowledge of his Life Style, identify the complementary portion of recollections.

Using the interpretation of early recollections as a starting point, the therapist can begin to formulate the client's Life Style. Usually, Life Style is expressed by the view the client takes towards himself or herself ('I am . . .'), the view of others ('Other people are . . .'), the view of world and life ('The world is . . ./Life is . . .'), and goals ('Therefore I want to . . . / I have to . . .'). Some therapists prefer, after careful deliberation, to write down their clients' Life Style explicitly in well-formulated sentences and to hand out a copy to them.

Dream interpretation

Adlerian therapists view clients' descriptions of their dreams largely in the same way that they do early recollections. At one level, dreams possess structural and functional features that are quite consistent with basic Life Style patterns because of the thematic unity that exists throughout the personality. As dreams are recalled or described, they again are interpreted through the contemporary Life Style filters and perceptive processes consistent with people's guiding lines. The Life Style themes are projected on to both early recollections and dreams because

> the person's imagination cannot create anything but that which his Life Style commands. His made-up dreams are just as good as those he genuinely remembers, for his imagination and fancy will also be an expression of his Life Style.
>
> Ansbacher and Ansbacher 1956: 359

The Adlerian approach to dreams differs from the methods associated with Freudian psychoanalysis in several ways. Most importantly, Adlerians believe that dreams reveal the current and forward-looking aspects of the personality rather than attempts to deal with past conflicts and experiences that were repressed into the unconscious. Second, Adlerian therapists recognise a distinction between the manifest and latent meanings of dreams, but do not become committed to overly symbolic interpretations of dreams. Drawing on the heuristic of Occam's razor, Adlerian therapists maintain that the simplest and most parsimonious interpretation of a dream is usually the best one. Finally, it can be said of both Adlerian and Freudian approaches to dream interpretation that symbols (e.g. water, clothing, houses, stairways, etc.) are used in highly individual ways – invoking universal interpretations to given dream symbols forces clients to fit into pre-existing moulds and may reveal little.

Adlerian therapists recognise that dreams may perform several, sometimes overlapping, functions for people (Adler 1998, Ansbacher and Ansbacher 1956), the first of which is simply to mirror the current Life Style. Problems, concerns, wishes or anticipations experienced consciously may appear again in dreams. Second, dreams may represent a bridge between clients' present situations on one side and the goals they are striving towards on the other. In this regard, dreams may recast current problems or obstacles in realising the goal in different, creative terms that may point towards an alternative path in waking life. Conversely, goals that clients experience as fleeting and unattainable may, through their dream imagery, omit salient details and constraints so that the goal is attained via the dream in compensatory fashion.

Adler also discusses an intriguing function of dreams in producing emotions or emotionally preparing people for life events. That is, dreams may not only point to alternative paths towards goals on a cognitive level, they may also emotionally prime people to take action. According to Adler, 'We have all the means ready in our minds to elaborate a Life Style, to fix it, and to reinforce it; and one of the most important means of doing this is the ability to stir up feelings' (Ansbacher and Ansbacher 1956: 361).

Armed with the knowledge that dreams may perform these or similar functions, along with emerging knowledge about the client's Life Style and his or her law of movement, Adlerian therapists may venture to interpret and share the impressions of the client's dream. As with the interpretation of early recollections, the interpretations of dreams should be phrased as tentative hypotheses that clients can either affirm or reject (i.e. the therapist should not become convinced of the accuracy of the interpretation and persist with it).

Oberst (2002) has developed a model of dream interpretation that recognises the functions of dreams outlined in Individual Psychology but that also views them as meaning-making opportunities, consistent with the emphases of constructivist psychology. In Oberst's model, dreams are interpreted segmentally in five stages, according to Kelly's (1955) cycle of experience. First the events or phenomena of the dream are anticipated, followed by the client becoming emotionally involved or invested in them in the implication stage. The anticipated events in the dream are encountered in the third stage, followed by an evaluation of the extent to which the anticipations about the dream are confirmed or disconfirmed. In the fifth and final stage of dream interpretation the client and therapist consider the implications of the dream's outcome for the client's view of himself or herself. Given the possibilities for the client's active and creative involvement in the dream interpretation process, we feel this technique particularly exemplifies the Individual Psychology approach.

Adler (1998) provided some overarching themes for interpreting dreams that may serve as a beginning framework. For instance, dreams that cannot be recalled or are only dimly recollected probably signal a relatively healthy person who does not regularly require or remember the work functions that dreams perform. Dreams of anxiety, fear, or dread may reflect apprehensions that people have that their current Life Style is being threatened, or that they may not be able to effectively respond to maintain their sense of self-esteem in the face of an upcoming challenge. Dreams of flying or attempting to fly or rise above may signal striving for superiority or that some important goal bearing on the self-worth was accomplished. Dreams of paralysis or an inability to move or respond could reflect indecision, conflict, or a lack of viable ways to proceed with some life problem. Other generalisations like this for initiating an interpretation are possible given Adler's (1929, 1968, 1998) descriptions, however the ultimate criteria for an interpretation are the extent to which congruence can be found between the dream and life themes observed in other areas (family atmosphere, psychological position, etc.). An illustration is provided in the following case example.

Less than a year after being promoted to regional sales manager, a client was told by the director of sales to prepare a summary of the year's business and to present it in front of about 400 people at the company's national meeting. The client, who had for some time been puzzled about why he was promoted and was feeling unprepared to manage his former peers, had become progressively more perfectionist and self-conscious. What he used to do without thinking (preparing sales reports, conferring with other salespeople) now was a detailed, ritualised, and painstaking process. The client was so driven to do a good job that he was behind with his reports and began to blame his 'profit-oriented company' for not thinking about the human side of the sales equation. Two weeks before his presentation to the national meeting, the client was struggling to finish his reports and to prepare his remarks. He reported the following dream at this time:

I was set to perform a comedy routine on a stage. But, for some reason, I had just learned about it and didn't have time to prepare. In fact, I didn't know how I would be funny to the audience, who I could hear in the background. Suddenly, I noticed that I didn't have anything on but a thin pair of polka-dotted boxer underwear. I couldn't go on like this! Just then, the curtain goes up and I am standing face to face with the whole audience looking at me and waiting for me to say something. I couldn't speak.

This dream reflects both the client's current Life Style and his concern about 'performing' in front of others at the meeting. The content pertaining to the 'late notice' for the routine and not wearing anything but underclothes vividly conveys the client's feeling of being unprepared and fear of being discovered as insufficient or a failure. This dream was consistent with other content gathered about the client. As a first child in his family of origin, he often felt responsible and in the hot-seat to perform. Although he frequently was able to stay on top of things, when he felt overwhelmed by life's requirements he would stop or slow down in making decisions, would let deadlines approach and expire, and would let the pace of events overtake him. The client either had to be completely on top of his life or would give in and be swept along by what he had left undone. In the current situation he was finding a 'middle ground' by learning to do what he could without giving up.

Quantitative measures of Life Style variables

The administration of tests and measures for clinical purposes should be guided by several considerations, the first of which involves the timing of test administration. Quantitative measures of Life Style variables preferably should occur very early in therapy. Most clients experience the completion of tests at the inception or early stages of therapy as a relatively routine effort to assess their emotional functioning. The completion of tests later in the course of therapy could be experienced as intrusive and as stemming possibly from the therapist's lack of trust in the client or from the therapist's feeling stuck or lost in conducting the therapy. The second consideration involves the extent to which the use of quantitative measures engages and fits with the client's view of the therapeutic process. For instance, some clients may expect or even request the use of objective measures to assist with their treatment. In such cases measures may be administered as much for their value in engaging the client as for the technical information they may provide. Alternatively, other clients may be offended by the use of tests that they see as reducing the complexity and richness of their lives to a series of numbers. In this regard, therapists should objectively evaluate their purposes for assessing clients and reconcile this with what their clients are wanting and needing in the way of therapeutic services.

In addition to the action- and process-oriented techniques described above, several quantitative measures exist for use either in assessing the Life Style in clinical settings or in conducting research on relevant Life Style variables. The first of these measures is the 65-item Basic Adlerian Scales for Interpersonal Success – Adult Version (BASIS-A; Curlette et al. 1999, Kern et al. 1996, Wheeler 1996). Five of the ten BASIS-A sub-scales assess Life Style themes that emerged early in life to meet the challenges of school/work, relationships, and friendships/community: (1) going along, (2) taking charge, (3) wanting recognition, (4) being cautious, and (5) belonging – Social Interest, which provides an indication of the respondent's overall level of interest and engagement with other people. The BASIS-A also has five supplementary scales (harshness, entitlement, liked by all, striving for perfection, and softness) that provide additional information about the five major Life Style themes. The BASIS-A has been validated against other known measures (e.g. the 16 Personality Factors, the Myers-Briggs Type Indicator, and the MCMI-II) and consequently is useful in understanding the Life Style, in planning and facilitating treatment, and in teaching Adlerian principles.

Several additional measures exist for assessing components of the family atmosphere. Among these is the 40-item Family of Origin Scale (FOS; Hovestadt et al. 1985) that assesses the overall level of dysfunction in the family of origin. Several studies have documented the reliability and the validity of the FOS (Capps et al. 1993, Hovestadt et al. 1985, Mazer et al. 1990). Higher scores on this measure correspond to greater levels of experienced dysfunction and disharmony. Because the FOS assesses specific family member behaviours rather than people's attitudes or opinions about their families, this instrument may be particularly useful for assessing components of family life that overwhelm and overburden children and ultimately lead to the development of faulty Life Style patterns.

The McMaster Family Assessment Device (FAD; Epstein, Baldwin and Bishop 1983) is a 53-item multidimensional measure of family behaviours and relationships whose seven sub-scales differentiate between emotionally healthy and unhealthy families. The FAD sub-scales assess the family's problem-solving abilities, expressive communication, maintenance of family roles, affective responsiveness, affective involvement with family members, rules for behaviour control, and a general functioning scale that assesses the overall health or pathology of the family. The latter scale correlates moderately with the FOS. The FAD sub-scales possess internal consistency estimates (α) that range from 0.72 to 0.92; the scales also moderately correlate with each other. The FAD differs from the FES in that the former is more process- and relationship-oriented while the latter possesses a greater focus on content such as active/recreational orientation, intellectual/cultural orientation, and so forth, in the family.

Although the FAD and FES assess some aspects of emotional expressiveness, the Self-Expressiveness in the Family Questionnaire (SEFQ; Halberstadt et al. 1995) provides a more thorough assessment of the positive and negative emotions that are expressed in the family. This instrument contains forty items that generate two factors (i.e. positive and negative emotions) that the respondent exhibits with family members. The valence of expressed emotions in families may be pivotal in affecting the orientation of the child towards encouragement and health as opposed to discouragement and distress. Such expression may affect children's abilities to model, label, and interpret the emotions that they observe in themselves and others. The SEFQ possesses good psychometric properties and is suitable for primary school-aged children through adulthood. A companion measure, the Family Expressiveness Questionnaire (FEQ; Halberstadt 1983), allows a respondent to rate the overall level and valence of emotional expressiveness in his or her family.

Finally, measures of Social Interest may provide valuable insight about clients' overall emotional health and their abilities to meet relationship and community life tasks. Measures of Social Interest can be employed during the Life Style assessment and also at the time of termination and follow-up to assess the amount of change towards emotional health. In this regard, Social Interest measures may provide a kind of therapy outcome assessment for Adlerian practitioners. Adlerian practitioners and researchers have used two Social Interest measures in addition to the Belonging–Social Interest scale of the BASIS-A. The first and more well-known of these measures is the Crandall Social Interest Scale (SIS; Crandall 1991, Crandall and Harris 1991). The SIS consists of twenty-four pairs of traits, fifteen pairs of which are scored to determine the level of Social Interest. Respondents read each pair and then circle or underline the term that describes how they would rather be. The items have a split-half reliability of 0.77 and a five-week test–retest reliability of 0.82 (Crandall 1991). Crandall reports correlational findings that generally support the content and construct validity of the SIS. That is, persons with higher levels of Social Interest exhibited lower scores on measures of hostility and depression, and higher scores on behavioural measures of co-operation and altruism. An advantage of this measure is that its response format of presenting equally attractive pairs of traits tends to minimise the confounding of social desirability with Social Interest.

Individual psychologists also have used the Sulliman Scale for Social Interest (SSSI; Sulliman 1973). This measure contains fifty statements that respondents evaluate as either true or false for their lives. Sulliman reports that the SSSI is internally consistent (KR-20 = 0.91) and was temporally stable (r = 0.93) for a sample of high school students. Although less research has been conducted using the SSSI relative to the SIS, at least two studies documented that Sulliman's measure is not biased by social desirability and that it correlated negatively and significantly with the clinical scales of the Minnesota Multiphasic Personality Inventory in a sample of hospitalised veterans (Mozdzierz, Greenblatt and Murphy 1986, 1988, Watkins 1994). The relationship of the SSSI with positive indicators of emotional health (e.g.

self-esteem, resilience, hope, optimism) has not been explored however. The SSSI is reprinted in Appendix 1 of this book.

Phase III: Insight

The purpose of this phase of therapy is to build an understanding about the self on at least two levels. The first level involves a cognitive, semantic, or factual awareness about the Life Style (e.g. life choices and consequences, problem and growth areas of the personality, etc.). This kind of understanding involves 'knowing that' as opposed to 'knowing how'. The initial phases of therapy may build or heighten this type of understanding. The Life Style analysis especially may increase clients' factual knowledge about the kinds of people they are and how their personalities have taken shape over time. This knowledge, while a necessary component of Adlerian therapy, is not sufficient by itself to produce enduring Life Style changes. Insights of a different sort must be achieved for clients to progress further in the change process.

The second level of understanding is the focus of work in the insight phase. In addition to 'knowing that', clients begin to 'know how'. This is a deeper form of understanding – perhaps one that exists more on a reflexive and emotional level. Although clients may understand their fictional goals, being able to observe them in process and to understand them in the moment is the objective of the insight phase. This means that the therapy takes on a greater process focus with interventions that are more experiential, interpersonal, and immediate. With the therapeutic relationship established, clients hopefully will feel safe and comfortable in being themselves with the therapist. During this phase therapists more directly contact their clients' maladaptive Life Style processes and help them to understand and change self-defeating patterns. We discuss three Adlerian techniques that can produce deeper insights in clients: confrontation, paradoxical intention, and spitting in the soup. This list is not meant to be exhaustive, but representative of the type of strategies and techniques available to individual psychologists. Obviously, strategies from other areas (e.g. interpersonal psychotherapy) also could be recruited in the service of building insight.

Confrontation

Dr Bernard Shulman (1973: 205) stated that 'confrontation techniques are intended to challenge the client to give an immediate response, make an immediate change, or examination of some issue'. The content of the confrontation usually involves some discrepancy or inconsistency in clients' lives. That is, clients may characterise their behaviour in one way, but actually respond in an entirely different, or even contradictory manner. Alternatively, clients may exhibit inferentially inconsistent behaviours or articulate attitudes or opinions that imply cross-purposes. The objective of confronting clients with these discrepancies is to make them aware of their responses and, while they are in the immediate situation that gave rise to their appearance, to find some way to respond that ultimately may lead to a positive change.

Clients can be confronted in several Life Style areas, beginning with their subjective views or perceptions (Shulman 1971, 1972, 1973). Here, the therapist first attempts to understand a particular position and then poignantly restates it to the client so that it is clearer and perhaps more starkly experienced. For example, a client with a history of participating in abusive relationships may state, 'I just don't want to give up on him. If I can make him happy enough, he'll change and like me so much that he'll never become angry enough to hit me again.' The therapist may respond with: 'How do you put that thought together with what you said last week: "If he gets drunk or angry one more time, I have no choice but to leave. It's the only way to save myself."'

Shulman also described the confrontation of clients' mistaken beliefs and assumptions about themselves or the world. Consistent with cognitive-behavioural theory, changes in mistaken beliefs can lead to affective and behavioural changes as well. Again, the confrontation can take the form of either a question or a statement that illustrates the absurdity of the client's attitudes. Suppose that a ruling type of client stated, 'It is absolutely imperative that the cashiers give me the correct change – I just lose it if they don't because matters of money must be exact!' A confrontation of this belief might be, 'You might have a point there. *You*, of all people, *must* be given the exact change because you deserve perfect service more than everybody else does. Honest mistakes by the cashier or a faulty change machine are simply not good reasons.' At this point the client must either defend or begin to relinquish the extreme belief that was articulated – either way, the therapist's statement calls for an immediate response.

Clients' private, unconscious goals can be targeted for confrontation as well. Typically therapists will have an idea of the client's laws of movement and can discern the client's goals before she or he can. Here, the therapist may phrase a tentative question designed to reveal the client's desired outcome. For example, a therapist might confront a procrastinating client with the following: 'Is it possible that by starting on your school work late enough you will avoid being really tested by the challenges of the work?' Alternatively, the confrontation could be phrased as a statement: 'When you start the work as late as you normally do, it really becomes impossible to tell whether the bad outcomes resulted from getting started late or from the problems you had in just doing the work.'

Finally, Shulman (1971) indicates that clients' destructive behaviours can be confronted. This form of confrontation was illustrated earlier in this chapter by the therapist's response to the client who kept incurring charges for sessions that he did not attend. Other Life Style problems can be the focus of this kind of forthright confrontation. For example, clients abusing alcohol or drugs may be informed, point blank, 'If you continue to drink this way, you are going to lose your job and your family. You have a problem here and you need help.'

Clients can respond in many ways to challenges, the most productive of which may be to admit to the discrepancy or problem and then work from there to find a solution. Other forms of recognition may be nonverbal, such as a knowing smile (i.e. recognition reflex), a transient, fleeting gesture or tic. Still other responses from clients may reveal they have heard the confrontation but choose not to respond to it. Here, clients may suddenly change the subject, wave the challenge away, or simply deny the discrepancy embodied in the therapist's confrontation. These can be signals to the therapist to follow up with another confrontation of the client's rejecting response. Alternatively, the client's hesitancy to respond to the confrontation may be signalling that that the therapist's timing was off or that the client did not feel safe at the time. The therapist must decide here whether to pursue further confrontation or to postpone it until a later time.

Paradoxical methods

Mozdzierz, Macchitelli and Lisiecki (1976) credit Adler with the discovery and use of paradoxical methods in therapy. These methods are used to reduce the occurrence of problematic symptoms, to help clients understand the role of the symptoms in their Life Style, to show clients that the symptoms are under their control, and to help clients to experience the humour and absurdity associated with toggling back and forth between their former symptoms and newer, more healthy responses. As West, Main and Zarski (1986) noted, a number of therapists from other theoretical orientations, such as systemic theory, have extended and refined the family of paradoxical techniques (e.g. Haley 1976) that Adlerian counsellors can add to their therapeutic repertoires. It bears noting that among the techniques we have been discussing thus far, the effective use of paradoxical methods (i.e. formulating the nature of the paradox for the client, timing its delivery, and responding to the client's reactions) requires considerable clinical skill and experience.

The primary component of this technique involves the therapist prescribing that the client should purposely attempt to make a problematic symptom appear on demand, appear more frequently, or manifest itself on a more severe or intense level. If the client heeds the prescription and is successful in invoking the symptom as directed, he or she may then learn that the symptom is not completely uncontrollable. That is, if the symptom can be turned on at will, perhaps it can be turned off at will. The process of following the prescription may help the client to learn about its role in the Life Style and the situations or events that formerly triggered the symptom – increasing his or her insight. This technique can be very effective – but can also be a complete failure, because there is a risk of the client being too compliant. Instead of promoting insight, the symptom simply worsens.

The use of paradoxical technique as described above is more likely to result in success for clients who are compliant with the prescription and who view the therapist as an experienced or expert change agent. Clients who tend to be non-compliant or who seek to defeat the therapist require a different approach (West, Main and Zarski 1986). That is, instead of prescribing the symptom the therapist counsels the client that he or she might as well adjust to it, make the best of it, give in to it, and so forth because it seems unlikely that the client will be able to alleviate it. This prescription challenge can stimulate non-compliant or oppositional clients to thwart the therapist's predictions or advice and to move against the symptom. In other words, the therapist's challenge creates an ordeal for the client such that dropping the symptom or reducing it deflates the ordeal (Haley 1976).

Another variation on paradoxical methods is found in Corsini's (1982) relapse prevention technique. Here, once a client has made some initial gains in reducing symptoms or problem behaviours, she or he is requested to try an experiment in which they will produce their former responses. As Corsini observed, many clients find this request puzzling or even silly and may argue against it given the gains that have been made. This technique is designed to help clients understand their symptoms and their role in the Life Style better because such knowledge may not develop initially as clients traverse from maladaptive responses to healthy ones. Purposely producing former responses raises clients' awareness about their Life Style patterns and may help to solidify the gains they have made. Further, predicting that a relapse will occur tends to normalise clients' behaviour so that when they do symptomatically backslide a bit, this has been predicted and is meaningful rather than alarming.

Spitting in the soup

Spitting in the soup, like paradoxical intention, is designed to make clients' characteristic and maladaptive ways of responding to challenges less effective than they formerly were. The significance of the name, 'spitting in the soup' is that if therapists can find a way to make clients' problematic behaviours ('the soup') less palatable (i.e. by metaphorically spitting in them or causing them to spoil in some way), clients will be less likely to benefit from them and, consequently, to perform them.

The use of this technique, like the others we have described, requires therapists to have some knowledge of their clients' ways of hesitating or safeguarding. By optimally mismatching how clients tend to use their dysfunctional behaviours, therapists can make them less viable as alternatives. Sometimes clients' behaviours or reasons for their behaviours can be lampooned or exaggerated to make them seem ridiculous. Also, spitting in the soup conveys that at some level the therapist understands what the client is attempting to accomplish with his or her symptoms. The use of additional techniques following spitting in the soup, such as confrontation, can build clients' awareness levels even further.

We can provide several examples of how this technique is used. Suppose that a child suspiciously comes down with a 'sickness' and is unable to go to school to give his book report or to take her test. Parents can make such sickness less palatable by saying, 'Wow! I think you are worse off than you know. You probably won't feel like going to the skating rink tomorrow either, so I'll just plan to cancel that, too.' Alternatively, a therapist may respond to a client who is known to 'conveniently' become ill to curry favour, sympathy, or exoneration from facing some task by responding in passing: 'That seems to be a bad cough, but if you could wheeze more deeply, it really would sound convincing.' Finally, one of us (AES) worked with a client who once took particular pride in getting attention and offending others by his body odour. The client was challenged by the following statement and subsequently changed his behaviour: 'I wouldn't just stop using deodorant, I'd go all the way. Why don't you stop bathing for a week and keep wearing the same clothes?'

There are several caveats to consider before using this technique. First, therapists should have a reasonably good idea of how their clients will respond to the challenges they pose by spitting in the soup. Second, therapists should be convinced that the response they are targeting is one that is contrived by the client and not due to a legitimate medical condition or the real worsening of a condition. Third, therapists should portray themselves as being curious about their client's behaviour, and respond openly to their reactions. For example, if some clients defend their behaviours, the therapist may respond along the lines of, 'Yes, I see what you are doing, I was just trying to help you do a better job of it.' Finally, a sound working alliance is necessary, with both the client and the therapist working towards to same goal of removing symptoms; such an alliance will help clients not to feel offended by the therapist's candid or challenging remarks.

Phase IV: Reorientation

The final phase of therapy involves helping clients to reorient and recommit towards the healthy fulfilment of the life tasks. This phase usually begins after clients have developed insights about themselves on both cognitive and emotional levels and have experienced sufficient encouragement from the therapist to make some initial changes in their Life Style. As these gains accumulate, clients may become progressively more ready to implement Life Style changes in contexts that reach beyond the therapy room.

The challenges confronting clients at this juncture take on particularly a social and existential colouring. Although clients have changed with the help of an encouraging therapist, how might attempts to implement Life Style changes in family and social relationships be met? To some extent, family, friends, and other associates have tuned their relationships to clients' pre-existing, maladaptive Life Style patterns. As clients venture new ways of being, perhaps by asserting themselves in new or effective ways, making more independent decisions, listening and responding rather than directing, and so forth, others necessarily must adjust to a change in the relational status quo. The resistance clients may meet because others are reluctant to change or do not know how to respond becomes the focus of the therapy during reorientation.

Therapy can give clients an increased and renewed sense of freedom and independence that, for some, raises existential issues. People who have changed their dependence or avoidance patterns in therapy may be left with the question of 'What kind of person do I want to be with others now?' Other clients could have questions such as: 'Now that I can truly be myself, what do I want to do with my life?' or 'Because I don't try to dominate others any more, how can I best fit in?' Indeed the freedom and choices that come with successful work in therapy can present their own dilemmas.

Adlerian scholars have developed several techniques to help clients with the social and existential 'growing pains' that they may experience in the latter phases of therapy. These involve the pushbutton technique, catching oneself, and acting as-if. Although we will discuss only these techniques, it is possible that many more could be recruited to assist with generalising clients' gains to broader life areas.

Pushbutton technique

Dr Harold Mosak developed the pushbutton technique as a device to show clients that they have control over what they choose to think about and, consequently, the emotional experiences that stem from these thoughts (Mosak 1985). Although Mosak described the technique as one he used to interrupt a depression, the pushbutton exercise can be used with a wide variety of psychological symptoms. Therapists can use this technique in either the insight or reorientation phases of treatment; we chose to discuss it here, however, because clients may benefit from realising that they have primary control over their feelings rather than the people or situations they encounter when reorienting to life's challenges.

The pushbutton technique is begun by asking clients to recall and then to visualise a very pleasant memory. This memory should be one in which the client was able to truly be himself or herself and was able to experience the memory as affirming and validating. Mosak (1985) instructs clients to project the image of the memory in front of them, with eyes closed, as if they are watching it on a television screen. As the memory plays from beginning to end, clients are instructed also to tune into the feelings and positive experience they had during the event. When this positive memory segment is completed, clients are asked to raise a finger as a signal to the therapist.

The second phase of the pushbutton technique involves asking clients (with eyes still closed) to recall and envision a negative memory – project it on to the mind's screen. Like the first phase, clients are asked to attend to the feelings they had as this negative scene is played out. When they give the signal that this memory has run to completion, the third phase begins by having clients recall either a new positive, self-affirming memory or the one that they produced earlier. Again, clients are instructed to envision the memory and to tap into its feeling components.

After recruiting and experiencing this third memory, the exercise is discussed. Clients are asked what happened to their feeling experiences during the three phases. Mosak (1985) discusses with clients that when they recall negative memories, they also invoke the negative feelings along with them. Similarly, when positive memories are recalled, positive feelings ensue. In this way, clients are made to understand that they play a very big role in deciding to push their happy/positive buttons or their unhappy/negative buttons – it is their choice.

This technique heightens clients' awareness that they have reflexive control over their feeling states. Some clients may not welcome this awareness because it implies that a significant proportion of the responsibility for initiating or maintaining Life Style changes resides with them. Once clients know that they can 'push their own buttons', the therapy can proceed to examine why some clients choose to continue engaging in negative or self-defeating thoughts that ultimately sabotage their happiness and reorientation.

Catching oneself

Clients may find it challenging to implement changes and to maintain the benefits of their changed attitudes and behaviours for a couple of reasons. First, thought–feeling–emotion complexes may have developed early in clients' lives and become ingrained and habitual through repeated use. Changing established maladaptive patterns requires conscious focus and energy because reliance on automatic processes may lead to engaging in dysfunctional patterns again. Second, people in the client's social network become accustomed to his or her ways of behaving and in many respects provide cues for these behaviours. Changes in a client's behaviour may meet with increased pressure, although implicit or subtle, to behave in the old ways.

The collection of techniques that focus on catching oneself have as their purpose making clients aware of the interpersonal or situational triggers that lead to maladaptive behaviour. The rationale behind the techniques is that knowledge of the mechanisms that produce an undesirable response can alert clients either to avoid the triggering events or, alternatively, to substitute a more productive or efficient response in place of the maladaptive one. Such knowledge of triggering events can be quite liberating and restore a sense of efficacy where formerly clients believed that they possessed no control and were at the mercy of other people or situations.

There are many possible variations of catching oneself, the most common form involving diaries of thoughts, feelings or behaviours that were experienced before, during and after particular events. Sometimes clients may initially catch themselves after the fact when reviewing the diaries and only catch themselves pre-emptively after cycling through several encounters with the problematic situation. Diaries and related aids can offer many helpful clues such as the time of day particular patterns may occur. For instance, is a particular client more likely to cave in to others' wishes at the beginning of the day or at the end? When is the client at his or her strongest? Next, where does the problematic pattern tend to recur? What people seem to trigger it? Asking these kinds of questions can help clients to identify problem areas and then to catch themselves.

An alternative form of catching oneself involves enlisting a reliable and reasonably impartial friend or associate to observe the client's behaviour and then to discuss, step by step the client's thoughts and feelings at various points along the way. If this method is feasible, it is particularly effective because another person may catch subtle signs that the client would otherwise have to eventually read on his or her own. The danger here is that if the observer is particularly sympathetic to the client then the feedback may be less candid and, consequently, less useful.

Living as-if

The living as-if techniques are effective in helping clients to transfer the gains they have made in therapy to contexts outside therapy. Instead of using insight to think or feel oneself into a new and less maladaptive way of responding, clients can make use of a number of strategies (e.g. fantasy, imagery, role-playing, etc.) to behave their way into new modes of thinking and feeling. Living as-if represents a kind of jump-start strategy that puts clients into a new situation and then has them work out the details of how to respond effectively in it.

Carich (1989) describes several variations of the as-if technique that can be adapted to clients' particular needs or their optimal modalities for assuming the as-if position. Some clients may benefit from closing their eyes and visualising a desired outcome to a previously troublesome situation. For example, a client who is self-conscious and fearful of public speaking may envision a performance in front of a large audience in which she or he is able to effectively deliver an address. Other clients who are not as skilled at picturing events with their mind's eye may benefit from writing or vocally narrating a story of such an as-if public speaking performance.

Another method for translating therapy-room gains to progressively wider contexts is George Kelly's (1955) fixed role technique (FRT). Although it has not been previously mentioned as an as-if technique in the Adlerian literature, FRT's active and constructive emphasis on generalising adaptive responses to clients' family and social contexts makes it a valuable resource. Briefly, this technique is initiated by cultivating clients' curiosities to participate in an experiment for finding new ways of behaving with others – it is an experiment that involves doing, being, and feeling as if one were another person. The first step after presenting these instructions and engaging the client is to ask him or her to write a self-characterisation from the perspective of a sympathetic friend. This is a paragraph or two in length and provides essential descriptive details about the client. Next, the therapist qualitatively and subjectively analyses this content and looks for ways of making subtle changes that optimally mismatch with the client's view. For example, if a client describes herself as shy, retiring, and demure, then the therapist's reframe would be that she is thoughtful, patient, and introspective.

The therapist continues to make changes in the self-characterisation that are viable and largely within the realm of possibility given clients' views of themselves. Eventually the therapist produces and then discloses to the client the 'new' characterisation and encourages the client to read it. An important element is that the client is given a new name in the therapist's revised characterisation. After briefly answering questions to clarify the main points, the therapist encourages the client to then immediately portray the person depicted in the characterisation – to try the role on for size. If this works, and after making some initial adjustments, the client is encouraged to continue the experiment by becoming the person in the role for a few weeks. Clients are instructed to feel, think, behave, and handle situations in the same way the person depicted in the vignette would.

At first, clients are encouraged to portray the role in safe and relatively peripheral relationships. With success and experience, the role, with the therapist's guidance, is engaged with progressively more central and close relationships – all without disclosing to friends or family that he or she is experimenting with new ways of being by assuming a new role. After three or four weeks, the therapist instructs the client to de-role and to assume his or her former role and identity. If the exercise has been successful, the client will be unable to completely shed the experimental role, but instead finds that beneficial attitudes and responses from the exercise tend to persist. That is, the as-if role has been incorporated into the client's dominant life role and identity.

The active ingredient of FRT is the guise or 'excuse' to temporarily assume another role identity for the sake of completing an experiment. Although the person in the characterisation sketch prepared by the therapist is not real, the client's portrayal of the role and the benefits reaped by living as-if are very real for the client. This technique is particularly useful not only in helping clients to anticipate changes in their Life Styles, but also to help them actively project these changes on to their current situations.

The FRT technique is quite powerful and should only be attempted with suitable clients. People with psychotic or dissociative tendencies should not participate in FRT, or only participate with great care. FRT typically provides clients the greatest benefits towards the end phases of therapy (i.e. in reorientation) because it helps them to consolidate and generalise gains they have made previously.

Chapter 4

Adlerian family counselling and family psychotherapy

It is not surprising that Individual Psychology stands as the progenitor of many contemporary child- and family-based interventions (Dagley 2000, Sherman 1993). An examination of some of the existing intervention models such as structural family therapy (Minuchin and Fishman 1981), strategic family therapy, and integrative, systemic approaches (e.g. Nichols 2000, Nichols and Everett 1986, Sayger and Horne 2000) reflect their Adlerian heritages. The broad expression of Adlerian ideas in these contemporary models stems from the core assumptions of Individual Psychology that people (family members) are socially embedded in a network of relationships (with partners or spouses, parents, siblings, extended family, and friends) in which we seek to meet the challenges of work, love, and community. Families and family life become quite important in affecting how children orient themselves towards others to meet life tasks. As a dynamic system, families also affect how partners and parents maintain their health and face the growth edges of their lives. In this section we provide an overview of the Adlerian approaches to intervening with couples and families. We begin with a brief review of the nature and purposes of such interventions and then address the stages and techniques of therapy that are specific to Individual Psychology.

Nature and purposes of intervention

We would like to make two distinctions in beginning our discussion of Adlerian family interventions, the first of which has to do with the question of who is the client. In traditional couples or family interventions, family members are seen together and, although each person is a client in the concrete sense, the object of the intervention is the relational unit comprising the family. Family members may be seen individually in various phases of the therapy to assess their unique perspectives in an uninhibited way, however, the focus remains on resolving the problems and improving the atmosphere of the family or couple as a whole. In other instances an individual family member is the client who is seen primarily alone over the course of treatment. This client's partner and other family members may briefly become part of the therapy to assess the familial origins and manifestations of the client's presenting problems or, with appropriate timing and purposes, to intervene strategically at the family level. Individual psychologists work comfortably in both of these modalities given their emphasis on the interpersonal and relational nature of problems that people encounter.

The second distinction, echoing that made in Chapter 3, is between Adlerian family counselling and family therapy. Although the distinction may frequently blur, we view Adlerian counselling as aimed at helping couples or families to successfully manage the challenges associated with the vicissitudes of family life. In general, Adlerian psychoeducational interventions and Adlerian family counselling interventions possess a primary- and secondary-prevention focus whose purpose is to help families maintain their emotional health or, alternatively, to help them with developmentally based issues (Ansbacher 1992). In this regard Adlerian counselling has enjoyed a long and rather rich history that dates back to Adler's establishing the first school-based child-guidance centres in pre-World War II Vienna in 1922 (Sherman and Dinkmeyer, Sr 1987, Hoffman 1994). This approach was expanded in the United States in 1937 to help parents and teachers in the family and child guidance centres (Dreikurs 1972). Marriage counselling and sex counselling centres appeared as early as 1926, followed by the family education and counselling centres (Dagley 2000). A unique component of the family counselling centres was that families would be invited to observe the therapist's work with a focus family as a way to illustrate Adlerian principles and to prepare them for their own time with the therapist. The STEP programme (Dinkmeyer, Sr and McKay 1976) for helping parents learn skills for effectively caring for children at various ages represents one of the more recent exemplars of individual psychologists' interests in providing broad-based services for families. Such an empowering orientation along with an emphasis on 'giving psychology away' is particularly consistent with Albee's (1982) community psychology orientation.

Adlerian family therapy is not only concerned with identifying problems or challenges that families face, but also with making more fundamental changes in family functioning so that the negative effects of family dysfunction can be minimised and more healthy relational patterns can be established, i.e. tertiary prevention (Sherman and Dinkmeyer, Sr 1987). Families that can benefit from Adlerian family therapy typically experience difficulties in multiple areas. Parents, for example, may have doubts or problems in their relationship that they do not face directly but instead through a relational triangle with their 'problem' child. This child, for his or her part, may experience the parents' focus as not being genuine and seek attention through a variety of self-defeating pursuits such as skipping school, experimenting with drugs or alcohol, and so forth. In addition to this, the family may infrequently express positive and validating emotions but regularly have negative and emotionally destructive exchanges that leave everyone depleted.

Consequently, family therapy may involve more intense and basic work with the family and its members, compared with family counselling, and also may be more lengthy regarding the time needed for the family to make the necessary changes.

Couples therapy may be necessary before the initiation of family therapy or, in some cases, as an adjunct to family therapy (Framo 1982). In the assessment phases of therapy it may become apparent that wider family difficulties stem from or are being maintained by a highly dysfunctional marital relationship. In such instances the therapeutic focus should be on the marriage first, or at least concomitantly, so that derivative problems in the family may be addressed. The partners, for instance, may be struggling with whether or not to dissolve their union and may be engaged in a variety of destructive behaviours that are designed either to test the strength of the union or to speed it to dissolution. Other family members or extra-marital partners may be triangled into this process. Helping the couple to resolve their issues (here, deciding to stay together, separate, or divorce) is a necessary prelude to therapeutic work with the wider family system.

Overall, the purposes of couples or family interventions parallel those of individual therapy: to increase the Social Interest of the family, to enhance their abilities to relate more meaningfully and productively, and to successfully engage the tasks of work and relationships outside the family. Adlerian therapists realise when considering these goals that families represent more than the sum of their members. Consequently their focus is not so much on pursuing individual therapy with family members en masse, but instead on working with the synergistic and emergent qualities that comprise family life. Improving the family's atmosphere, altering established relational patterns that contribute to problems or dysfunction, and cultivating the family's interest in their emotional health as well as others' well-being would all represent interventions at the 'community level' of the family. Adlerian therapists may help families to work towards developing additional healthy characteristics such as cohesion, encouragement, clear but flexible roles, distinct separation of generational boundaries, open and honest communication, quality time together, some kind of religious or spiritual orientation, and autonomous identity development of family members, among others (Framo 1982, Krysan, Moore and Zill 1990, Satir 1983).

Phases of family intervention

Adlerian therapists have discussed the intervention process with families or couples as spanning four stages, similar to the ones Dreikurs (1967) articulated in working with individuals (Dagley 2000, Dinkmeyer, Sr and J. Dinkmeyer 1982, Sherman and Dinkmeyer, Sr 1987). These phases are intended to: (a) form a relationship with the family and its members, (b) assess the collective family life style, (c) promote the family's insight about their difficulties, and (d) reorient the family towards developing and maintaining a healthy and socially interested Life Style. Rather than reviewing the characteristics of each phase and describing the therapeutic strategies associated with each (as we did in Chapter 3), we will discuss the salient issues for conducting Adlerian family counselling and therapy in each phase. We also will describe how selected techniques used in individual therapy can be adapted when working with families.

Phase I: Establishing and maintaining the therapeutic relationship with families

As in individual therapy, Adlerian therapists working with families realise the important role of a therapeutic frame to guide the development of the relationship. Several aspects of this frame merit discussion, beginning with the question of who exactly is the client (or who the couple or family believes to be the identified patient). This implies that the Adlerian therapist should decide in collaboration with the family whether a bona fide family intervention is required or whether an individual within a family requires adjunctive treatment. Second, once these issues have been sorted through, the therapist should clearly communicate his or her procedures for working with the family as a whole as well as with its individual members. What rules or procedures will the therapist follow in disclosing information revealed by one or more family members to the entire family? On what grounds would a therapist working with a teenage client share information with the parents? Making these guidelines explicit, especially at the inception of therapy, will avoid problems later. Third, it is very helpful to explain the therapeutic procedure itself. That is, the therapist may meet first with the family or couple as a whole, followed by separate sessions with individual members and then more joint sessions. Telling families what to expect and striving to maintain an equidistant position from each member will build the family's overall trust in the therapist and will minimise perceptions that the therapist favours or is in alliance with particular family members.

Once the parameters of the therapeutic contact have been established, the next step in this phase involves the family elaborating its views of the presenting problems. What brings the family to the therapist and why did they consult the therapist at this particular time? Because the family members cannot all speak at once (although in our experience families regularly try to do so!) it is important to note who speaks first to convey this information and what their orientation to the problems seem to be. Such observations may begin to reveal information about who is the 'communicator', 'symptom-bearer', 'identified patient', or the 'emotion-showing' member of the family, among many other possible roles. Other family members will also share their perspectives and contribute to the emerging narrative that the family has developed, either implicitly or explicitly, to characterise its functioning.

Beyond the content conveyed in the initial interview, Adlerian family therapists attend to process issues that arise between family members. As each member discusses his or her view of the family and its problems, how do other members react? Does an egalitarian and acceptant atmosphere emerge as the family works on this issue or, alternatively, do the communications seem telegraphic and censored by the anticipated reactions of disapproving family members? Who strives to have the last word and what effect does this have on the family? Further information about process-related issues can be gathered in interviews with individual family members. Here, it is possible to ask questions such as, 'What was going on with you when you were talking and then looked over at your older brother?' Overall, the process focus will help the Adlerian therapist to begin experiencing what it might be like to be a member of the family (i.e. to experience the family atmosphere).

Within the first three sessions the therapist and family (or couple) should come to an agreement about the goals for the treatment. This will focus the family's work on salient issues and also provide criteria for when the family's treatment is completed. This task, like many associated with couples or family work, is more complex because the family's views of their problems, the work needed to address relevant issues, and the ultimate outcomes of such work must all be, in most cases, socially constructed by the family. That is, a consensus about such issues must be reached, although the dynamics and process of achieving consensus takes more time and requires more from the family therapist. Further, all goals and objectives for therapy may be subject to revision as the family's understanding of itself deepens and reveals previously unseen dynamics or issues requiring intervention. In this regard Adlerian family therapists remain focused, but fluid, in their work.

Phase II: Family lifestyle assessment

The goal of this phase of couples or family therapy is to help the family members become aware of their collective private logic and life plans. Family interactions represent movement and such activity has one or more goals that frequently are unknown to the family members. What beliefs or myths guide the family as it meets day-to-day challenges (Nicoll and Hawes 1985)? How does it view itself, its members, and the wider world of relationships? Each family member or spouse may contribute uniquely to the movement towards the family's fictional goal. Elucidating the various roles family members play in this regard and helping the family to understand the patterns that underlie their goals will position them for making changes in the insight phase of family therapy. We discuss selected life style assessment techniques below and have emphasised methods that require members to construe shared or common family experiences.

Genograms

Completing a genogram with a family can reveal much about their relational dynamics (McGoldrick and Gerson 1985). This exercise is adapted for couples or family therapies simply by soliciting information from all the participants. The kinds of information that family members supply will range from factual to the purely evaluative or attitudinal. Although family members may not disagree about the givens of their family such as the members' ages, gender, or birth order, the nature of the relationships between people may become the subject of deliberation. For example, one or two younger siblings may feel that the parents favour the oldest child. Conversely, the oldest child may feel particularly constrained by the parents' attention and may experience it as a position not of privilege but of scrutiny and obligation. The act of completing a genogram allows family members to more or less candidly share their perspectives about the different possible relationship pairings in the family. Similarly, the family may discuss salient events such as the birth or death of immediate or extended family members. These discussions enable family members to make their private meanings of family events and relationships public and also make it possible for new and consensually validated meanings to emerge from the honest sharing of different perspectives.

The therapist should attend to several issues during the genogram exercise. First, the exercise is greatly facilitated by the presence of a co-therapist, if this is possible. With one therapist drawing the family structure at the easel or board and posing questions, another therapist can attend to the process issues that occur between family members at this time. Second, it is informative to take note of the content that generates disagreements between family members. For example, persistent arguments over apparently factual material such as significant dates may underlie issues of control and power in the family. Alternatively, disagreement over more subjective content may suggest different life goals or guiding lines for family members. Third, what families do not say about the structure and relationship of their family can be just as revealing, if not more so, than what is verbalised (McGoldrick and Gerson 1985). Do family members avoid talking about certain people or relationships?

Family time lines

The family time line exercise provides another intervention-oriented assessment method that is useful in Adlerian family therapy, although this technique does not have exclusively Adlerian origins. A similar technique exists in Satir's (1983) family life chronology assessment. The family time line procedure involves placing significant events in the lives of the couple or family on a line that is drawn on a board or flip-chart to indicate their temporal relationship to each other. Similarly, significant events in the family members' lives (births, deaths, developmental milestones, moving from home, career promotions, etc.) are also depicted on the time line. As the significant events are identified, family members are asked to talk about themselves and what their families were like during those events. Photographs or photo albums can be used in conjunction with the time lines to provide a visual stimulus for discussing life in the family at particular time points (Sherman and Dinkmeyer, Sr 1987). Families may also be asked to reflect on how events that occurred earlier in the time line may have affected later events and experiences. Finally, the time line allows temporally repetitive patterns to be identified, similar to the way that intergenerational patterns appear on genograms.

The appeal of completing the family time line is that it provides an impetus for the family to construct jointly a narrative history of their lives together. Adlerian family therapists find more value in the constructed history than in attending to the historical accuracy of those events. Similar to early recollections, the family time line reflects a projection of the family's current goals and fictions on to the past (i.e. the family interprets its past according to its present concerns). Consequently, it is informative to observe the level of consensus or disharmony among the family members as they provide factual data about past events or their interpretations of them. Significant disagreements about the meanings of events may underlie a non-shared or discrepant set of goals operating among different members of the family. Finally it is also informative to note how family members resolve their differences of opinion regarding the time line. Is there an 'official family history' to which all members subscribe or is there a fragmented, disjointed history that garners little agreement?

Early recollections (ER)

A similar assessment–intervention technique exists in soliciting and discussing the early recollections of the family. This technique is adapted for work with families by asking them to recall earlier events that were experienced by all or most of the family members. Because a considerable age range may be represented among the siblings, it is not possible to have the family recall its *earliest* recollections; the focus should instead be on recalling events that occurred within previous family epochs (i.e. when the family was in a psychologically different position than currently exists). The ER process with families involves generating approximately five memories by first focusing on a specific event or interaction and then recalling the thoughts, feelings, sensations, and behaviours associated with it. Similar to the ER technique with individuals, the single and collective constructions of these events represent current family goals and concerns. The repetition of the same or similar themes across several memories reveals much about the family's operating dynamics and may begin to build their awareness of these patterns as well.

Belove (1980) has adapted the ER technique for use with couples and calls it First Encounters of an Emotional Kind (FECK). This technique is useful for helping couples learn how challenges or problems in their marriages began and also to provide hope and encouragement for their continued lives together. The couple are asked to recall the earliest interactions that they had together and to focus on the sensorial and emotional components of the memories. As with other ER work it is important for the couple to recall and focus on specific memories rather than generalities from the past or their impressions of memories. Once the recalled memory is in focus, each partner is asked to reflect on the feelings and meanings of the interaction. An interesting result that frequently emerges from this exercise, as Dreikurs (1946) keenly noted, is that the very behaviours and characteristics that attracted partners to each other, over time and with repeated exposure, become the source of difficulties. For example, what is initially viewed as a partner's thoughtful, methodical approach to problems may later be experienced as compulsiveness and hesitancy; attracting virtues are later transformed into repelling vices. Each partner discusses their recollections of corresponding events, addressing discrepancies or differences in meanings that appear along the way. Ordinarily four or five memories may serve the purpose in helping a couple understand their relational dynamics and individual/collective goals.

The three aforementioned techniques all involve the interactions of family members to construct a portrait of their relationship patterns. In most cases the material that families discuss is more evaluative and attitudinal than factual or logical. Adlerian therapists therefore are sensitive to the subtle or overt forces that families exert on individuals to make their accounts consistent with the dominant, prevailing family narrative. Even if the family does not possess the psychological acuity to discern its fictional goals and the necessary guiding lines, these may nonetheless be operative and create 'rules' of reporting or story-telling that other family members enforce. Although this phenomenon is present in almost all families, its pervasive operation to constrain family members' narratives indicates a high degree of control, and perhaps rigidity, in the family. Appropriately timed and executed process commentaries about such control may help to reveal both its sources and the sanctions for violating it. Further, finding a way to relax such control may give family members the increased semantic 'manoeuvring room' that they need to relate in healthier ways.

Birth order and family roles

An analysis of the family members' birth order and resulting family roles can also reveal information about relationship dynamics that contribute to the maintenance of family problems (Ackerman 1958). Although actual birth order may provide a starting point for such an analysis, the family members' perceived or psychological positions within the family are more meaningful for understanding their goals and behavioural tendencies (Adler 1927). One method for ascertaining the psychological position is to observe how family members interact in completing the aforementioned exercises, especially the genogram. Who seems to be the leader and initiator? Who seems the most popular and charming? Who seems always to be left out or observing from the periphery? Who is scrutinised, interrupted, or intruded on? Looking for these patterns during the initial interviews with the family and as they interact may provide some indication of the roles and role functioning that exists.

Two alternative methods exist for assessing the psychological position in the Psychological Birth Order Inventory (PBOI) and the Birth Role Repertory Grid (BRRG; see Chapter 3 and Appendix 1 for a fuller description of these instruments). The PBOI and BRRG may be used in several ways to facilitate the family's investigations of the roles that members occupy. One approach involves having family members separately complete the PBOI first and then later discuss their scores on the four roles with the other family members. A richer, but slightly more complex approach involves each family member completing a BRRG. As discussed previously, the BRRG differs from the PBOI in that the former requires the respondent to apply the birth/family role constructs not only to himself or herself, but to all the family members.

Once the BRRGs are completed, the therapist surveys each one to assess the predominant roles ascribed to each member. For instance, two older siblings may attribute characteristics of the youngest child (being a charmer, initiator, popular, etc.) to a younger sibling. Alternatively, the younger sibling may experience the attention he or she receives as intrusive and characterise himself or herself more in the only child role. After the therapist has examined the BRRGs, they are then redistributed to the family members and a discussion can ensue, round-robin style, about how each member perceives the role behaviours of other members. As with the other process- and intervention-oriented techniques, the discrepancies that exist in family members' perceptions of the others' roles, along with the discussions that ensue to substantiate their perceptions and impressions, help to make private or infrequently shared meanings more public. Further, these discussions can lead to the objectification and resolution of role conflicts and to a greater appreciation of the subjective experiences that each member has in occupying his or her niche within the family. A role analysis, along with the information gleaned from completing the genogram, will reveal how family members achieve their collective goals through either co-operating or failing to co-operate.

Other quantitative measures

Adlerian family therapists may choose to blend several of the above methods with more objective measures of the family's functioning. In this regard, many of the instruments we discussed for use with individuals in Chapter 3 may also be used with family members. Perhaps the most useful among these would be the Family Environment Scale (FES; Moos and Moos 1986). This instrument can be used to characterise the family's present atmosphere along ten dimensions (real form) and can also be used to assess how family members would like their family to be in the future (ideal form). Having family members complete the FES and then discuss their scores on scales such as family cohesion, control, conflict, and so forth may help them to learn how their family functions. The ideal form of the FES can be used to establish goals for the family sessions and possible criteria for termination. Other measures such as the Family Assessment Device (FAD; Epstein, Baldwin and Bishop 1983) can be used for similar purposes.

An evaluation of the family's collective orientation towards or away from Social Interest can be made by having family members complete one or more of the measures of Social Interest that we described in Chapter 3 (e.g. the Social Interest Scale, Sulliman Scale of Social Interest, Basic Adlerian Scales for Interpersonal Success (BASIS)). A multidimensional measure such as the BASIS may be particularly revealing of how the family, both individually and as a unit, has oriented itself towards valuing and participating in meaningful relationships with others. In actually assessing Social Interest the therapist could survey individual members' responses to the instruments used and then have the family discuss the levels of their scores and what Social Interest means to them. Alternatively, an overall Social Interest score for the family could be calculated from the individual measures, which could then be used to characterise where the family stands regarding their collective Social Interest orientation. This discussion would involve what the family seems to be doing well (e.g. giving their time and resources to help others) and what seem to be growth edges for the family's Social Interest (e.g. relaxing the need to be seen by others as the 'most charitable' family in the community).

Phase III: Promoting insight

Use of the above techniques with couples or families will begin to help them understand, at least on a cognitive level, the source and nature of their difficulties. Such an awareness, while necessary, is not sufficient, however, to cause the family to change. More than is the case for individuals, families especially will attempt to maintain the status quo of their relationships and the problems that are associated with them. This stems in part from the fact that the family defines its own reality and the members continue to play their respective parts in this reality until almost everyone becomes aware of the need to revise the family's script and to actively portray different parts in it. The family members need additionally to build a reflexive, procedural awareness of how they function or fail to function. Adlerian family therapists can actively intervene at this level to both build this awareness and help the family to develop more adaptive ways of meeting the tasks of life. In this regard we describe several selected techniques that promote family insight and subsequent change.

Confrontation of family dynamics

As therapists observe or directly experience the operation of dysfunctional family processes they can pose questions and challenges that produce an immediate response from the family. As we discussed in Chapter 3, such confrontations may target: (a) clients' subjective views or private justifications, (b) their mistaken beliefs, or (c) their private goals or guiding lines (Sherman and Dinkmeyer, Sr 1987, Shulman 1973). Additionally, therapists may confront family members regarding their behaviour with other family members to the extent that such behaviour is significant for moving the family towards its fictional goals. For instance, if the therapist noticed that a spouse repeatedly interrupted and then talked for his or her partner when the therapist posed a question, the therapist could respond with the confrontation:

> Have the two of you noticed that whenever I ask Marcia a question, Ken stops her and speaks for her? Ken, is there something that you don't want Marcia to say or that you are afraid of hearing from her? Marcia, I guess you can get by without thinking or doing too much since you always can rely on Ken to be your mouthpiece. Someone who does not know you might think you don't have a mind of your own or that you're afraid to speak up.

In practice, an Adlerian family therapist would not fire such an uninterrupted barrage of questions at the couple or family, preferring to keep the confrontation as succinct and poignant as possible. In this brief example, it is possible that the observable behaviour stems from the husband, Ken, needing to maintain tight control over himself and his wife – even to the point of speaking for her. For her part, Marcia's fictional goal may be to avoid taking responsibility and having to deal with the consequences of decisions she makes autonomously. In this regard, is it no surprise that she may seek and then engage in a partnership with a much more dominant partner. Overall, such process-oriented commentaries and queries both interrupt a particular dynamic mid-stream, making the couple or family more aware of themselves in the present, and also demanding some kind of action or response. In many respects these kinds of interventions represent the active ingredients in individual, couples, and family treatment.

Making family roles and experiences concrete

Several additional therapeutic procedures exist for making hidden or implicit roles and experiences concrete and readily observable to the family. Under this heading we place the techniques of family sculpting and role reversal (Bitter 1987, Sherman and Dinkmeyer, Sr 1987). With the assistance of the therapist, sculpting requires family members to assume physical positions and postures that exemplify their roles in the family and their relationships to other people. Here, family members take into account the closeness or distance in their relationships, their orientation towards or away from other people, and their manner of contacting and relating to others. The family members may assume positions relative to another person (i.e. a dyad) or relative to the family as a whole. Further, family members can be asked to sculpt themselves according to the problems or distress they experience or, alternatively, according to the kinds of relationships they would like to experience with others. As family members sculpt their relationships they are asked to describe what the sculpted position is like for them: how does it feel now and what would it be like to maintain the position? Further, they can be queried about the behaviours of others that caused the posture or position that was taken (e.g. 'What might happen if you weren't holding on to his arm with both of your hands?').

If the couple described above, Ken and Marcia, were asked to sculpt their relationship, we might see Marcia standing limply with her hands beside her while Ken stands behind her and to the left with his left hand grasping her left arm and his right hand on her back, as if operating a puppet. Alternatively, if Marcia's dependencies were more salient and Ken experienced less of a need to control or dominate, we might see her with both arms desperately wrapped around Ken's torso, and her face and eyes searching for his while he looks forward and reaches for things other than Marcia. Of course, many other variations are possible. The poignant component of sculpting, in part, is that it allows people to say with their body language what it is difficult to communicate verbally or even emotionally. Similar to the way that some clients gain awareness by listening to themselves talk, family members may experience entirely new dimensions of their existing relationships by attempting to concretely depict them.

Role reversal is another technique that can be quite useful for helping couples or family members to appreciate how their behaviour is perceived by others and also what it is like, at least in a limited way, to fill the shoes of their partner, parent or sibling (Sherman and Dinkmeyer, Sr 1987). The technique is particularly useful when two members seem entrenched in their conflicted positions such that it is difficult for them to de-centre themselves and appreciate the other's perspective. Role reversal is initiated by asking each family member to think, feel, and respond as if he or she were the other person and then to respond to the other as honestly as possible without letting the 'old' identity colour the responses. This technique, if successfully performed, allows the conflicting pair to feel that they have been understood and that their concerns have not been dismissed. In concretely enacting the roles and experiences of another, each person develops a new appreciation for the concerns and burdens the other may feel.

For example, one of us (AES) worked with a mother and her teenage son on his progress in high school. The therapist used the role-reversal exercise to help each of them understand the other's position. In this family the mother performed a substantial caretaking function in the family by preparing meals, reminding other family members about their obligations, and attempting, unsuccessfully, to get the son to complete his homework, among other things. His mother adopted the son's role of making numerous requests of his mother for money, permission to stay out later than the curfew, and preparing his favourite clothes for school. The exercise stimulated the son on several fronts, the first being that he did not realise what 'work' it was being his mother and feeling so obligated to everyone else. It was almost as if she did not have a life of her own. Alternatively, he found that his mother's portrayal of him was humorous. His constant grinning seemed to convey a recognition that he attempted to avoid practical responsibilities for himself on most occasions. The mother, realising how easy she made life for her son at the expense of her own time and effort, seemed committed to doing less for him and expecting more in return.

Symptom prescription

Symptom prescription techniques are another alternative to help family members understand the control they have over their problems, relationships, and symptoms. This method may be particularly beneficial when used in family work as the members begin to leave old patterns behind and experiment with new ways of being with each other. The core component of symptom prescription, which sometimes is referred to as paradoxical prescription or paradoxical intention, is to require that before the next session the couple or family should attempt to re-instantiate the symptoms and problem behaviours that occasioned their visit to the therapist. A variation of this technique may involve helping family members to reduce or contain the free, unbridled expression of a symptom by requesting that the symptom be expressed regularly at a certain place and time (among other possible parameters). For couples or family members who still display dysfunctional symptoms, this technique may help them to realise that they have control over their behaviour with the family: if they can induce the problematic interactions and symptoms, then they may well be able to stop them. As we discussed in Chapter 3, however, care should be taken in applying this technique to families lest they interpret it as the therapist's permission to continue 'solving' their difficulties in the usual unproductive manner. In addition, there are limitations to what should be prescribed, especially for families that previously engaged in verbal or other forms of physical abuse. Clearly, nothing can be gained from a reversion to this kind of behaviour.

For families who have begun to change their behaviour, the symptom prescription functions as a relapse prevention technique (Corsini 1982). As family members experience the benefits of changed relationships and new alternatives, the request to produce their initial problems may well be met with protests and disbelief; this is a sign that the family has invested in continuing the change process. Such prescriptions, especially if rationalised as a way to compare the present behaviour with the way it was at an earlier time, also acknowledges that families may 'backslide' on occasion and that this is to be expected.

Phase IV: Reorientation

As the family begins to relinquish some of its dysfunctional characteristics and patterns, family members will experience the need to develop new ways of behaving and relating to each other. The objective of the reorientation phase of Adlerian therapy is to help the family re-form itself in ways that promote the development and maintenance of emotional health. We describe several techniques below that have been useful in this regard. Each technique can be practised in the family therapy sessions so that the family can learn the essential features and also can discuss their experiences of the exercise.

Family council meetings

Family council meetings involve the entire family getting together each week to discuss the important events that have transpired in the family and in the members' lives during the previous week (Dreikurs 1972). The meetings typically occur at the same time each week and are intended to become a regular, ongoing part of the family's life. The family council meetings, if conducted properly, have myriad benefits that include building a sense of cohesion, fostering trust, providing tangible or emotional support, recognising accomplishments, and encouraging initiative, among others.

There are several elements that must be included in family council meetings for them to be successful and to become a resource for, rather than a hindrance to, the family's forward movement in life. First, the family members within each generation should be made to feel that they are on an equal footing. Adlerian psychology in general (Adler 1927, Ansbacher and Ansbacher 1956), and family interventions in particular, emphasise a democratic, egalitarian approach to family relationships. As leaders of the family and facilitators of the family council, the parents should model a level and equal give-and-take in their discussions in front of the children. In relating to the children, they should strive to treat everyone equally and to not show favouritism to one or more children. Further, although the parents should govern the family in a firm but gentle authoritative manner, they should always avoid authoritarian, autocratic rule whereby they dictate to each other or to the children. Finally, parents should moderate the children's inter-actions so that these retain an even-handed and fair nature. Older children should not be allowed to impose their way or will simply because they are larger or can verbally argue in ways that their younger siblings cannot.

A second important characteristic is that the communication process in the family council should be honest, expressive, and open to all members. Family members will be helped by being able to verbalise their significant experiences and feelings in a forum that includes the other important people in their lives. This means that family members should be made comfortable to share these experiences and that other family members who do not have the floor should be able both to listen and to hear on a deeper level. In this regard, it is very important that the communications in the family council not be allowed to degenerate into arguments that merely involve the exchange of damaging or hurtful messages.

Finally, the parents as moderators of the family council meetings should reserve their private or more adult concerns for meetings that they can have with each other. For instance, although the family council may discuss the implications and changes that will ensue from a parent losing his or her job, this parent's expression of worry or more intense display of emotion is more appropriately expressed privately to the other partner. In other words, sad-dling younger children with fully fledged adult emotions probably creates more problems than it solves in instantiating children's insecurities and the corresponding needs to 'parent' or 'caretake' mother or father.

Communication skills

Along with learning how to conduct family council meetings, families will also benefit from learning how to communicate effectively with each other. Although we have encountered a number of clients who characterised their presenting concerns as 'poor communication' or 'lack of communication', we believe that working on communication styles and skills is premature until the underlying difficulties and dynamics that create dysfunctional communi-cations are addressed. Consequently, a focus on building or enhancing com-munication skills during the reorientation phases of Adlerian family therapy seems more appropriate than merely addressing poor communication as a symptom.

At the outset, family members should be helped to understand the pur-poses of communication to express information and feelings that they have for important family events. In practice this means that family members express themselves honestly while avoiding the temptation to convey delib-erately hurtful or destructive material. We have observed that even couples that strongly desire to stay together can dissolve their relationships with continuous and damaging verbal exchanges. On the other side of the equation, honest communication also means that family members earnestly attempt to understand another's perspective and experiences. Making another person feel understood reduces the need to retaliate with negative comments.

Beyond the minimising of negative communications, family members should be taught the benefits of encouraging one another when appropriate opportunities arise (Dagley et al.1999). Encouragement is conveyed in a variety of ways that may include recognition of work done well at either school or at home, celebrating accomplishments, telling a family member what one likes or appreciates about him or her, instilling a sense of faith and hope regarding challenges that family members face, and so forth. Family members should strive to honestly express their sentiments rather than letting encouraging communications seem contrived or inauthentic; modelling and practise of encouraging communications and exercises by the therapist can help in this regard.

Another aspect of building communication skills involves learning how to resolve conflicts that may arise during family council meetings or other interactions. Pepper and Roberson (1982) propose a four-point process that can be adapted for use with adults as well as children. First, and consistent with our recommendations above, the conflict should be approached by a show of mutual respect by each family member; people should neither fight nor give in. Second, each person should strive to pinpoint the personal issues that the conflict threatens. Does the conflict stem from a threat to one's sense of control or superiority? Is comfort or equal treatment being challenged? Identification of the position that each person strives to protect will help to resolve the conflict. Third, each family member should be made aware that only they can control his or her behaviour. Fights, bickering, or destructive statements occur because both people agree to interact on such levels (Pepper and Roberson 1982, Sherman and Dinkmeyer, Sr 1987). Finding a common, but adaptive ground, is necessary for successful conflict resolution. Fourth and finally, each person should mutually participate in making the decisions about how to resolve the conflict by neither imposing one's will nor submitting. The decided course of action should faithfully represent the interests of both persons.

Caring behaviours

Families should supplement their enhanced communication abilities with behaviours that are consistent with their new insights and attitudes. Adlerian family therapists can help families develop and practise caring behaviours on two fronts. First, family members should develop some concrete, real ways of taking care of themselves. For couples, this could mean scheduling a weekly date to a restaurant or a movie; this may also include setting aside time for physical intimacy. Parents should also be assisted in identifying venues that allow the family to spend quality time together. This may include playing some sport together as a family (e.g. basketball, water-skiing, etc.), participating in a family hobby, or attending a religious service, among others. This time, regardless of its content, should facilitate meaningful and restorative interactions among all the family members.

On the second front, the family should be assisted to develop Social Interest for people beyond its boundaries. Caring for others may be demonstrated in a variety of ways, some of which could include participating in school-based fundraising projects for particular causes, making gifts of toys that children have outgrown to less fortunate children, and the parents' demonstration of a benevolent and socially interested orientation towards other adults.

Chapter 5

Child guidance and parenting

The psychoeducational approach of Rudolf Dreikurs

One of the most important contributions to Adlerian Psychology was Rudolf Dreikurs' psychoeducational approach to child guidance, classroom counselling, and counselling for families. What Dreikurs called 'Democratic Education' is not only a counselling and psychotherapy method of intervention with children who have behaviour problems, but also a general educational style that can be taught to parents and educators in order to prepare them for preventing behavioural problems in children and for a better education in general.

The role of a psychoeducational therapist is similar to that of a teacher who teaches pedagogical and interpersonal skills and who facilitates self-help and the possibilities of growing. A psychoeducational therapist has a preventive function and does not wait until a pathological process has taken place, but starts on an educational basis, by teaching more efficient pedagogical techniques to parents and teachers in order to avoid a psychopathological development of smaller behavioural problems.

In his time, Adler worked with children, teachers, and families. In the early 1930s he founded child guidance centres in Vienna, where doctors and psychologists worked together with schoolteachers and parents. The aim of these centres was not only the treatment of children with problems, but also the teaching of alternative educational styles with a clear preventive idea. The concept of Parenting or Parent Education is meant to help parents to bring up their children to be psychologically healthy personalities with Social Interest and with fewer psychological problems by teaching them more 'democratic' techniques.

Dreikurs' 'Democratic Education' can be conceptualised in three major lines of intervention:

1 Indirect psychological intervention by training parents and teachers how to bring up and educate their children and pupils more efficiently, being able to intervene in a preventive and corrective way with their children and pupils.
2 Direct psychological intervention with children who have psychopathological and behavioural problems. Here, the Adlerian counsellor works

with the children themselves trying to correct maladaptive behaviour and treating psychopathological disorders (e.g. enuresis).

3   Preventive and therapeutical intervention on a community level by fostering interdisciplinary collaboration (physicians, psychologists, teachers, parents, etc.) in order to improve the quality of teaching and counselling with normal and problem children in general.

What Dreikurs and his co-workers used to call 'traditional education' prevails in schools and families that use an authoritarian or autocratic teaching and parenting style, as for example the use of praise and punishment for motivation. According to Dreikurs, Democratic Education goes along with a general and progressive democratic development in our society; instead of authoritarianism, democratic values such as co-participation, dialogue, self-determination, shared responsibilities, etc. have emerged and spread widely in families, in schools, in society, and in communities in general. With respect to teaching, the teacher is not only supposed to transmit knowledge, but also to stimulate and motivate the class, to foster their understanding of human values and living together. Instead of simply receiving instruction, pupils now seem to have a right to enjoy learning and to take responsibility for their own learning progress.

When reading Dreikurs' publications (e.g. Dreikurs 1968, Dreikurs and Soltz 1964, Dreikurs, Grundwald and Pepper 1971) some of his thoughts and insights might appear obsolete and trivial to the modern reader; this impression may exist because many of Dreikurs' and Adler's revindications have, slowly and tacitly, found their way into the family and into the classroom. For instance, most parents do not consider spanking their children an effective measure to correct misbehaviour, and the great majority of contemporary teachers make efforts to hold interesting and stimulating lessons and would refuse to punish their pupils physically. In the same way, the educational politics of democratic countries are based on human democratic values, such as freedom, autonomy, participation, co-operation, solidarity, tolerance, dialogue, initiative, critical spirit, and so on, and they aim at preparing their students for a life of responsible maturity. But these well-meaning politics are based on the belief that it is the teachers and the parents who know perfectly how to implement these values, which is not always the case, and therefore there is still a discrepancy between the educational ideal (which used to be perfectly 'democratic' in the Dreikursian sense) and everyday upbringing practice at home and in the classroom. Furthermore, providing 'Democratic Education' can be relatively easy when well-meaning parents and teachers deal with 'normal' children who, except for minor 'misbehaviour', typical for some developmental stages, do not present deeper psychological problems. But unfortunately, and in spite of an increasing democratic consciousness in education, behaviour problems in children and adolescents have not decreased. On the contrary, they seem to get worse, and juvenile violence is a constant topic in the media. Consequently, the question can be posed: does Democratic Education really work? Has it been implemented incompletely or erroneously? Maybe the authoritarian educational style has been substituted not by a really Democratic Education, but by a highly permissive 'laissez-faire' attitude, not only in confused and overstrained parents and schoolteachers, but also in society in general.

What is a 'problem child'?

When talking about a 'problem child' or a 'child with problems', we used to refer to behaviour problems (problems of discipline, obedience, violence, etc.), but in many cases these children also have learning problems. Difficulties with learning can be a result of misbehaviour (the child bothers a classmate, disrupts the class and therefore distracts himself or herself from paying attention to what the teacher says), but frequently learning disabilities like dyslexia, low attention span, hyperactivity, etc. are a breeding ground for behaviour problems (a hyperactive child has the tendency to bother the others and to disrupt the class). Most often we find what we would like to call a 'psycho-organic problem' at the base of learning disabilities, and a 'psychosocial problem' at the base of misbehaviour; but psychosocial difficulties such as paternal neglect or violence in the family can lead to both violent reactions in the classroom *and* learning disabilities. In any case, behaviour and learning troubles develop to form a complex network that is difficult to diagnose in all its manifold aspects and even more difficult to treat.

Neuropsychological aspects of the problem child

When we talk of the 'psycho-organic problem', this is in reality a varied collection of brain dysfunctions along with psychological effects. These neuropsychological dysfunctions have sometimes been integrated into the common denomination of 'minimal brain dysfunction' which presents a variety of combinations of different symptoms, the most common of which could include hyperactivity and attention deficit, impulsivity, impaired fine motor movements, hyper- or hyposensibility to sensorial stimulation, etc. In many cases a neurological examination reveals the presence of so-called neurological 'soft signs', for example difficulties in movement coordination and balance. Such a child can show impairment in learning performance and in behaviour: slow learning, low frustration tolerance, immature emotions, clumsy movements, impaired awareness of danger and impulsive acts. In many cases no distinction can be made as to whether these problems are a direct result of a neurological dysfunction or if they are the child's psychological reaction to perceiving him or herself as different from and inferior to the others, just as a physically or sensorially handicapped child can feel inferior and react with behaviours that strive to overcome these inferiority feelings.

Chronic medical illnesses, such as diabetes or asthma, or simply poor health can have the same effects. As a result of these conditions, the child can develop a variety of difficulties, from simple 'naughtiness' and occasional disobedience to learning disability and violence. The negative reaction of adults and peers can aggravate the situation: criticism, rejection, or scorn contribute to the child's existing inferiority feelings so he or she tends to withdraw or to overcompensate for these feelings with striving for superiority. The child can turn passive and resigned, or hostile and aggressive. He or she can also try to get attention by becoming the class clown or by exaggerating his or her problems and needs, demanding immediate satisfaction. These problems, when they reach a certain point of escalation, can result in phobia of attending school, truancy, depressions, psychosomatic symptoms, violence, substance abuse, delinquency and suicide.

As for the psychosocial problem, the parents' erroneous educational style is often exacerbated by a socially deteriorated environment with all its associated aspects: economic problems, poverty, immigration, violence, neglect, alcohol and drug abuse, and margination in general. But even in relatively good social conditions, many parents have difficulties in giving their children a 'Democratic Education' in the sense of Dreikurs. While in Adler's and still in Dreikurs' times parents used to raise their children with authoritarian methods, imposing their rules and values with severity and punishment, without the possibility of being questioned, today many parents and other adults who work in education complain of educational methods that are too permissive and too 'laissez-faire' to deserve the terms 'education' or 'method'. Many parents, inexperienced and insecure about how to bring up their children, on one hand tend to overprotect and pamper them, and on the other, spoil them and anticipate their every wish. This permissive attitude goes along with a society that seems to hide, under the cloak of freedom and individualism, an unlimited permissiveness. For instance, in Spain, a country with traditional tolerance with respect to alcohol consumption, the sale of alcoholic drinks to people under 16 is not allowed, but in practice there are no restrictions for individuals of any age to purchase and consume alcohol, and at the moment there is an ongoing discussion in the media about what to do about the kids (some of them only 12) who gather in the streets on Friday and Saturday nights and consume great amounts of cheap wine, beer and all kinds of risky mixtures of soft and hard drinks. It appears that the former authoritarian and repressive upbringing has changed into its opposite. In view of the increasing violence among children and adolescents, voices arise that demand a return to the former authoritarian values.

In an Adlerian view, it is obvious that not only repression and severity can produce inferiority feelings in the young person; permissiveness is negative too. Children who never learned to make efforts to overcome obstacles, who never had to fight for anything, will always believe that there has to be somebody in their lives who removes all the obstacles from their path and who grants them all of their whims. And they will never experience the satisfaction of achieving something by their own efforts. That is why they feel inferior to their 'governing slave' (parent). Both authoritarian and permissive upbringing can produce discouraged children who have difficulties in developing Social Interest. Nonetheless, we want to point out that neither the psycho-organic nor the psychosocial complex of problems, neither neuro-psychological dysfunctions nor erroneous educational style alone, are enough to produce discouraged children; more important is what Adler used to call 'the opinion', the personal stance the child takes with respect to what happens to him or her. Obviously, a girl with dropout drug-dependent parents and a cognitive deficit as a result of her mother's substance abuse during pregnancy has a high probability of becoming an adolescent with many troubles, but 'everything can also be different', as Adler used to say. In the Adlerian view, the girl's opinion is her free, though not always conscious, decision, which can make her, instead of becoming a delinquent (strive for power), a fighter against social injustice (Social Interest). Thus even a child raised in unfavourable conditions can compensate for discouragement with personal effort and in a 'useful' way by viewing difficulties as challenges and obstacles that can be overcome (striving for perfection or striving for compensation). As we have pointed out in former chapters, this striving for compensation or 'usefulness' implies, in the Adlerian sense of Social Interest, that this individual does not only try to overcome his or her personal misfortunes, but will also contribute to help others in some way. In the psychological literature, resilience is known as the concept that describes how children can overcome negative childhood experiences and become psychologically healthy individuals (Cyrulnik 2002).

Unfortunately, in many cases, the discouraged child has not enough willpower and resources to develop a high degree of Social Interest and remains on the path of striving for superiority. If it is an active and strong-minded child (a male, in many cases), he will tend to seek power and dominance over the others and become a 'tyrant', in the extreme. A more passive child can go for the line of the least resistance and seek a certain power by getting admiration and being the centre of attention (being pretty, having certain abilities); or she can try to seek compassion and pity by showing and exaggerating her sufferings. Traditionally, many young girls decide on seeking attention and compassion instead of seeking dominance, as our society is still more tolerant of power-hungry males and females who are anxious to please, rather than vice versa.

Encouraging a child to develop more Social Interest requires a great amount of time and dedication, so Adler and Dreikurs always insisted on the preventive value of their method: if more and more parents and teachers are trained in their method, small problems can be detected at the beginning and treated more effectively before they become pathological. Following the educational line traced by Adler, Dreikurs designed a systematic classification of behaviour problems in children according to one of four goals the child pursues with his or her behaviour: attention, power, revenge or display of inadequacy. Many normal children during their development have stages where they seek undue attention or superiority over the adult, and normally, these phases pass by spontaneously; but they may also lead to more problematic attitudes such as revenge or withdrawal, and these are problems that require a more careful intervention. In this chapter we will detail what Dreikurs called 'the four goals of the maladapted child' and then present, with some updates, the possible corrective measures he proposed.

The four erroneous goals of childhood misbehaviour, according to Dreikurs

Before any intervention, we must detect the goal the child pursues with his or her misbehaviour in any moment. The most efficient way to guess the child's goal is to observe our (the educator's) own emotional reaction to the child's behaviour. In this way, we can also have an idea of the erroneous belief behind that goal which pushes the child to behave in that way. In the following we summarise the four possible goals in a systematic way by pointing out (a) the adult's spontaneous and impulsive emotional reaction to the child's misbehaviour and his or her usual attempts at correction, (b) the child's erroneous beliefs that make him or her act like that as an overcompensation for inferiority feelings, (c) the child's emotional reaction to the adult's attempt at correction, and (d) the possible alternative educational measures along the lines of Democratic Education. Of course, what we call the child's erroneous beliefs are not conscious thoughts; more exactly, they are unconscious perceptions of the child about him or herself and his or her relations with others, acquired through former experiences and in interaction with his or her attitudes to them. Some of the alternative educational measures will be detailed later, in the section on intervention with the problem child.

Goal 1: Attention seeking

An example of a typical situation is a child whining and niggling; or a pupil causing a disturbance by making noises during the teacher's explanations, bothering classmates, etc. The educator constantly feels annoyed and bothered by the child's behaviour (a). It seems that the child only feels appreciated when somebody gives him attention or does something for him. But because it is often difficult to obtain attention by doing something 'good', something positive and valued by the adult, the child, for fear of being overlooked and neglected, prefers to seek any kind of attention, even when it takes the form of a reprimand or punishment (b). The educator's usual reaction is to disapprove and to rebuke the child's behaviour, telling him to 'be quiet', 'stop bothering', 'stop fussing around'; the child, in face of this kind of 'attention', receives what he wanted: attention, and pauses for a moment. But as soon as the teacher continues with her lessons or shares her attention among the other pupils, the child, invariably, resumes his disturbing behaviours, and even tends to intensify them (c). As corrective measures we recommend: withdrawal from the child's radius of action; doing something unexpected; ignoring the misbehaviour and giving attention when the child behaves or does something positive (d).

Goal 2: Seeking power

An example of a typical situation is a child defying the adult's order, refusing to do something or doing something the adult does not want her to do. The educator feels very annoyed, provoked and challenged, and feels the need to impose his will on the child, preserve his authority and make the child obey (a). The child who seeks power and superiority is more discouraged than the one that only seeks attention, though in some developmental stages, minor attempts at seeking power can be considered to be a normal reaction, as long as they do not give rise to fights for who imposes their will. The child wants to compensate for a strong feeling of inferiority by proving that she is 'somebody', that she does her will and not the will of the educator (b). In many of these situations, the adult tends to use not only criticism and reprimand, but also punishment in order to impose his will, and a struggle for power may start on both sides. If the child 'wins', the educator has the feeling of pedagogical and personal defeat, but sometimes it is easier for the adult to let the child have her way instead of imposing his will. If it is the adult who 'wins', the child feels defeated, humiliated and infuriated; she might stop her behaviour and obey in face of the adult's stronger force and power, but usually she will resume her fighting with him in order to re-establish her 'self-esteem'. And she may use more and more violent and complicated ways of fighting, and is at risk of ending up seeking the goal of revenge, to win at any price (c). As alternative measures we propose refusing to be challenged and refusing to fight; continuing to be gentle and friendly, but consequent; acting instead of preaching; avoiding punishment and using natural and logical consequences; and diverting the child's negative impulse to something positive and productive (d).

Goal 3: Seeking revenge

An example of a typical situation is a pupil who hits another after being punished; damages or destroys the property of others (especially the educator's). The adult victim of the child's vengeance act feels sad and hurt, often also full of hatred for the child who did this to her (a). This child is really very discouraged, because in many situations he has had to suffer the humiliation of punishment and of adults imposing their will. He has abandoned overt struggling for power because he knows that, finally, it is the adult who 'wins'. He only gets a certain satisfaction and imaginary superiority by hurting and damaging (b). The adult tends to use severe punishments and to seek help from other adults against the child; in many cases, the educator tends to abandon all attempts at correcting the child's misbehaviour, she gives him up for lost. She refrains from pedagogical actions with respect to that child, as it is a 'hopeless case' (c). Punishing the child severely or abandoning him only reinforces the child's inferiority feelings; he may continue seeking power and revenge and ending up with violence and delinquency, especially when his normal environment rejects him; then he may look for the company of people with antisocial attitudes. But he also may give up all attempts at compensation and withdraw from any active participation, falling into the goal of withdrawal. Therefore, it is important not to give in to the temptation of punishing the child. These children need constant encouragement by patient and caring teachers, parents, and other caregivers (d).

Goal 4: Withdrawal or display of inadequacy

An example of a typical situation is a pupil who seems to be unable to attain any learning target; when asked to do something unusual, she does it clumsily and fails even in apparently simple tasks. In these cases it is indispensable to exclude any neuropsychological impairments, as these behaviour patterns are frequently due to, or at least exacerbated by, a brain dysfunction. If there are neuropsychological problems and learning impairments, these have to be treated first by adequate interventions. If no neuropsychological problems can be assessed, it is important to explore the family situation (possible existence of neglect, domestic violence, sexual abuse, etc.). In some cases, withdrawal and the display of complete inadequacy are the endpoint of the child's running through the first three stages of 'erroneous goals', but more often these children, due to an extremely negative family situation, were so discouraged in their early attempts at getting attention that they end up directly in withdrawal. In these cases, the teacher's educational measures have necessarily to be accompanied by a multidisciplinary sociopsychological approach.

When a child withdraws from activity or displays inadequacy, the educator despairs of the child's clumsiness and constant failure and tends to abandon her attempts at improving the child's problems (a). As all her attempts at attaining superiority have failed, the child is convinced of her worthlessness and incapacity to attain anything positive, and gives up completely (b). She may withdraw from any activities that can challenge her self-esteem and thus has no possibilities of making positive experiences. The adolescent may become a drug abuser or suicidal. Some children opt for demonstrating their incapacity by giving up all attempts at showing their worth and usefulness; it seems that they intentionally seek failure (in school or in their relationships). As the adults have given them up for lost, there is hardly any reprimanding, criticising or punishing. Both adults and child have withdrawn (c). These children need high doses of constant and never slacking encouragement and extreme patience. Alternative corrective measures are 'positive eyes', empathy and unconditional acceptance, and faith in the child's capacity to change (d).

The adapted child, in the Adlerian and Dreikursian sense, is not a child that never defies the adult, nor a child who always obeys to any of the adult's demands. Frequently, we find attention and power seeking behaviour in adapted children too, but hardly ever do they present the goal of revenge or withdrawal. The adapted child is collaborative, tolerant, and interested in other people; he or she takes an active part in activities and respects the rights of the others. An important aspect of a child with a high degree of Social Interest is his or her capacity for giving encouragement to others.

Intervention with the problem child

Psychoeducational intervention with a problem child has two axes: the long-term strategy with a multidisciplinary programme and – hopefully – collaboration with the parents, plus tactical measures in critical situations. The tactical intervention to correct an inadequate behaviour in a specific situation (e.g. a child hitting another) only works adequately within a general psychoeducational frame.

The intervention should comprise the participation of psychologists, doctors, teachers, parents and, if necessary, other specialists such as neurologists, speech therapists, physiotherapists, etc. In cases where a possible neuropsychological impairment is suspected, a thorough neuropaediatric and neuropsychological assessment is required; if impairment and/or a specific learning disability are present, they must be treated by appropriate specialists. The treatment of the behaviour problems of a child with learning disabilities is not basically different from the intervention for behaviour problems without a neurological basis. Although it is necessary to account for the specific deficits, these children should not be treated differently from their classmates; giving them special attention can enhance their inferiority feelings. It may be necessary to make fewer intellectual demands (but without understimulating them), but they should not be pampered or pitied. It is important to give them the possibility of having positive experiences and tasks with an adequate degree of difficulty, so that they can experience situations of success. Edwards and Gfroerer (2001) for instance, have made some suggestions on how to intervene successfully with children diagnosed with attention deficit/hyperactivity disorder (ADHD); their school-based intervention programme emphasises the importance of the children's need to belong and to feel accepted. Taking care of these needs, such as by peer tutoring and positive group experiences, can increase these children's concern for others and thus decrease impulsive and aggressive behaviour (typical in ADHD).

It is also necessary to explore the family situation and emotional problems of the child due to possible traumatic experiences. The teacher observes the child's behaviour in the classroom. In order to elaborate an effective intervention strategy it is desirable to ensure the collaboration of the parents, but unfortunately this is not always possible, due to their refusal or incapacity to participate, especially in those cases where the family situation is the source of the child's conflicts. In any case, the parents should be informed and oriented with respect to the educational measures to be taken with the child.

The basis of Adlerian intervention with children is the unconditional acceptance of the child and the view of his or her behaviour problems as 'mistakes' that can be corrected. The child is not 'bad', but discouraged and mistaken, in the same way as the adult with psychological problems is discouraged and mistaken and not 'sick'. It is also important that the adult keeps working with a respectful and friendly attitude even when, at first, the problem child provokes a negative reaction in him. Instead of being too severe or too soft with the child (fighting or losing), the adult must try to understand and want to help.

Intervention in the family and in the classroom

In order to deal efficiently with behaviour problems, parents and teachers must not only observe the child's misbehaviour but also observe their own spontaneous emotional reaction. As we have shown above, this is the way the teacher can detect the child's 'secret' goal and react more efficiently. If the teacher feels that the child is getting on her nerves, the child is seeking her attention; if she feels challenged and defied, the child wants to have power over her; feeling hurt and hatred means that the child has been taking revenge; and despair and abandon is the teacher's reaction to the child's withdrawal. A child usually only pursues one goal at a time; but of course, the same child can pursue different goals in different situations.

In the following, we present Dreikurs' basic rules of intervention in Democratic Education in our slightly updated version. The objective of Democratic Education is not that of 'eliminating' undesirable behaviours that bother the educator, but the fostering of Social Interest in the child.

Basic measures of Democratic Education

1 Taking action instead of lecturing and preaching

Many educators with good will make considerable efforts to 'speak' with the children, trying to make them see reason, explaining to them the reasons why they should do or not do certain things; they want the children to understand those reasons and make them see why it is better, even for the children themselves, to wash their hands, tidy up their room, do their homework, not hit other children, etc. But in many situations, the child has already perfectly understood but has his or her own reasons (Adler's private logic) which are stronger than the adult's 'reasonable reasons'. It can be more important for a child to keep his mother busy with preaching hygiene (getting her attention) than brushing his teeth, or feeling superior to an angry father by constantly 'forgetting' to take out the garbage. The adult then has the tendency to give more and more extensive explanations of why these things have to be done in order to make the child see sense, but as this is just 'more of the same', usually it does not work: instead of giving the sufficient amount of necessary explanation, the adult lectures and preaches, while the child turns deaf for these repetitive discourses. In the case of attention seeking, the adult 'chases away flies' by repeating phrases like 'Stop touching this!' 'Don't do this!', 'Stop niggling!', but just as when one tries to chase away an annoying fly by gesticulating vehemently, the fly comes back again and again until more drastic measures are taken. The child knows perfectly what he is supposed to do, but while he receives attention (even in the form of reprimands or telling-offs) he will not stop. The adult must take action.

One of the most important rules is not to pay attention to the attention seeking behaviour; as far as possible, these behaviours have to be ignored. But it is important to keep in mind that children have the need to receive adequate attention, and the younger they are, the more attention they need. Thus it would be a mistake to simply ignore the child who is misbehaving (and of course, it is not always possible, e.g. when she is about to strangle her baby brother); the child has to get attention when she is 'good', or simply when she needs it (because she has a little problem, or needs hugging, or in many other situations). In the classroom, the teacher can ignore the noise-making of a slightly hyperactive boy (but not the hitting of a classmate, of course), but give attention in other situations, for example asking him a question to which she supposes he knows the answer, or asking him to do a task she knows he likes, etc. The teacher can also use a 'distracter', asking the boy to do something 'important' (socially 'useful'), for example helping a classmate to draw a picture, etc. In this way, the boy is not only prevented from continuing with his attention seeking behaviour, but also softly introduced into Social Interest.

2 Encouraging

In contrast to what is meant by 'social reinforcement' in behaviour modification (giving praise or reward in contingency to the performance of an
expected behaviour), Adlerian Psychology does not recommend praising
children when they have done something 'good' (or simply obeyed the adult's
demands). Although in theories of behaviour modification positive
reinforcement is considered to be an adequate stimulus to increase the occurrence of an expected behaviour, we recommend moderation in rewarding
children, be it with something material (money, gifts, sweets, etc.), or with
verbal appreciation. Praise expresses the adult's evaluation and approval of
the child's behaviour (I like what you did, you have accomplished what I
expected from you) and implies comparison with other people (other children); praise is given when the child has reached his or her goal, has been
successful, and little attention is paid to the efforts the child had to make to
get there. Encouragement, in contrast, avoids giving too much emphasis to
the child and the educator as individuals, giving it instead to the social or
functional value of the child's behaviour or product; it acknowledges the
effort more than the result and is still given when the child fails or has problems in reaching the goal. Instead of focusing on the child, encouragement is
task-oriented. Instead of saying 'I'm glad you have managed to tidy up your
room', or 'I'm proud you finally made it' the adult may say 'I think you are
happy now to find your stuff more easily' or 'That was quite a difficult task!'
The differences might appear very small, but in some cases (attention-seeking
children) they can be very important.

In the education of problem children, the adult has the tendency to focus
on what the child did wrong or where the child failed. The concept of
encouragement implies avoiding criticism and emphasising the positive
aspects; to do this, the adult has to pay less attention to the child's shortcomings and more to his or her strengths, which means developing a bias for the
child's strong points (having 'positive eyes', in Dreikurs' words). It is also
important to 'believe' in the child, in his or her capacity to improve constantly. Without this faith it is nearly impossible to encourage another
person, child or adult, and to foster Social Interest.

3 Using natural and logical consequences instead of punishing

Punishment, specially physical punishment, as a method of imposing the
adult's will and of eliminating undesirable behaviours fortunately is falling
out of use, but apparently has not been supplanted by more efficient measures. That is why adults still resort to more or less arbitrary punishments. The
use of punishment is never positive, as the child will give in to the adult's
stronger force and obey for fear of punishment. Punishment provokes anger
and hatred, feelings of humiliation and inferiority and does not help the child

to develop a new behaviour. In contrast, the use of natural and logical consequences aims at correcting the maladaptive behaviours at the same time as aiming at increasing Social Interest.

A natural consequence is what happens as a result of the child's behaviour when the adult does not intervene. A young girl who does not want to eat her lunch will soon get hungry as a natural (in this case biological) consequence and, if her mother does not give in to her whining and prepare her a snack, she has to suffer the uncomfortable feeling of hunger until the next full meal. Thus, the next day, the girl may want to eat at the proper mealtime. In daily life, though, there are few real possibilities for natural consequences to occur, because the educator cannot allow them to happen (a young boy who runs away from his mother's hand and into the street would have an accident as a natural consequence); in most situations, we must give in to logical consequences.

Logical consequences are the result of the educator's intervention, not as an individual but as a representative of the social order. To apply logical consequences correctly and efficiently, it is indispensable to have previously established a series of basic rules – known and accepted by child and adult; anybody who does not stick to these rules has to accept the consequences. The use of logical consequences therefore is not the adult's more or less arbitrary imposition – it is a necessary and objective result of the child's acts. Just as adults who are late for work repeatedly have to face being fired, pupils who do not do their homework or do not hand in their papers may receive an entry in the class register. The pupil who has not finished her drawings because she was 'busy' chatting with her neighbour might have to stay in the classroom during the break and finish her work, because this is what the rules say. An adolescent girl who does not pick up her clothes and put them into the washing box, might not find clean clothes by the end of the week when she wants to go out, because her parents only wash the clothes they find in the box. A boy who does not want to learn how to tidy up his room is at risk of losing objects in all that mess. In this case, his parents secretly may help things to 'get lost' and be difficult to find.

In all these cases it is indispensable that the adult, when using one of these measures, does not adopt a punishing attitude such as 'See? As you haven't done your homework, you must stay in the classroom and do it!' or 'It's your own fault that your things have got lost!' 'You didn't put your clothes into the box, so I refused to wash them.' These attitudes are interpreted by the child as being punishing, threatening, or extorting. The adult's reaction must come up in a neutral and casual way, as a passing remark, in a friendly voice and with respect for the child. Of equal importance is the existence of a basically positive relationship between adult and child and that the consequences are not used in the midst of a struggle for power among them both; it is only when these conditions are given that the child will not confuse logical consequences with punishment.

A variation of the use of consequences is to apply them to all the children present (to the whole class, to all the siblings) and not only to the 'miscreant'; Dreikurs and Soltz (1964) called this technique 'to put them into the same boat'. As an example, we suppose that there is a rule that all the pupils of the lower classes have to queue while going down to the schoolyard in order to avoid stumbling and falling on the stairs; if one of the children leaves the queue and runs down, not only must he come back and queue again, but the whole class must do so. The probability that the others get angry with their classmate who obliged them to go back (possibly several times) can be an efficient regulator of the boy's behaviour.

Even normal children will always try to violate the established rules with different tricks and promises, excuses and prevarications, but the adults must stay affectionately firm and unshakeable (without falling into rigidity); it can be quite difficult for the adult to stay firm and say no, without wanting to dominate on one hand or falling into the temptation of giving in resignedly on the other. A warm voice, an affectionate attitude and respect for the child's dignity are essential for the use of any logical consequence. As we said before, it is necessary to establish previously general rules of living together, to check them from time to time and revise them if necessary.

The use of physical force is only allowed if the child's behaviour represents an immediate danger for somebody else or for himself or herself, and even then it must be applied with the maximum of respect the educator is capable of in such an extreme situation.

4 Avoiding critical situations

Critical situations arise when the child defies openly the adult's authority, by refusing to obey an order or by doing something that has been forbidden. In these situations, adults often feel the impulse to maintain or impose their authority at any price because they are afraid that children, once they have 'won the battle' will continue fighting and defying in the future. But this is actually the beginning of a continuous fight for superiority: both want to win, no matter how, and the 'defeated' one will have a strong sensation of humiliation or failure. Although it is usually the adult who finally imposes his will (especially when the child is young), he does not always have the sense of having won the whole battle. And the older the child the more difficult it is to make him obey; fighting with a rebellious adolescent can be disastrous. In these cases it is not recommended to impose one's will at any cost; we do not even recommend the use of logical consequences in these situations, because they will be interpreted as punishment or revenge by the older boy or girl and may be accepted stoically, but without any positive effect for the future. In the beginning of a fight for power, it is better for the adult to withdraw from the child's radius of action, at least for the moment, as far as it is materially possible, for example leaving the room. This can be easy when at home, but in the classroom it is far more difficult for the teacher to leave the class alone, though in specific situations it might be an emergency solution. Although the adult's withdrawal apparently looks as if the child has won the fight and the educator has failed in her educational attempt, this is not the case. The child's goal, in these situations, is to defeat the adult by demonstrating that he is stronger than his adversary; but if there is no enemy, there can be no victory (or defeat). The child's destructive energy evaporates.

To make this happen, it is important that the adult does not act in personal interest and for fear of losing her authority; she only loses it when she insists in maintaining it. But a will one has voluntarily resigned cannot be broken. Of course, later, when the tempers have fizzled out, the teacher or parent must find a moment to discuss the child's behaviour, find out what happened and why, what the child's needs are, what can be done in the future, etc. In those moments, rules can be checked and revised (an older child can have more privileges, more pocket money, more time to stay out, etc.).

Another measure for pressing situations can be described as 'doing something unexpected'. This method requires a certain creativity and presence of mind even in critical situations: the adult must repress his direct impulsive reaction to the child's provocations and act in a way the child does not expect. What the child expects is 'more of the same', an increase of reprimands, rebukes, punishments, etc., but if the adult refuses to enter the vicious cycle and if she is capable of doing something completely different that confuses the child, his destructive force vanishes. The ideal solution is to do something that makes the child laugh – against his will – or diverts his negative energy to something constructive; then, the battle turns into collaborative action. Once a teacher told us that one of her pupils, a usually very rebellious boy, defied her by sitting on the table and refusing to come down so that she could start her lesson. She did not want to fight and decided spontaneously to sit on her table herself. Even more, she invited the whole class to follow their (her and the boy's) example. Surprised and amused, all the pupils sat on their tables and our teacher gave her whole lesson from the table, without further incidents.

Collaboration, as opposed to fighting, is what should be achieved when educating children, but collaboration cannot be created by giving orders. Giving orders is an invitation for fighting, for the child to say no. We have to convince children of the usefulness of certain behaviours and the uselessness of others. To do so, we must foster the child's autonomy (when children know how to do things by themselves, it is less necessary to give orders), demand only what is fair (neither overload nor understimulation), avoid criticism by correcting mistakes with an affectionate and passing remark, and, of course, set a good example.

5 Living together

For adequate living together it is essential to establish elementary rules; some rules will be universal, valid for any human community, and some will be specific for every family, for every class or every group. As the child grows up, he or she will take a more and more active part in establishing these rules. Establishing rules also implies working out the (logical) consequences of their infringement, so that every member of the group knows what is expected of them and what happens if they do not carry out their duties. Although the rules may be different for adults and children and for children of different ages, everybody has to come up to their tasks. It is recommended to form a Family Council (or Class Council in school) which gets together on a regular schedule or on demand of one or more of its members in order to establish, check and revise the rules, to discuss existent problems, to plan upcoming events, etc. In this Family Council every member of the family takes part (even the babies) and it is recommended to establish an agenda, a list of speakers, to elect a president (who can also be designated by rotation), someone to take down the minutes, etc. While in school, a tutorial period can be an appropriate hour for the Class Council in its formal application; families tend to be more reluctant to formalise their get-togethers and use strict procedures. They might prefer to talk about concerns as they come up. This is perfect, but in families with many problems it has been shown to be better when the family follows a somewhat stricter procedure, because it avoids temper outbursts and heated debates when dealing with critical aspects. Councils, like all the measures we propose according to Dreikurs, require time. Recently it has been said that it is not so important how much time parents devote to their children, but the quality of their interaction; but without a minimum of time, a reasonable quality cannot be achieved. And Democratic Education requires time, effort and steadiness. It requires time to talk with children (not TO children), to listen to their needs and desires, to let them tell their stories in their own way, and to enter in an interaction that is imbued with respect. And it is important also to have a good time together, to play and experiment, not only to spend time when something goes wrong. Having a good time together is the best basis for a good relationship, for increasing trust and respect for each other and for intervening efficiently when a problem arises.

Contemporary developments of Adlerian education

Several authors have written excellent manuals for child guiding and classroom/parent counselling. Dreikurs himself wrote practical books for parents and teachers (e.g. Dreikurs 1968). *Children: The challenge* (Dreikurs and Soltz 1964) is one of the most interesting books for parents and has been translated into other languages and re-edited several times. A manual for teachers is *Maintaining sanity in the classroom: Illustrated teaching techniques* by Dreikurs, Grunwald and Pepper (1971). Other authors also discuss interesting approaches of Adlerian family and classroom intervention. Mosak (1971b) participated in a programme that introduced Adlerian methods into an entire school system. Corsini (1979) also describes in detail the application of Democratic Education based on Individual Psychology to a school run by nuns. Don Dinkmeyer, Don Dinkmeyer Jr and others have also dedicated many publications to the psychoeducational approach. They have developed a systematic training programme for parents and teachers, which is used in different settings (Dinkmeyer, Sr and McKay 1976, Dinkmeyer, Sr, McKay and Dinkmeyer, Jr 1997).

An interesting line of application of Adlerian principles in the classroom could be the relatively new approach of conflict resolution and mediation. In face of the increase in uncontrollable violence among adolescents, mediation is becoming more and more popular in school settings. The Dreikursian psychoeducational approach is, though democratic in its principles, a top-down approach: it is something that the adult (teacher, parents, counsellor) does with the child. The child is the object of education, and it is the adult who guides him or her out of supposed ignorance and into a community of adults who know what is good for them. This implies that the adults have the knowledge of what is right and wrong.

In contrast, the conflict resolving and mediation approach is designed to achieve major involvement of the young person in his or her educational process and in the resolving of problems. The idea of conflict resolution is to manage disputes between pupils or students through the intervention of trained mediators. This corresponds to the changed attitude towards children in our society. The lack of orientation with respect to their own lives has put the adults in a position where they are no longer able to advise their children of where to go and what to do, and what are the purposes of education. A higher co-participation of children and adolescents in this process can be a possibile way of helping to resolve the problem of violence in our society. This means that it is no longer exclusively the adult who fosters Social Interest. Social Interest is not yet exclusively something that adults teach, foster, or waken in the child, but it is something that develops and grows among the children themselves. That is why the idea of the mediator being another child (older child, peer, classmate) and *not* the teacher or school counsellor is so appealing. The mediator intervenes between two (or more) opponents in order to avoid fights and uncontrolled discussions by establishing rules (only one person may speak at a time, no interrupting, no insults, etc.), pinpointing the issue, and helping the disputants to explore alternatives and make decisions. The mediator never takes part in the conflict.

As Clark (1994) mentions, numerous school districts in the USA include conflict mediation training in the classroom as an integral part of the curriculum, and these programmes are widely acknowledged as effective means against hostility and violence. They aim at developing more effective, more creative, and of course, less conflictive problem-solving strategies in children and adolescents. Clark also mentions that the implementation of these programmes reduces the frequency of fights, suspensions, and discipline referrals. The author traces out a conflict resolution programme based on the Adlerian values of co-operation, social equity and mutual respect. According to this author, conflict resolution programmes provide a viable alternative to the traditional punitive-based discipline procedures. He also points out the positive effect mediation has not only for the learning process of the disputants and the general school climate, but also for the mediator himself or herself. The mediator enhances his or her own Social Interest by means of his or her own positive acts.

As a conclusion to this chapter we argue that the Dreikursian approach of the 'four goals of the maladaptive child' is still useful in everyday family and school settings. It is an excellent preventive measure to avoid smaller misbehaviours turning into big problems. But if the Adlerian and Dreikursian educational ideas are to stay alive, they have to keep pace with the challenges of education in a postmodern society. We think that Individual Psychology has much to offer in this sense, and some encouraging efforts have been undertaken by contemporary Adlerian authors who deal with child guidance and therapy; they emphasise, quite consistent with the Adlerian idea of community, the positive influence of group experiences based on social equity, feelings of belonging and taking care of each other. For example, Sonstegard and Bitter (1998) outline the basis of child counselling in groups; Newbauer and Blanks (2001) propose Adlerian group therapy as part of the treatment of adolescent sexual offenders; and Popkin (2000) analyses youth violence and prevention of youth violence, and strongly recommends mentoring among children of different ages as a powerful means to help violent children, together with conflict resolution and mediation programmes. This author suggests that some children do not need counselling or educational measures, but 'a big brother' (or sister) who guides them. In the author's view, mentoring is one of the strongest resilience factors for helping children to cope with society's demands. So, all these authors insist on positive dyadic and group experiences as an antidote for isolation, loneliness and feelings of inferiority and, consequently, as a firm basis for healthy development.

Chapter 6

Adlerian therapy and its relationship to other psychotherapeutic approaches

In this chapter we present an integrative review of how Adlerian theory and practice relates to existing theories and intervention methods. Our review was guided by several premises, the first of which is that we believe Individual Psychology and the therapeutic approaches it inspires still possesses contemporary value for clinicians. The insights that Adler described in his classic works do not cease to be valuable simply because time has passed or because more modern counselling theories have emerged (Adler 1927, 1931, Ansbacher and Ansbacher 1956). The usefulness and validity of Adlerian constructs are supported by their reflection and incorporation in the theories of Adler's contemporaries and those who worked afterwards.

The theory and methods of Individual Psychology also are supported further by the fact that they continue to generate research and appear in various forms in the contemporary literature. For instance, Baumeister and Leary (1995) presented a comprehensive review of attachment theory that supported Adler's primary assumption that people have a need to contribute and to belong meaningfully with others. Recent work also revealed that the epistemological position of Individual Psychology and some of its methods for assessing and changing the Life Style were particularly consistent with the burgeoning constructivist approaches (Carlson and Sperry 1998, Jones 1995, Jones and Lyddon 1997, Oberst 1998a, Shulman and Watts 1997, Watts 2000). Overall, we believe that the similarities and potential areas of convergence between Adlerian psychology and other approaches are of greater interest and are clinically more compelling than the nature of the existing differences. Identifying such commonalities among theories could expand the range of clinical conceptualisations and therapeutic techniques that clinicians would have at their disposal.

In this chapter we examine the relationships between Adlerian theory and practice and Freudian psychoanalytic theory along with more recent psychodynamic formulations of personality and counselling. We also compare Adlerian theory with several current and representative cognitive-behavioural and humanistic psychotherapies. Finally, we explore the rich integrative possibilities that exist between Adlerian psychology and the emerging

constructivist approaches. We begin our analysis of each perspective by identifying the important similarities and differences with Adlerian psychology
at the level of personality and counselling theory. Next, we examine the
implications of these similarities for assessment and intervention methods.

Freudian psychoanalytic theory

Among the theories we will consider in this chapter, Freudian psychoanalytic
theory in its original and modified forms holds less promise for convergence
with Adlerian theory and practice. This initially may appear somewhat surprising given that Adler and Freud were contemporaries who spent the better
part of eight years together in the Vienna Psychoanalytic Society before
Adler's 1911 exodus to create his own theoretical school. As we have indicated elsewhere in this volume, the existing scholarship on the Adler–Freud
relationship more strongly suggests a collegial relationship among relative
equals, albeit a steadily deteriorating one, rather than the usually suggested
relationship of Adler being a disciple, student, follower, or a generally
uncritical adherent to the corpus of Freudian theory (Hoffman 1994). The
differences that exist between Adlerian and Freudian theory would seem to
support the idea that Adler's thinking was independent of Freud's and that if
anything his relationship with Freud caused Adler to develop his theory
along very different lines.

To briefly characterise some of these differences, Adler and Freud took
opposing views of human nature. Freud maintained that because of the
unbridled nature of instinctual-based impulses, people operated according to
the pleasure principle to maximise instinctual gratification and obtain pleasure while minimising pain, punishment, and guilt. This focus on wish fulfilment and instinct gratification suggests that human nature is essentially
hedonistic and that the potential for bad, negative, or brutal consequences
stemming from hedonistic pursuits is quite high. Further, Freud divided the
psyche along both structural (id, ego, superego) and dynamic (unconscious,
preconscious, conscious) lines and gave causal primacy to the role of the
unconscious. If not being driven by the fulfilment of a wish or need,
behaviour may be overdetermined by people's efforts to defend against the
emergence of content (e.g. wishes, repressed memories or experiences) from
the unconscious.

Alternatively, Adler viewed people as less susceptible to the influences of
instinctual or other unconscious forces. Although Adler admitted that people
had aggressive and destructive capabilities, he also emphasised, contrary to
Freud, that people have unselfish needs to contribute to, care and provide for
others, and to promote the betterment of humankind. Further, Adler
emphasised a holistic perspective (versus an intra-psychic division) in understanding the self. In this regard, Adler's emphasis on growth and adjustment
in the personality makes his conceptualisation and use of ego functioning

particularly consistent with that of Hartmann (1958). Although aspects of self-functioning may be unknown to the person or lie outside of awareness, Adler believed that unconsciousness as a place within the psyche did not exist. In other words, Adler assumed a simple lack of awareness or insight about aspects of the life plan or style of life whereas Freud's perspective emphasised the motivated or purposive lack of awareness.

For Freud, the ability to be gainfully employed and self-sufficient along with the establishment of an intimate emotional relationship with an opposite-sexed partner constituted somewhat elusive endpoints that marked the healthy functioning of the personality. In addition to love and work, Adler also believed that contributions to one's wider social network in the community, here broadly conceived as encompassing many possible realms in which benevolence and support may occur, played a pivotal role in the emotional life of the person. In fact, the demonstration of Social Interest at both attitudinal and behavioural levels exemplifies a healthy mental life. Further, instead of simply being benchmarks for emotional health, Adler viewed work, love, and community as tasks that people strive to meet in creative, individualistic ways. That is, rather than behaviour being overdetermined by instincts and drives that can trace their origins to rather objective, bodily based causes, Adler viewed people's psychological processes as being pulled by subjective and fictional goals that emerge from efforts to meet the three tasks of life. Although other differences exist in the personality theories of Freud and Adler, the present review should provide an indication of the more fundamental points of divergence.

Some interesting similarities and differences also exist between Freud and Adler at the level of practice. Regarding similarities, both clinicians developed largely insight-oriented psychotherapies that had as their objectives building the client's awareness of the hidden or unconscious forces that shaped the personality and also occasioned their distress. The goal of Freudian therapy was to elucidate via interpretation, dream analysis, and analysis of the transference the true nature of the client's defence mechanisms, repressed memories, and unconscious drives and to thereby diminish the power of these phenomena to determine behaviour. Again, Adler did not envision the unconscious as so much of a storehouse of unacceptable drives and experiences but more as a descriptive term that conveyed the lack of awareness people experienced regarding their fictional life goals and private logic. For Adler, insight about the style of life was accomplished through examining earliest recollections, gathering information about the family atmosphere and constellation, gentle guessing about the possible causes for life problems or dilemmas, and posing of 'the Question' to assess the role of the problem in maintaining the style of life.

The building of insight alone, however, is not the final objective of Adlerian counselling. Once the client has developed cognitive and emotional awareness of the private logic, therapy may proceed to examine how attempts to meet the tasks of life may be mistaken, dysfunctional, or otherwise self-defeating. For instance, knowledge that a client experiences feelings of inertness and powerlessness may render interpretable his or her failed attempts to achieve control and mastery through aggressive, domineering, or threatening behaviours. At this juncture in therapy, the inappropriate and exhaustive goal-striving for personal superiority over others may be addressed and modified along healthier and more socially useful lines. That is, life goals are realigned so that the client no longer is working against others but is able to find a place among others and to contribute to others so that life is experienced as fulfilling and rewarding.

Several noteworthy differences exist between Psychoanalysis and Individual Psychology regarding the therapist's relationship with the client. In traditional forms of Psychoanalysis the therapist and client occupy different positions in the power and insight hierarchy. The psychoanalytic therapist possesses more power because his or her insights about unconscious drives or conflicts lead in time to the client's nascent awareness of this material. Further, the therapist's well-timed interpretation provides the client with an external, 'objectively based' explanation for the meaning of a behaviour, feeling, or attitude.

In contrast, Adlerian therapists relate to clients more as collaborators working at the same level to understand the private logic and to reorient the client's method of addressing life tasks. This egalitarian orientation is embodied in the use of the stochastic method of gently enquiring and tentatively suggesting possible explanations for behaviour in contrast to outright interpretation. In addition, the client's reactions are useful in guiding this method of problem exploration and elaboration, whereas such behaviour from a psychoanalytic perspective may be discounted as resistance or as deriving simply from unconscious conflicts. Similarly, Adlerian therapists do not promote or encourage the formation of transference relationships, which is the primary vehicle for producing therapeutic movement in a wide variety of psychodynamic therapies (Adler 1931). Individual psychologists instead emphasise the real and working aspects of their relationships (see Greenson 1967) with clients and view the formation of a transference as an unproductive way of relating that can detract from the tasks of detecting and altering a client's basic mistakes and dysfunctional goals.

Finally, although short-term and problem-focused psychoanalytic approaches exist in the work of Sifneos (1987) and Davanloo (1996), psychoanalytic therapy generally is comprehensive in scope and lengthy in its duration compared with the versatility allowed by the Adlerian approach. Adler emphasised helping people with a wide variety of problems ranging from depression and psychosis to child-raising and education. This implies that practitioners of Individual Psychology may engage in comprehensive, personality-reconstructive interventions and, just as frequently, provide practical guidance and psychoeducational interventions that address relatively circumscribed difficulties stemming from developmental and existential causes (e.g. choosing a career path, developing a healthy parenting style, etc.). In other words, rather than being pseudo-problems that mask more fundamental unconscious conflicts, Adlerian therapists realise that life problems and dilemmas are frequently just that.

In the sections below we discuss some more recent developments in psychoanalytic and psychodynamic approaches and relate them to the theory and practice of Individual Psychology.

Neo-psychoanalytic theories

Horney's psychoanalytic approach

Although we do not have any evidence that Adler and Horney may have influenced each other directly, the two theories share some striking similarities at theoretical and practical levels regarding the development of psychological problems (Mosak 1989). That two keen clinical minds would converge on such similarities in describing and treating neurotic (e.g. generalised anxiety disorder, obsessive-compulsive disorder) and somatoform disorders (e.g. conversion disorder), among other life problems seems to validate at some level the theoretical conceptualisations of each approach. To begin, Horney attributed the root of neurotic behaviour, the experience of enduring basic anxiety, to the familial and social contexts. Basic anxiety represents the experience of feeling alone and vulnerable in a harsh and unforgiving world (Horney 1937). Although Horney never fully articulated a construct in her theory that corresponded to Adler's Social Interest, she seems to understand the profound difficulties created when one lacks a secure sense of community with others. A number of influences such as harsh, authoritarian, abusive, or neglectful parenting may underlie the creation of basic anxiety and give rise to subsequent efforts to use neurotic strategies (moving towards others, moving away, moving against) to reduce these anxieties.

Although Adler enumerated several aetiological routes by which problems in life may develop, such as failure to meet community responsibilities or seeking a kind of personal superiority over others, he also placed primacy on the causal roles of the family atmosphere in contributing to the development of problematic Life Styles. Adler's overburdening situations in childhood were cited as influences that thwarted a child's efforts to find a place among his or her family members and that may lead to pervasive discouragement (Ansbacher and Ansbacher 1956). Such situations included neglected, abused, or unwanted children and today are subsumed under the rubric of dysfunctional family environments. The enduring operation of these influences may make disruptive, attention-getting behaviour a more salient way of belonging in a dysfunctional family (Dreikurs and Soltz 1964). The further development of the Life Style along these self-defeating lines may render the person brittle and hesitating, compromised (gravitation towards the useless side of life), and somewhat one-dimensional in interpersonal relationships (e.g. dominant versus submissive). The establishment of such problematic Life Style themes is quite similar to Horney's characterisation of life led through the use of neurotic strategies.

Although Adler eschewed typologies, the ones he created to illustrate pernicious Life Style themes map quite well on to a similar typology that Horney (1937) developed. People who fundamentally fear inertness and helplessness may attempt to dominate and rule over others. Such a ruling type for Adler is consistent with Horney's aggressive or moving-against type. Those who fear responsibility and a decisive approach to life may characteristically defer, depend, and cling to others. This getting type of personality embodies Horney's moving-towards or compliant type of person. Finally, people who see interpersonal relationships as so fraught with problems and disappointment (i.e. the 'No!' response to social responsibilities and relationships) that they back away from significant relationships comprise the avoiding type for Adler. This orientation corresponds with Horney's moving away or avoiding type as well. In summary, Adler and Horney envisioned similar routes to psychological distress and also specified similar interpersonal manifestations of this distress. What similarities and differences exist between the two clinicians at the level of psychotherapy?

Adler and Horney also made similar use of the idea of the unconscious. For both, unconsciousness represented a general lack of awareness of self or personality functioning rather than the aforementioned warehouse of unacceptable drives and experiences. Horney's incorporation of the construct was somewhat more involved in that people not only were unconscious of their strategies of managing basic anxiety, but also were largely unaware of the ensuing basic conflict of these strategies. Further, Horney maintained that people were unconscious of their efforts to stabilise the sense of self and to shore-up their eroding self-esteem through pursuing an idealised image. In this way, Horney envisioned layers of events and manoeuvres that people were unaware of as their vicious cycles of neuroses developed. Adler's use of the unconscious was somewhat more straightforward in that people largely were unaware of how they viewed and responded to the multiple life forces (e.g. family atmosphere, genetic endowments, establishing a career path) en route to seeking completion and belonging with others. Also, lack of awareness of forces affecting the Life Style was perhaps more broad than the unconscious envisioned by Horney insofar as her theory addressed lack of awareness of specific aspects of the neurotic process and not broader life themes.

For both Adler and Horney, the objective of therapy was to build a gradual awareness of how the self operates, either in developing and maintaining the Life Style and problems in pursuing mistaken Life Style goals, or in developing and maintaining a neurotic orientation. Again, Adlerian methods for assessing the Life Style were meant to elucidate broader areas of personality functioning. Therapy from Horney's perspective would first target building an awareness of the most recent psychological structures that contributed to the vicious cycle of neurosis – that is, the defences used to maintain the idealised self, such as blind spots, compartmentalisation, arbitrary rightness, and so forth. Once the need for the idealised self and image were neutralised, a focus on the more distantly developed neurotic strategies could occur with the ultimate goal being both an awareness of the root causes for basic anxiety and a healthy manner of managing the inevitable anxieties of life.

Erikson's ego-analytic approach

Expressions of Adler's theory also appear in the ego developmental personality theory of Erik Erikson (Erikson 1951, Erikson and Erikson 1997). Erikson, like Adler, recognised that people face existential challenges about how to meet the requirements for work and livelihood, intimate and pro-creative relationships, and community or societal responsibilities. In some respects, Erikson's work extends Adlerian theory by examining how people meet these challenges as a function of both the passage of time and the transformations of the ego associated with cumulative life experiences.

Erikson (1951) contended that the experiences underlying the ability to take a place among others, and to find gainful employment and meaningful relationships, occur quite early in the life span. In the first stage of his model, Erikson maintained that the infant's predominant orientations towards either basic trust or mistrust of people are set before the first birthday. Between the ages of 3 to 6 years, Erikson believed the family of origin significantly affected the cultivation and channelling of the child's sense of initiative and goal-directedness. The outlines of how a person may begin to productively belong with others in dealing with both successes and disappointments appear in resolving the school-age dilemma of industry versus inferiority.

The tasks of choosing a career or vocation in life become salient in the adolescent stage (i.e. ages 12–19 years). Here people finish their formally required education and can elect either to enter the workforce directly or to pursue more advanced studies at a university to prepare them for a career. Erikson believed that the extent to which individuals developed a solid sense of identity significantly affected their abilities to pursue both work and intimate relationships. That is, the sense of identity that emerges from being oneself in multiple roles underlies the capability of choosing a satisfying line of work and also of pursuing satisfying intimate relationships in the young adulthood stage.

Expressions of Adler's Social Interest construct appear in the adulthood stage (25–65 years) where people must decide how to become generative and give back to others as against self-centred and developmentally stagnant. In particular, the ego strength of care for others and a desire to give something back appears especially consistent with the ideal of Social Interest.

Although Erikson's theory is primarily descriptive of the developmental process and includes less in the way of meaningful guidance for clinicians, his recognition of life tasks, and particularly caring for community and society, recapitulates Adler's theory and extends it along developmental lines. Given the relatively early emergence of tendencies to address life tasks and the ways in which such tendencies may change with physical experience and maturity, Erikson's model offers a particularly useful paradigm for integrating Adlerian and developmental theories. Consistent with the observations made about Horney's contributions, the fact that different psychologists working at different times and levels of analysis identified the same salient existential issues and ways of addressing them speaks to the timelessness of Adler's work.

Interpersonal approaches

Interpersonal approaches describe how the personality emerges from the nature of the dyadic relationships that people experience. These approaches also place correspondingly less emphasis on the intrapsychic phenomena (e.g. repression of id-based wishes) that characterise Freudian psychodynamics. Sullivan (1953) is the generally recognised founder of this approach and maintained that the meeting of all human needs depends on transactions with others. The nature of one's relationships, and the ways in which the self-system coordinates the meeting of needs while minimising the experience of anxiety, contributes to the structure and function of the personality. Sullivan particularly emphasised the socially embedded nature of the person, the role of the family context, and the importance of co-operation in satisfying people's needs.

Subsequent theory and research in this area has focused on the interpersonal circumplex as a way of understanding the varieties of interpersonal needs and the possible roles that people may adopt to meet those needs (Leary 1957, Benjamin 1974, 1993, Kiesler 1996). Most circumplex models create a two-dimensional interpersonal space that is bounded by dominance versus submission on one axis and love (attraction/affiliation) versus rejection (attack/antagonism) on the other. Benjamin's Structural Analysis of Social Behavior (SASB; 1974, 1993) is particularly elegant in this regard and articulates how the interpersonal behaviour of one person instantiates a complementary or reciprocal response in another and also contributes to the introjection of another's interpersonal reactions to the self. Incorporating interpersonal scholarship, Klerman et al. (1984) have developed a comprehensive interpersonal psychotherapy that targets role loss, role disputes, and transitions, and interpersonal skill-building to treat depression, among other disorders.

Adlerian and interpersonal perspectives offer some exciting opportunities for theoretical and practical cross-fertilisation. These opportunities stem primarily from the fact that both theories maintain that the personality is moulded by the roles and relationships that people experience in transacting their lives. Beyond this assumption, the basic circumplex variables are also highly meaningful to the work of individual psychologists. The dominance–submission dimension is salient in that it approximates the pull to a position of power, significance, perfection, or completion versus a hesitating or wasting orientation to life. The love–rejection dimension also is relevant in that it conveys the extent to which people are productively and supportively engaged with others, which goes to their level of Social Interest. Further, the quadrants generated by these interpersonal dimensions bear striking similarity to the four general personality types (i.e. socially useful, getting, avoiding, ruling) that Adler described for illustrative purposes in examining combinations of Social Interest and level of life activity (Ansbacher and Ansbacher 1956).

Within the realm of practice, both the interpersonal and Adlerian therapies clearly distinguish between healthy, supportive interpersonal roles on one hand, and dysfunctional, self-defeating roles on the other. A primary goal of each therapy is to help clients build awareness of their relational styles and of the incipient goals that motivate their interpersonal transactions. The two approaches diverge somewhat in the methods used to achieve this awareness, however. Adlerian therapists may provide direct feedback about the nature of a client's mistaken goals. Similarly, they may highlight discrepancies between the content of clients' interpersonal messages and the behaviours they ultimately exhibit. Finally, Adlerian therapists may use a variety of in-session strategies to render dysfunctional interpersonal behaviours less salient for clients (i.e. spitting in the soup). The interpersonal approaches more actively use the therapeutic relationship to provide an optimal mismatch with the client's interpersonal portrayal so that it may be understood and altered. That is, interpersonal therapists, more than Adlerians, would be likely to foster projections and transferences, among other phenomena, so that the therapist could experience complementary or reciprocal reactions to the client and subsequently work to alter dysfunctional patterns. Despite these differences, both approaches exhibit compatible vocabularies, conceptualisations, and objectives for intervention.

Object relations perspectives

More contemporary psychodynamic models of personality include the object relations approaches of Kohut (1971, 1977) and Winnicot (1988). As a group, these approaches also focus less on the relationships of intra-psychic phenomena and more on how personality develops from infancy through adulthood as a function of the real and internalised relationships that are developed with other people (i.e. objects). These perspectives view people as seeking a middle ground in their efforts, 'to live independently without feeling lonely . . . to cooperate and give without being used, . . . and to live with others, receive from them, and rely on them without being engulfed or stunted' (Cushman 1991: 51). The infant's relationship with the mother plays a pivotal role in designing the relational templates through which subsequent object relationships will be managed later in life. In this regard, the mother does not need to be perfect or error-free in her provision of care for the child, but must be sufficiently available, both physically and emotionally, to become a 'good-enough mother' for the child. The essential ingredients for this type of parenting involve the mother and child functioning as a single unit, with the mother being preoccupied with the needs of the child during infancy. Further, the mother must function as a mirroring figure that reflects the good and positive qualities that the child exhibits. Mirroring such affirming experiences precludes the formation of a predominant sense of emptiness that could underlie the creation of a basic fault (Balint 1968).

With physical and emotional maturity comes the child's ability to split the phenomenal field on the basis of real or imagined experiences. The mother may be experienced primarily as 'bad' or 'good' at any particular time given the situational transactions that occur between the mother and the child (e.g. a withdrawn breast, a scolding mother, etc.). This normative splitting may be projected on to others and also introjected based on the child's mirroring experiences. Healthy development in infancy and very early childhood depends upon being able to synthesise these disparate good and bad parts into an integrated representation of others and the self (Winnicot 1988). From Kohut's (1971, 1977) perspective, increased maturity is heralded by a move from narcissistic omnipotence to a more balanced experience of the self in which one's needs and limitations are realistically acknowledged (Vakoch and Strupp 2000).

Individual Psychology and the object relations perspectives share some interesting similarities at the level of theory. To begin, both perspectives view the maintenance of balanced relationships with others as a hallmark of emotional health. Similarly, the failure to establish a meaningful role for oneself in a social group such that normative narcissistic needs characteristically remain unmet may lead to the formation of faulty life goals and basic mistakes (e.g. striving after a fleeting sense of dominance and superiority over others or constantly seeking approval and affirmation). Further, family constellation variables that are frequently the focus of Adlerian assessment and therapy such as family size, actual birth position, and the perceived role in the family (i.e. psychological birth order) all may have some effect on the extent to which each child in the sibship is able to experience the mother as 'good enough' and to have a sufficient quantity and quality of mirroring experiences with her. We could identify no studies, however, that have examined these relationships empirically. In Adlerian parlance, the mirroring of such affirming and validating messages to the child could be construed as the provision of encouragement, among other things (Dagley et al. 1999).

Despite these parallels and potential areas of theoretical convergence, disparities between Individual Psychology and object relations approaches exist at the level of practice. Adlerian therapists work at the level of the real relationship (Greenson 1967). That is, they attempt to be appropriately encouraging and challenging while avoiding the more extreme positions of spoiling the client on the one hand or being antagonistic and provocative on the other (Adler 1931). From this real relationship the therapist and client proceed to understand the private logic and to effect beneficial changes in the Life Style. Because object relations work necessarily emphasises relationships between people, therapists working from this perspective encourage the formation of transferences and projections so that these may be used therapeutically to create reparative interpersonal experiences. For instance, a client may respond to a female therapist in ways to try to win her approval and admiration, especially if this was precariously provided by the client's mother. Adlerian therapists may label such self-defeating relational patterns as stemming from clients making basic mistakes about what must be done to achieve a position of significance (i.e. by being ingratiating). Rather than fomenting the client's transference of the rejecting mother onto the therapist and examining the history of this relationship, Adlerian therapists would maintain a focus on the more contemporary manifestations of this style of relating. For instance, an Adlerian therapist may pursue how the portrayal of a rejected child role maintains a sense of discouragement and simultaneously precludes taking more responsibility in meeting the tasks of life.

Humanistic and person-centred theories

Some interesting connections and points of divergence exist between Individual Psychology and the humanistic and person-centred genre of counselling theories (Watts 1998). The more intriguing possibilities for integration may be found in the personality theory of Maslow (1962, 1987, 1979) and the theory and techniques that Rogers developed (Rogers 1959, 1961, 1972, 1977, Rogers and Sanford 1984).

The parallels between the personality theories of Adler and Maslow are not accidental because Adler functioned as a mentor for the young Abraham Maslow after he moved back to New York from the University of Wisconsin in the mid-1930s. In fact, Maslow's dissertation on the role of dominance in the mating behaviour of primates was designed to test Adler's contention that superiority and power were more fundamental motives than the need for sex (Hoffman 1994). The success of Maslow's studies in this regard led him to, like Adler, view people as being pulled along by large, over-arching life goals rather than being pushed or victimised by unconscious drives. Maslow's

(1943) classic paper outlining the hierarchy of human needs and the pursuit of self-actualisation goals followed shortly thereafter.

Although the personality and counselling theories of both Maslow and Rogers have as their core statements the maintenance and enhancement of the experiencing organism (Maddi 2001), Maslow placed more particular emphasis on the basic or maintenance needs of the person compared with Rogers. This emphasis more closely aligns Maslow's thinking with that of Adler regarding the social embeddedness of the individual and the need to meet responsibilities involving others. Specifically, the third rung of Maslow's hierarchy above physiological and safety needs is that of belongingness and love. As a basic or maintenance need, Maslow asserted that people need to feel that they are part of a group that is larger and more powerful than themselves (they need to belong). This can be accomplished on multiple levels as people find different domains and realms of activity that involve taking a meaningful role among other people. The emphasis here is on both getting along with others and also contributing to and with others. Thus Maslow's need for belongingness bears some noteworthy resemblance to Social Interest and to the goal-striving for belonging that Adler described.

The fourth need Maslow articulated, self-esteem, may be viewed as the outcome of occupying a meaningful role relative to others. That is, by finding a way to make a unique contribution while also taking one's place among others, the net effect is a validation of one's role in the group and corresponding perceptions of the self as being a valued and important member of the group or community. Such experiences may underlie, at least in part, the striving for completion that individual psychologists have identified. Certainly, heightened feelings of inferiority can create the need for self-enhancement and for restoration of self-esteem in ways that preclude meaningful and productive relationships with others and the subsequent pursuit of perfection or completion (Ansbacher and Ansbacher 1956).

It may be more challenging to integrate Individual Psychology with the humanistic perspectives beyond this level because of the apparent difficulties in reconciling the humanistic emphases on self-actualisation and individual growth with the social and community emphases embodied in Individual Psychology, and particularly in Social Interest (Kvale 1992, Wallach and Wallach 1983). Several possible routes exist, however, for pursuing integration.

First, theoretical integration in this area may be possible to the extent that individual psychologists recognise the existence of additional life tasks beyond work, relationship and community. In this regard Dreikurs and Mosak (1977a, b) proposed two additional life tasks that involved (1) developing the sense of self and getting along with the self, and (2) spiritual and existential efforts to developing life meanings. Each of these tasks bears more on individual needs to seek fulfilment and to actualise inherent potentialities and may be broached as people pursue completion and perfection. No theoretical or empirical research, however, has been conducted to explore the viability of adding these extra tasks (Mansager and Gold 2000). Consequently, the status of these needs in Individual Psychology is unclear.

If self-fulfilment needs are postulated in the context of either the Adlerian or humanistic perspectives, theoreticians will need to specify how both the individual and collective needs are pursued. Maslow's (1962, 1987) work reflects this essential tension between the social and community commitments expressed in the basic need of belongingness on the one hand and the growth and self-actualisation needs that occupied the top of his hierarchy on the other. In fact, his recognition of a kind of 'Jonah complex' in which people experience guilt in transcending their social embeddedness to pursue uniquely personal goals and activities conveys Maslow's awareness of competing tendencies.

Maslow achieves at least a partial solution to this dilemma by indicating that people must meet the requirements of their growth needs prior to addressing self-actualisation concerns. Further, people will cycle into and out of actualisation and fulfilment experiences as a function of time. That is, self-actualisation is not an end-state from which people never return, but instead involves brief, fleeting experiences of fulfilment from which people return to meet responsibilities for life maintenance (work, love, and community). Current scholarship on peak or flow experiences supports the temporally limited nature of self-actualisation and also implies a foundational importance for basic needs (Csikszentmihalyi 1990, 1993).

Additional fronts for possible integration exist in Rogers' concept of the actualising tendency (Rogers 1959, 1961, Rogers and Sanford 1984). Compared with Maslow's use of actualisation, Rogers focused more broadly on the tendency of humans to actualise their inherent potentialities, which could involve pursuits within many domains of activity. This comprises the fundamental, primary motive of Rogers' approach. An additional learned or acquired need that all people experience is to be positively regarded by others. This pair of motives (i.e. to actualise and to be positively regarded) implies that people will pursue at least some measure of their growth and development in relationships with others. That is, what people can do with their talents in conjunction with their needs to receive approval, affirmation, and validation with others begins to approximate to Adler's conception of Social Interest. Alternatively, the need for approval implies the need to assume a meaningful role relative to others so that the successful portrayal of that role garners the approval and validation of others. Even Rogers' construct of self-actualisation does not imply self-absorption and a lack of focus or engagement with others (i.e. diminished Social Interest). Instead, self-actualisation merely reflects the tendency of all people to grow in ways that are consistent with their evolving self-concepts. Although self-actualisation can go awry when too much time and energy are devoted to the self at the expense of maintaining meaningful relationships with others, the primary focus is on being oneself with others – fulfilling our true natures in the context of others. In this regard, the self-absorbed person rather than the self-actualised person is one who in many respects parallels the person whose life goal is to establish personal superiority over others.

The possibilities for integrating Adlerian and humanistic psychotherapies exist on several fronts, although differences in the ultimate therapeutic objectives of the two perspectives will pose some challenges. First, Adlerian and humanistic approaches both exemplify an open therapeutic stance that assumes the client knows more about his or her life problem than does the therapist. The task of the therapist, at least in the earlier stages of intervention, is to understand the client's subjective perceptions of self and of the world. In this regard the Adlerian therapist's embrace of Social Interest 'to see with the eyes of another, to hear with the ears of another and to feel with the heart of another' (Ansbacher and Ansbacher 1956: 135) comes very close to the Rogerian objective of developing an empathic relationship with the client (Watts 1998). In other words, rather than just providing interpretations or analysing transferences, Adlerian and Rogerian psychologists work to understand how the client perceives his or her own form of misery, dysfunction, or stuckness. In addition to empathy, Adlerian therapists also would agree, as would clinicians from other orientations, that behaving genuinely with clients and providing unconditional positive regard for them comprise essential ingredients of the therapeutic relationship.

Second, these psychologies also assume that people are inherently good or at least neutral in their overall natures. That is, if provided the proper supportive environment, people will pursue generally healthy goals that assure their individual and collective survival. Within this common positive orientation, some differences exist between the two theories in that, for Rogers, the tendency to pursue positive, growth-fulfilling tendencies was focused more on the self than on providing such experiences for others. Somewhat differently, Adlerian therapists emphasise people's good natures in their capacities to become socially interested and involved with others, with correspondingly less inflection on self-growth.

Although the relationship-building and assessment phases of therapy may be open and non-directive, Adlerian and humanistic practitioners diverge in their uses of emerging insights about the client. Individual psychologists will use their knowledge of the client to actively and somewhat directly help them to understand the basic mistakes they have made in their Life Styles and how this is manifested in their private logic. This insight may be broached in a number of ways, some of which may involve examining repetitive maladaptive life themes and dysfunctional relationships in search for common causes or alternative outcomes. As the client's insight about self builds, the therapist may more directly comment about or confront the client's faulty assumptions about himself or herself, about others, or about important life goals.

Humanistic therapists, while not inert or inactive with clients, will assume a more non-directive stance that involves redirecting clients' solicitations for feedback and advice back to them so that they can develop their own awareness and insights.

A similar level of activity and directness exists in the reorientation phases of Adlerian psychotherapy. To guard against the resumption of previous maladaptive behaviours or goal-seeking, individual psychologists attempt to collaboratively work with clients to identify and instantiate Life Style alternatives that do not eventuate in hesitating or wasting attitudes, among others. For instance, if a previous Life Style goal in the domains of personal and community relationships involved a deferential, self-sacrificing orientation to others, then after the client becomes aware of how his or her private logic works to maintain this status, the therapist may actively portray an interpersonal stance in the sessions that precludes the client's return to a compliant and dependent role. That is, the Adlerian therapist may make the client's one-down position unpalatable and less attractive by making the tendency appear more extreme than it actually is or clearly identify how the tendency meets a secondary need to avoid one or more life tasks. Alternatively a similar effect may be achieved by burlesquing or lampooning the maladaptive tendencies. After rendering previous dysfunctional or maladaptive strategies less useful to the client in this regard (i.e. 'spitting in the client's soup'), Adlerian therapists may then orient clients to healthier Life Style goals. In the case of the deferential client, this may take the form not only of educating the client about the importance of taking more active responsibility for important relationships, but also giving the client more of these responsibilities experientially in the sessions.

Such strategies typically are not found among the methods of humanistic therapists. Rather than providing a reorienting influence, humanistic therapists assume that the sense of agency and empowerment that comes from providing the therapeutically facilitative conditions (i.e. genuineness, empathy, unconditional positive regard) will help clients to discover their own inherent tendencies toward health. These methods reflect the humanistic emphasis on self and self-growth while Adlerian therapists assume that an important component of emotional health involves developing the capability for co-operation and the assumption of meaningful roles among others. Again, however, finding a way to contribute and belong involves some sacrifice of the goals and behaviours that people otherwise might find uniquely rewarding and growth-producing. In this regard, the emphasis on belonging meaningfully with others, apart from the exclusive pursuit of self-actualisation, embodies the Adlerian goal of treating the whole person and restoring the sense of integrity that comes from meeting the life tasks.

Cognitive-behavioural theories

Although the cognitive-behavioural therapies (CBT) have no direct heritage in Adler's Individual Psychology, at least some of the principal exemplars of the cognitive restructuring therapies such as Beck (1976) and Ellis (Ellis and Dryden 1987) can trace their origins to the same semantic and linguistic (Korzybski 1933) and philosophical works (e.g. Vaihinger 1925) that inspired Adler. Because a variety of CBT approaches currently exist (e.g. Dobson 1988), it would be difficult here to comprehensively examine the relationship of each one to Individual Psychology. Instead, the major assumptions and methods common to many of the cognitive approaches will be reviewed.

To begin, CBT makes several assumptions regarding psychological structure and operation (Robins and Hayes 1993). First, cognitions play a mediational role in structuring and processing life experiences to coordinate affective and behavioural responses. That is, problems in behaviour or in experiencing negative, dysphoric emotions stem from cognitive origins, although most CBT practitioners now acknowledge that behaviour and emotions mutually affect each other and exert feedback on cognitive processes. Second, particular kinds of psychological problems and disorders result from particular manifestations of cognitive disturbances (i.e. depression from thoughts of hopelessness and defeat, anxiety disorders from thoughts about feared situations, schizophrenia from a generalised decrement in integrative and executive functioning, etc.). Third, CBT assumes that client knowledge about the underlying cognitive basis of the problems is a prerequisite for effective therapy, followed by active efforts to change maladaptive cognitive processes. Fourth, people are assumed to be rational and goal-directed such that once their faulty or maladaptive cognitive processes are understood, they will relinquish dysfunctional patterns and work towards more adaptive outlooks of themselves and the world. These assumptions appear to be common features in several of the more well-known CBT approaches (e.g. Beck 1995, Burns 1989, Ellis 1995, Meichenbaum 1990). It follows that if psychological treatment can target and change maladaptive, dysfunctional cognitive processes then changes in behaviour and affect will result.

The general cognitive model of psychopathology maintains that processing anomalies exist on at least two levels. Automatic thoughts and beliefs comprise an outer layer of cognition and involve the assumptions or characterisations of the self, others, the situation, or the world that occur without people's effort or, sometimes, their awareness. Automatic thoughts may be fleeting or momentary in their duration. The content of automatic thoughts characterises the particular type of problems that people experience. People with generalised anxiety disorder, for instance, may experience automatic thoughts about the lack of control they will experience in an upcoming event, such as feeling vulnerable or self-conscious around unknown others, etc. Cognitive-behavioural therapists often choose a client's automatic thoughts as an initial area of intervention because a careful articulation, examination, and rational analysis of the thoughts typically renders them inoperative and subsequently decreases their ability to cause the client further distress (Ellis and Dryden 1987).

Schemata form the deeper cognitive representations of the self and the world and often operate implicitly or unconsciously. Schemata are local and segmented models of the situations and relationships that people have encountered in the past. Schemata that misrepresent the world or conflict with core, self-defining schemata lead to distress and other symptoms. Once a person, event, or context triggers the activation of a schema, it can significantly affect the encoding as well as the retrieval of memories. For instance, people who experience generalised anxiety disorder may perceive and encode largely harmless, innocuous stimuli as anxiety arousing because their relevant schemata bias the processing of stimuli in this way. Information that is schema-consistent is encoded and recalled more frequently than data that are discrepant with a schema (Goldfried and Robins 1983, Mandler 1984).

The continued operation of maladaptive schemata, in part, underlies the persistence of psychological problems and their self-fulfilling nature. Beyond eliminating dysfunctional automatic thoughts and other symptoms such as arbitrary inference, catastrophising, and dichotomous thinking, CBT aims to alter the nature and use of clients' maladaptive and self-defeating schemata. This typically is accomplished through a variety of therapist-guided exercises such as Socratic questioning, the downward arrow technique (Burns 1989), direct testing of beliefs, relaxation training, rational disputation, and clients' self-administered exercises between sessions (e.g. dysfunctional thought records or diaries).

Adlerian therapy and CBT share several points of convergence, beginning with the basic assumption that problems in living stem from erroneous cognitions and faulty beliefs that people develop about situations and the mistaken, self-defeating ways in which people respond to them (Freeman and Urschel 1997, Shulman 1985). Further, both approaches assert that knowledge about the nature of dysfunctional beliefs and the people and situations that trigger them will lead to the client's rational decision to develop more healthy cognitive processes.

Adler's theory of tendentious (or **biased**) **apperception**, the recognition and linking of new perceptions in terms of an existing mass of knowledge, bears remarkable similarity to CBT's conceptualisation of schemata. Adler maintained that new or novel stimuli were perceived in terms of their implications for people's fictional life goals. That is, people's ways of understanding themselves, others, and their environments are overdetermined or biased by what they have been trying to accomplish in life (i.e. their particular paths toward success, belonging, and completion). He also recognised that people recalled events from their pasts in terms of their present life goals and guiding lines. In fact, early recollections and exercises that are designed to solicit them (e.g. Dinkmeyer, Sr, Dinkmeyer, Jr, and Sperry 1987) reveal how people reconstruct their pasts in terms of their present goals. In this regard, biased apperception processes tend to function in a manner that is indistinguishable from CBT's notion of schemata both in terms of rendering contemporary experiences meaningful and in reconstructing prior lived experiences.

Adler's (1931) theories about apperception also relate centrally to certain ideas in problem-solving therapy (PST; D'Zurilla and Nezu 1999). PST views life as a series of decisions or dilemmas that present themselves to people for action or resolution. Problems in living or even psychopathology result from ineffective problem-solving approaches and poor coping strategies (i.e. effects stemming from mistaken life goals). In the PST model, two processes (problem orientation and problem solving) affect people's abilities to deal effectively with life challenges. Problem orientation refers to how people prepare themselves to deal with challenges and encompasses variables of problem perception, problem attribution, problem appraisal, perceived control, and time–effort commitment. Problem solving refers to attempts to achieve a useful, adaptive solution to life challenges by defining the problem, generating alternative solutions, making decisions, and implementing strategies (D'Zurilla and Nezu 1999).

Biased apperceptive processes can affect multiple variables in the PST model, beginning with the ability to perceive or recognise the existence of problems. For instance, if a person has grown up in a hostile and abusive family of origin, it may be difficult to recognise that his or her overly compliant and submissive Life Style in extra-familial contexts is contributing to the person's manipulation by others. Such biased apperception may also affect the person's ability to determine the locus of the problem. That is, she or he may believe that a passive and inert style is a stable, enduring feature of the personality (i.e. internal problem locus) and that the problem does not lie in being surrounded by harsh or manipulative people (external locus). **Antithetical apperception** also can impede effective problem solving by limiting the variety or range of potential solutions that are generated and in deciding which solutions to implement.

Both PST and Adlerian therapy focus on diminishing the effects of biased and antithetical perception processes so that alternative, new approaches can be used to adaptively complete a task. The two methods achieve therapeutic ends through different means, however. PST works somewhat more narrowly within the problem context and views the presence of life difficulties as stemming from poor problem-solving skills. Presenting problems, consequently, are couched in problem-solving terms and clients' awareness of problem-solving variables and skill in addressing them become the focus of therapy. Alternatively, individual psychologists see impediments to effective decision making and problem solving as emanating from basic mistakes and faulty methods of achieving significance and belonging.

Developmentally oriented cognitive-behavioural clinicians have begun to focus on the role of maladaptive schemata that emerge earlier in clients' lives as these may result from dysfunctional family experiences, abuse, and so forth (Young 1994, Young and Lindemann 1992). The significance of early maladaptive schemata in the creation of psychopathology resonates particularly well with the emphasis that individual psychologists place on the shaping influence of the family atmosphere in affecting people's initial efforts to find a way to belong. That is, children that are abused, hated, neglected, or pampered may develop, very early, core schemata of themselves as damaged, unworthy, deserving of negative treatment, and so forth. The private logic of these individuals may evolve and operate in ways that perpetuate the dysfunctional and self-defeating Life Styles resulting from the experience of distress early in life (Adler 1927, Ansbacher and Ansbacher 1956, Meunier 1990, Toman, 1993).

The operation of early maladaptive schemata may be revealed in several phenomena that individual psychologists have described (Young 1994, Young and Lindemann 1992). First, maladaptive schemata tend to maintain themselves by thwarting the incorporation of experiences and awareness that would lead to change (i.e. schema maintenance). Biased and antithetical apperception both exemplify characteristics of schemata that are resistant to change in this way. Antithetical apperception may reveal itself in one of several ways that CBT practitioners have variously referred to as all-or-nothing thinking, 'musturbation', catastrophising, and over-generalisation, among others (Burns 1989, Ellis and Dryden 1987). These self-defeating processes tend to perpetuate themselves and to create vicious cycles. Second, the behavioural avoidance components of people's hesitating or safeguarding tendencies may reflect their efforts to avoid triggering negative or painful schemata (e.g. 'I'm not going to be able to succeed') that Young (1994) noted. Although a memory or awareness is present in the person and can be accessed with the appropriate cues, behavioural patterns become progressively more constrained to prevent this from happening.

Third, Young (1994) observed that people frequently will strive to compensate for the negative effects of early maladaptive schemata and discussed numerous ways in which such 'reparative' strategies may produce negative results. This conceptualisation is particularly consistent with Adler's (1927, 1931) discussion of how the Life Style becomes maladaptively transformed to achieve a fictional goal that would compensate for perceived weaknesses or deficiencies. Reminiscent of Horney's (1937) conceptualisation of neurosis, the attempted solution becomes part of the problem.

Both Adlerian and developmentally oriented CBT practitioners may focus on the early, conscious decisions that people made about how to respond to their distressing experiences as a way to build insight about their private logic or their maladaptive schemata. That is, Adlerians (Dreikurs and Soltz 1964) and some cognitive therapists (e.g. Young and Lindemann 1992) believe that clients, even as children, make conscious decisions about the meanings of

challenging events they experience and about how they will respond emotionally and behaviourally. Although these decisions may elude discovery as
they are covered over by the passage of time and with the evolution of subsequent schemata, Adlerians believe it is important to help clients trace back
at least some of their contemporary problems to decisions they made about
their lives in the past.

For instance, an adult who presents for counselling with a history
of dependent relationships on others along with self-defeating, self-
handicapping Life Style themes may have decided during childhood that if he
or she could not garner care and encouragement through success or achievement then attention from others may be obtained through complete failure
and inadequacy (the mistaken childhood goal of inadequacy, see Chapter 5).
Contextualising the emergence of this early life decision may serve two functions, the first of which is to allow feelings about the decision and the client's
life situation at the time to be expressed or vented. These feelings may be
articulated for the first time during therapy. Second, the examination of an
early decision in the client's contemporary life may reveal how the decision,
although appropriate or inevitable at the time it was made, has now outlived
its usefulness given the current circumstances. Such an awareness may help
the client to become more open in considering alternative ways to understand
self and the world.

Several differences exist between the Adlerian and CBT approaches, the
first of which concerns the presence of an organising, core tendency for the
personality. CBT may be unique in that no single or well-defined theory of
personality exists, beyond perhaps the early work of George Kelly (1955), on
which to place its primary psychotherapeutic assumptions. Consequently,
CBT is not informed by any kind of underlying principle that is hypothesised
to operate within people. Maladaptive schemata are presumed to function in
particular situations and contexts. In contrast, Individual Psychology is quite
explicit in assuming that people are pulled in unique directions by the ways
they attempt to achieve completion and belongingness by fulfilling the tasks
of life. Positing such goal-directedness provides an interpretive lens for
Adlerian therapists to view the cognitions, behaviours, and emotions that
clients display. In fact, Individual Psychology may benefit from supplement-
ing its more molar focus on life goals with the conceptualisations and
strategies afforded by the bottom-up perspectives available in the CBT
approach.

A second difference between Adlerian and CBT approaches concerns the
strategies that are used to change underlying cognitive processes (i.e. maladaptive schemata, antithetical perception, mistaken goals, etc.) that mediate
between lived experiences on the one hand and affective and behavioural
responses on the other. The family of CBT interventions focuses rather
exclusively on the mediating cognitive processes as the object of intervention.
That is, the emphasis is not so much on the person who has the difficulties,

but on the problematic cognitive processes that exist within the person. In contrast, Adlerian therapists emphasise the whole person and would be less likely to target cognitive or perceptual processes exclusively but instead would focus on the interconnectedness of symptoms with the Life Style. It is not just the maladaptive cognitive processes that are of interest to Adlerian therapists, but the ways in which clients use such processes in the service of life goals.

The implications of a holistic emphasis are that Adlerian therapy incorporates more relational and experiential components than most of the existing CBT approaches. Instead of objectifying a client's rigidified, all-or-nothing thinking and attempting to change it through procedures such as keeping a record of triggering mechanisms or disputing this form of thinking through Socratic questioning, Adlerian therapists may go beyond these exercises and attempt to bring the client's maladaptive styles of thinking into the therapeutic relationship. That is, the therapist may deliberately invite a client's tendencies to categorise him or her so that dysfunctional cognitive patterns can be addressed and disputed in the immediacy of the relationship. Similarly, Adlerian therapists may attempt to directly change people's safeguarding tendencies as these appear within the therapy hour by interpreting them or making them less useful (i.e. 'spitting in the soup').

Third and finally, Adlerian therapists emphasise the historical context from which the Life Style emerges along with its current status and functioning, while a majority of the CBT approaches (with the exception of Young's therapy) do not find it necessary to pursue such history due to their problem- and solution-oriented focus. Individual psychologists believe that the cognitive manifestations of more basic Life Style problems do not emerge arbitrarily or simply from situational causes, but can be traced to the compromises and decisions that people made earlier in their lives, especially during their years in the family of origin. Although contemporary symptomatic expressions of problems may not require a focus on clients' developmental histories, such an emphasis does help to educate them about the origins of some of their difficulties. In addition, to the extent that it is important to identify situations or people that trigger clients' dysfunctional responses, an examination of significant developmental experiences may both reveal the origin of life problems and enable clients to catch themselves at the outset of a maladaptive response pattern.

Kellian and constructivist theories

As opposed to what is usually called objectivism, which implies that there is a reality that can be interpreted in a correct way, constructivism in psychology involves people constructing their own realities by selectively assembling pieces and fragments presented by sensory and perception processes. Both Adlerian and Kellian psychologies (Kelly 1955/1991) embrace a constructivist epistemology in conceptualising the mental processes of both clients and therapists (Carlson and Sperry 1998, Jones 1995, Jones and Lyddon 1997, Shulman and Watts 1997, Oberst 1998a, Watts 2000). Both positions further maintain that the constructive process is not completely data or 'bottom-up' driven, but instead involves the organising influence of existing constructions and perceptual templates on the creation of new meanings. That is, an existing apperceptive mass gives shape, form, and order to the incoming flow of sensory and perceptual data. Adler's constructivist epistemology can be traced to his incorporation of Vaihinger's (1925) *Philosophy of 'As-if'* and, further back, to the work of Steinthal (1881).

Kelly's personal construct psychology

Both Adler and Kelly adopted a representational form of constructivism in that they assumed that a real world existed and that people, through the process of successive constructive approximations, were gradually coming to understand it. This recognition of an ontologically substantive world whose subtleties and nuances are progressively represented as life experience develops makes Kelly and Adler the same kind of positivistic idealists as Vaihinger.

Kelly (1955/1991) calls representations of reality 'constructs', that is, the patterns people create to make meaning of their experiences. The relationship of constructs to reality is not always a close one, although Kellian and constructivist perspectives emphasise that the functionality of a construct system can be judged to the extent that it allows a 'good-enough' or viable representation of the world. An absolute, perfect construction cannot be achieved, only successive approximations, which are tested with respect to their predictive validity.

We note a striking similarity between Kelly's concept of constructs and Adler's fictions. In Kelly's words:

> We take the stand that there are always some alternative constructions available to choose among in dealing with the world. No one needs to paint himself into a corner; no one needs to be completely hemmed in by circumstances; no one needs to be the victim of his biography. We call this philosophical position *constructive alternativism*.
>
> Kelly 1955/1991: 11

This reasoning is essentially Adlerian. As we have stated in former chapters, Adler also refuses determinism. Individuals always have the possibility of responding alternatively to their experiences (Adler's notion of the 'opinion'). Adler suggests in a quite constructivist way:

> No experience is a cause of success or failure. We do not suffer from the shock of our experiences – the so-called trauma – but we make out of

them just what suits our purposes. We are self-determined by the meaning we give to our experiences, and there is probably always something of a mistake involved when we take particular experiences as the basis for our future life. Meanings are not determined by situations, but we determine ourselves by the meaning we give to situations.

Ansbacher and Ansbacher 1956: 208

Kelly affirms that people develop constructs as hypothetical representations of their universe in order to test them against the reality of this universe in terms of their predictive efficiency. Kelly gives us the following example:

A man construes his neighbour's behaviour as hostile. By that he means that his neighbour, given the proper opportunity, will do him harm. He tries out his construction of his neighbour's attitude by throwing rocks at his neighbour's dog. His neighbour responds with an angry rebuke. The man may then believe that he has validated his construction of his neighbour as a hostile person.

Kelly 1955/1991: 9

This example could be drawn from Adler. Instead of constructions, Adler would have spoken of erroneous fictions and tendentious apperceptions. In Adlerian terms, this man is to be considered 'neurotic', because instead of adapting his private logic to reality (the manifold manifestations of the neighbour's behaviour) he maintains 'useless' (maladaptive) fictions, which impede him from interacting adequately with other people (lack of Social Interest). He uses ('unconsciously' but deliberately) a test (throwing rocks at the dog) to convince himself that his construction (fiction) of the neighbour as being a hostile person is correct. This puts him in a position of moral superiority over his neighbour (fictionate goal of striving for superiority).

These similarities notwithstanding, Adler and Kelly incorporated constructivism somewhat differently in their theories of intervention. Adler believed that people constructed their individual, unique meanings of the self and of the world but that inevitably such meanings always had to be reconciled with the requirements to meet the tasks of life. Although Adler's concept of the creative self conveys that there are many viable ways to respond to the myriad influences on one's life and many different ways to successfully approach the life tasks, some methods for doing so are clearly healthier and better than others: those that are guided by common sense and Social Interest. Regardless of the particular path chosen, life requires people to relate meaningfully to others, to work, and to contribute to the community in some way. Consequently, an active and mediational tone exists in Adler's constructivism that is consistent with his psychology of use, which could be phrased in this discussion as: 'it's not what we construct, but what we do with our constructions (or how we use them) that matters'.

The goal of Adlerian intervention is to help clients to become aware of their dysfunctional Life Style paths and early decisions so that they may be changed. Individual psychologists sometimes refer to clients' basic mistakes or mistaken life goals. Here, the terms 'mistake' and 'mistaken' refer to ways of orienting to the life tasks that have caused people to experience problems, unhappiness, discomfort, and so forth. These terms also imply that for a given individual, different ways exist for pursuing life tasks that do not entail such problems. For example, although a demoralised, unhappy client may not realise that attempting to solidify one's self-esteem by disparaging and degrading others creates more problems than it solves, a therapist may recognise this pattern and predict that it will continue to cause problems.

Although Adlerian therapists may understand how clients perpetuate their problems and what needs to happen for the problems to resolve, given their clinical experiences and knowledge of personality (i.e. seeing the 'reality' of the clients' problems), they do not impose or force their realisations on clients. Such a strategy would make Adlerian therapy clearly objectivist much in the same way as the cognitive-behavioural approaches. Instead, clients are helped to discover the nature of their present Life Styles through exercises such as early recollections and the completion of genograms. As this awareness builds, clients are helped to forge new ways of responding to others through therapeutic techniques such as well-timed confrontations, discussions of client beliefs, and the use of the therapist's interpersonal style to render mistaken goals useless or pointless, among others.

If with time and work the therapist's construction of the client's reality is not moving the therapy in a productive direction, the therapist will have to relinquish former constructions of the client and develop new ones. That is, although individual psychologists may agree there is 'a reality' that they can discern in their professional work with the client, they remain only provisionally bound to it insofar as it contributes productively to the therapy process.

Kelly also acknowledged that a real world existed, but focused more on the relationships of individual constructs with each other, with how constructs changed, and how constructs were used to understand other people, among other things. Kelly's assessment method, the repertory grid technique, clearly demonstrates this emphasis on construct interrelationships. Although Kelly recognised that constructs must be regularly revised and replaced when invalidated by experiences in the world, lest one engage in a particular kind of cognitive rigidity that he termed hostility, he does not acknowledge that any other constraints or requirements are posed by reality. Perhaps Kelly implicitly assumes that people must meet these tasks. Nonetheless, the world and one's place in it essentially remain to be construed according to Kelly.

Rather than emphasising the feed-forward and feedback relationships between people's constructed meanings and reality, Kellian psychotherapy focuses more on problems as they are manifested through the operation of people's constructs. Here, the therapist functions less as an exemplar or representative of some real-world issue but more as a commentator and guide that examines how the client's construct system functions regarding some life problem. In this regard, Kellian and constructivist therapists may refrain from characterising a client's life patterns as mistaken or believing they have some access to the reality of a problem that is unknown to their clients.

Working from this position, Kelly's (1955) therapeutic strategies typically involved discussions with the client aimed at either loosening or tightening the extent to which constructs are applied to various people or situations. For instance, if a battered spouse always and invariantly applied the bipolar construct 'wants me for sex' versus 'will hit me' to all men that she encountered, such a construction might be tightened by talking about particular male figures known to the client that may defy characterisation with this construct. That is, this construct may be tightened so that it becomes more appropriately impermeable to some people that the client encounters. Outside an ongoing abusive relationship, this construct ultimately may become completely impermeable to all relationships with men. The opposing process, loosening a construct so that it applies to a wider range of experiences the person encounters, will increase the construct's range of convenience and render a wider variety of events as potentially meaningful.

This talking-out of constructs resonates particularly well with Adler's emphasis that the only meanings that exist are the ones that can be publicly articulated and, thereby, examined (Ansbacher and Ansbacher 1956). In addition, similar to the repertory grid method, the systematic examination of a client's family of origin through genogram completion or other structured methods may result in a client becoming both more aware of and more circumspect about important Life Style beliefs. An Adlerian therapist working with the female client above may similarly note and discuss the highly dichotomous ways she has of understanding men (i.e. her antithetical apperceptions of them). Beyond this, the therapist, especially if male, may interpersonally orient himself with the client in a way that defies her 'successful' or typical use of her dominant 'male construct'. At this point the client may experience anxiety in letting go of her former way of experiencing men as she transitions and experiments with new ways of perceiving them in preparation to meet the tasks of relationship and love in a more adaptive manner.

Kellian therapy may also involve dilating or expanding the client's perceptual field in a careful and controlled manner with the goal of either invalidating a construct or creating the experience of anxiety, signalling the need to forge a new construct to represent the newly experienced aspect of reality. Here, a wide variety of methods may be employed to create the dilation, one of which may involve the therapist actively representing some aspect of reality to the client (e.g. the need to pay one's child support). Pointing out inconsistent, contradictory, or inferentially incompatible constructs also may dilate the client and signal the need to create new constructs. Kelly's fixed role therapy technique (see Chapter 3) may help a client to revise constructs and to form new ones under the guise of enacting a new, optimally dissimilar role crafted by the therapist.

Contemporary constructivist approaches

Modern constructivism emerged largely from Kelly's (1955/1991) personal construct psychology and has become somewhat variegated as constructivist themes have been articulated in other lines of theory and research that include the cognitive-developmental constructivism of Kohlberg and DeVries (1987), Loevinger (1987), and Selman (1980), the experiential approach of Greenberg and Safran (1987), and the narrative work of Daigneault (1999), Howard (1991), Neimeyer and Stewart (1999), Sarbin (1986), White and Epston (1990), among other variations. Constructivism also encompasses an additional area of scholarship known as social constructionism which focuses on meaning-making as this occurs in groups and wider societal contexts (Gergen 1994) rather than on individually derived meanings. Although the historical origins along with the theoretical and practical differences between constructivism and both Kellian and Adlerian approaches could be the subject of an extended discussion, only the main points of similarity and divergence will be reviewed here.

Many of the principal differences between the Adlerian and constructivist approaches, as broadly conceived, again stem from their respective emphases on the role of reality and a real world in affecting the client and the therapeutic endeavour. Constructivism embodies at least two assumptions about reality, the first of which is that, although reality and a real world exist, people's constructions of themselves and of the world rather than the world itself should frame all psychotherapeutic interventions. This is the same assumption, essentially, that Kelly (1955) made about reality.

The second assumption uniquely defines the contemporary constructivist psychotherapies and asserts that although a real world may exist, there are no definite, enduring, or cross-contextual meanings inherent in reality apart from the person who creates them (i.e. no meanings in and of themselves). The world essentially is unknowable other than in a fleeting or situational way. This assumption forms the core of what is known as postmodernism (Anderson 1990, Neimeyer and Mahoney 1995). One immediate implication of the postmodern or constructivist approaches is that clients must create their own meanings for experienced events and that no readily supplied, pre-existing meanings (available from friends, family or the psychotherapist) for life problems will resonate well with the network or hierarchy of meanings that the client has developed.

Constructivists vary in the extent to which they subscribe to the second assumption. Some psychologists exemplify a radical form of constructivism that is difficult to distinguish from Kantian idealism insofar as they assume the only true reality that exists consists of the set of perceptions and constructs created by the person (von Glasersfeld 1984). Other psychologists subscribe to a more representational form of constructivism (i.e. critical constructivism) that views the meanings for things, people, and situations in the world as more enduring and less dependent on time or contexts (Neimeyer and Mahoney 1995).

At this time, the various pedigrees of constructivism represent more of an attitude or philosophy about how to conduct psychotherapy than a well-defined set of specific psychotherapeutic techniques. This philosophy informs the rationale, timing, and ultimate use of many existing techniques from other orientations (e.g. empathy, genuineness) along with those that possess more traditional constructivist or personal construct origins (i.e. laddering exercise, biographical repertory grid technique, mirror time, etc.). In this regard, many postmodern therapists are constructivist in their theoretical commitments and eclectic in their use of specific strategies and techniques.

Several constructivist therapeutic techniques have emerged since the publication of Kelly's (1955) theory, one of which is the laddering exercise (Neimeyer 1993). This exercise produces a controlled elaboration of a client's constructs or beliefs by having him or her systematically list important beliefs about some issue or problem and then answer therapist-posed questions about what these beliefs imply. Another technique is the biographical repertory grid (Neimeyer and Stewart 1996). The biographical repertory grid is as much a therapeutic device as it is an assessment tool. One purpose of this exercise, although the technique is very adaptable, is to have the client create a narrative as the grid is completed that integrates how she or he has handled difficult situations or circumstances at various times in life, spanning from childhood to the present. That is, the self at different ages and during different trying times comprises the elements of the grid. Again, just like the genogram exercise, the act of completing a biographical repertory grid produces insights and consolidates systems of meaning that previously may have been only implicit or largely unintegrated.

Adlerian theory and practice share some features with the modern constructivist approaches, mainly regarding the needs to incorporate and manage the givens of one's life (e.g. birth order, talents, abilities, hereditary background, early family atmosphere, etc.) while forging a way to seek completion and belongingness. Adlerians and constructivists would probably agree that people are more likely to develop healthy Life Styles to the extent that they develop their own unique meanings and methods for pursuing the life tasks rather than simply accommodating themselves to some pre-existing structure of meanings or opportunities or conforming to the Life Style paths taken by their parents or siblings. Further, given the diverse goal-directed striving that exists among people, Adlerian therapists probably would recognise a kind of 'personal postmodernism' in that a particular object, event, or outcome could possess very different meanings for people as a function of their life goals and guiding lines.

These similarities in theory and practice methods notwithstanding, constructivist and Adlerian therapists display some noteworthy differences that stem from how they construe their professional roles. As an example, we will consider how the two approaches may tackle a client's problem or presenting issue. To begin, constructivists would refrain from characterising a client's life problem as a sign of having made a 'basic mistake' in the Adlerian parlance and would not label it as such in therapeutic dialogues. They may even go so far as to not point out or identify dysfunctional behavioural patterns that exemplify the problem. Perhaps most importantly, constructivists would not presume to know or recognise the realities that originated or maintained a particular client's problems. To do so would put the therapist in the one-up position of representing reality, being more objective, or presuming to know more about the client than the client does.

Beyond this initial stance, constructivists would examine the semantic implications of the constructs comprising the problem for other areas of the person's life. The goal here would be to have the person examine the viability (as against the correctness) of his or her current way of constructing self and the world. This is largely a process of self-discovery guided by how the therapist construes the meaning-making system of the client. Although the client may not develop the meaning structures and ways of getting by in the world that ultimately lead to optimal health, the constructivist emphasis is on developing a viable or 'good-enough' way of understanding self, relationships and the world. Instead of reorientation, constructivists work towards an adaptive and workable reconstruction of problem areas in life.

In contrast to the constructivist approach, Adlerian therapists maintain that clients do make mistakes in their constructions of events or situations to the extent that the constructions underlie behavioural or emotional problems when clients use, enact, project their systems of meaning. Clients may fail to recognise the need to meet the tasks of love, work, and community or construct largely self-defeating lines of movement towards these tasks. This implies the existence of 'better' or more adaptive constructions of various life situations, some of which may be recognised by the therapist as possibilities for the client to incorporate. Although Adlerian therapists may rely on their constructions of client and clinical realities to guide their interventions, they do not foist their insights or 'recipes' for change on clients. Instead, individual psychologists understand the most important insights are the ones that the client develops himself or herself.

Adlerian therapists may identify and highlight clients' problem areas and attempt to deepen clients' awareness of how their current ways of approaching life have not worked for them. They may do this by forming hypotheses about the nature of symptomatic difficulties and the mistakes that may underlie them and pose these as tentative explanations that clients may either refute, affirm, or elaborate on (i.e. the stochastic method). That is, clients are assisted in discovering the details of their mistakes along with their implications. The ability to articulate foundational assumptions about self and others builds the client's insight into his or her private logic.

Once insight about the client's private logic is developed and articulated, the therapist may then begin to reorient the client towards the tasks of life by characterising his or her current or previous behaviour as mistaken attempts at meeting these tasks. For instance, the client whose dysfunctional family stifled her emotional expression may view others outside the family (even years afterward) as somewhat hostile and disinterested. Once the client understands the persistence of this construction into new interpersonal contexts, the therapist may characterise this orientation as a mistake insofar as others (the therapist included) do not behave in a hostile or disinterested way. Further, any passive or compliant orientations the client portrays in his or her love or community relationships similarly may comprise a mistake.

In summary, Adlerian, Kellian, and constructivist therapists all espouse a constructivist epistemology that is applicable to clients and clinicians alike. Although Adlerian and Kellian therapists maintain that a real world exists, Adlerians probably believe more than the Kellians that people are affected by the necessities of the real world to meet the tasks of life. The existing varieties of constructivism de-emphasise the question of a real world and focus principally on clients' construction of meanings and helping them to forge new meanings in the face of life problems. Relative to both the Kellian and constructivist approaches, individual psychologists place greater emphasis on their constructions of reality and use such constructions to organise the therapy process rather than simply to communicate the content of 'objective reality' to their clients.

Some possible directions for cross-theoretical research

Our review of the similarities and differences that exist between Individual Psychology and other theories of personality and psychotherapy suggest several promising areas for cross-theoretical research. We conclude this chapter with a brief review of some of these areas and suggest possible routes through which the research may be pursued and the theory advanced.

The last ten years have witnessed an increasing interest in positive psychology, optimal functioning, and personal growth (Csikszentmihalyi 1990, 1993). Individual Psychology, along with other perspectives such as Maslow's self-actualisation theory, had variously addressed what it means to be emotionally healthy and to lead a well-adjusted, happy, or meaningful life. For Adler (1931), the possession and use of Social Interest to meet relationship and community tasks is an important indicator of psychological health. Similarly for Maslow and other humanistic theorists (e.g. Csikszentmihalyi 1993), the ability to experience self-actualisation, peak, or flow experiences is a hallmark of emotional well-being.

At this time no prior studies have examined the relationships between the Social Interest and self-actualisation constructs insofar as these are benchmarks of health for different theories. As discussed previously in this chapter, Social Interest and self-actualisation are quite different conceptually, especially given the transcendent quality of peak experiences. In the extreme, a deep level of Social Interest may even preclude a more exclusive focus on self that seems necessary to achieve actualisation regularly. Nonetheless, the empirical relationship between these constructs, as operationalised by existing measures, remains unknown.

It is possible that the Social Interest construct is subsumed in Maslow's (1962, 1987) hierarchy under the need or task of belonging with others and somewhat under the need for self-esteem, to the extent that such esteem stems from assuming productive roles in social settings. Some Adlerians (Dreikurs and Mosak 1977b) also believe that the additional tasks of meaning and spirituality lie beyond the cultivation of Social Interest; however, no measures exist for assessing these tasks within Individual Psychology. In this way, Social Interest would occupy a more fundamental role in emotional health and would function as a prerequisite for the development of self-actualisation abilities.

The relationships between Social Interest and self-actualisation could be evaluated using the existing measures to operationalise each construct in a structural equation modelling design (see Chapter 3 for representative measures of Social Interest). The empirical question here would be: What are the contributions of Social Interest and self-actualisation to happiness, satisfaction, and fulfilment in life? In this design, measures of Social Interest and self-actualisation would be used to predict happiness/satisfaction/fulfilment. If Social Interest functions at a more basic level than self-actualisation, then its contribution to the criterion variables would be either mediated or moderated by self-actualisation. If Social Interest contributes independently to the measures of emotional health and life satisfaction, then its causal path would not go through self-actualisation exclusively.

This is important research to pursue because it would address the extent to which Social Interest is the *sine qua non* of mental health. The results may support the existing conceptions that health stems from meeting the three life tasks. Alternatively, this research may suggest that Dreikurs and Mosak (1977b) were supported in proposing an increase in the number of life tasks. Regardless of the ultimate nature of the empirically observed relationships, pursuing this research would create a bridge between two complementary theories of intervention and personality and may well spur adherents in each area to conduct further studies.

Psychological birth order provides another front for integrating Individual Psychology with research lines in sociology, social psychology, and personality. As noted in Chapter 3, the morass of confusing and equivocal findings in birth order may have stemmed from ignoring Adler's (1927, 1931) caveat that psychological or perceived birth role in the family is a more salient variable for analysis than is actual (or ordinal) position. Although much of the research in birth order has not been motivated by Adler's ideas, a re-emphasis of psychological position may prove fruitful for integrative purposes.

Both the theory and measurement of psychological position remained relatively unelaborated beyond Adler's discussion until recently (Campbell, White and Stewart 1991, Stewart and Campbell 1998, Stewart, Stewart and Campbell 2001). Theoretically, the emergence of psychological roles is anticipated by a symbolic interactionist variant of role theory, the role identity model (McCall and Simmons 1978), when this model is applied to the family context. Several predictions can be made on the basis of this theory, the first of which is that an organised and coherent set of behaviours is associated with an identifiable position within the family (Stryker and Stathan 1985). This prediction has largely received support in psychological birth order research that has established the construct validity of at least four psychological positions (Stewart and Campbell 1998, Stewart, Stewart and Campbell 2001). Second, roles are interactional in nature such that the thoughts, feelings, and behaviours associated with a role occur in the context of the complementary or reciprocal roles that are portrayed by other family members. Third, observing and experiencing the self in the process of repeatedly portraying a role cultivates a sense of role identity that embodies internalised standards for that role (McCall and Simmons 1978, Stryker 1983). The latter two predictions remain to be evaluated. Pursuing this research, however, will involve some interesting syntheses between Individual Psychology and role theory.

Another area in which Individual Psychology may productively inform research is in the study of how birth order relates to personality. Again, the results have been largely equivocal with both large, well-conducted studies (e.g. Jefferson, Herbst and McCrae 1998) and thorough reviews (Ernst and Angst 1983) revealing few meaningful relationships. Recent research using the psychological role, however, has discovered statistically and practically significant relationships between scores on the White–Campbell Psychological Birth Order Inventory (Campbell, White and Stewart 1991; see Chapter 3) and the Personality Research Form (Stewart, Stewart and Campbell 2001). In addition, ongoing studies will reveal how psychological birth order mediates the relationship of actual birth order to personality traits.

Finally, Individual Psychology's emphasis on the family as a potent influence that shapes personality processes augurs well for current work that examines how families affect the learning and socialisation of children's emotions (Halberstadt 1986, Saarni 1999). In fact, there is a growing awareness that the emotional expressiveness in the family can characterise the overall family atmosphere and also affect how children choose to express their feelings (Yelsma et al. 1998). Individual Psychology is unique among personality and counselling theories in placing a strong emphasis on the psychology of the family. This, along with Adlerians' interest in case-based and qualitative research, may help to identify the variables and mechanisms through which families come to influence both their children's personalities and overall emotional health. The use of quantitative measures that are relevant for family atmosphere variables (e.g. the Family Environment Scale, see Chapter 3) in this area may also promote the cross-fertilisation of theory and research between Individual Psychology, developmental psychology, and theories of emotion.

Overall, the possibilities for integrative research stem in part from Adler's prescience in identifying important personality and family process variables as he developed his theories (Adler 1927, 1929, 1931, Ansbacher and Ansbacher 1956). Although modern psychology has moved beyond the era of the 'big schools' and is now more problem and question driven, Adler's observations about human nature can be translated into valuable research questions and hypotheses that are relevant for current work in personality, development, and social psychology. To do this, clinicians and scholars will need to discern Adlerian themes in current research lines and also identify areas of contemporary interest that Adler addressed during his career and in his writings.

Chapter 7

Adlerian Psychology: Further developments and relevance in a postmodern world

Evolution of Adlerian Psychology

Adler published more than 300 books and articles and gave countless lectures and public demonstrations of his techniques in Europe (especially the German-speaking countries) and in the United States. The Nazi regime fought his ideas and had the child guidance centres closed. Just like many German and Austrian intellectuals, Adler had to emigrate to the USA, where he found friends, promoters, and disciples, but also detractors. To a certain extent, his ideas were received with high interest, but the pre-eminence of Freudian Psychoanalysis also led to resistance to the expansion of Individual Psychology. It was Adler's disciple Rudolf Dreikurs who founded the Alfred Adler Institute of Chicago and who contributed significantly to the growth of Individual Psychology in the USA and in other countries. There was also a certain interest in Adler's ideas in South America and in Spain, mainly promoted in the 1940s by Oliver Brachfeld (Brachfeld 1970, Mestre and Carpintero 1988, León 2000), but later this interest decreased. Although Individual Psychology was met with a certain resistance, it continued to spread mainly in the USA, and after World War II, in Germany, Austria, and Switzerland.

Many Adlerian principles found an explicit or implicit acceptance in other theories. Some psychologists who had been initially interested in Individual Psychology incorporated Adlerian constructs into their own theories of personality or psychotherapy; for example Victor Frankl, Rollo May, Albert Ellis, and others. As we have said in the preface of this book, the lesser influence of Adlerian Psychology compared with Freudian Psychoanalysis and Jungian Analytical Psychology is probably due, at least in part, to the fact that Adlerians have a tendency to prefer clinical practice to discussing theoretical issues in academia. On the other hand, Adler's commonsensical way of expressing his ideas made it easy for other authors to incorporate his concepts into their own systems.

After its temporary decline, Individual Psychology is now recognised as an important theory of both personality and psychotherapy. In many countries,

Individual Psychology is officially recognised, taught and practised. At present, there are Adler schools and associations in the USA, Canada, Germany, Austria, Switzerland, Great Britain, Italy, France, Hungary, Japan, and Lithuania. In the USA and Canada, the North American Society of Adlerian Psychology (NASAP) is Individual Psychology's central organisation. It publishes newsletters and a quarterly journal, and has an annual convention. There is also an International Association of Individual Psychology (IAIP), which sponsors international meetings once every 3 years for people interested in Individual Psychology. As Dinkmeyer, Jr and Sperry (2000) state, Adlerian Psychology continues to grow around the globe.

But there are also signs of a crisis in the Adlerian community. In its spring 2000 edition, the *Journal of Individual Psychology* presented a discussion among important Adlerian authors about the present and the future of Individual Psychology and NASAP (Carlson 2000, Dreikurs Ferguson 2000, Watts 2000, among others). On one hand, there are Adlerians who think that Individual Psychology is still 'ahead of its time' (Dreikurs Ferguson 2000); others, however, have a more pessimistic attitude towards the future of Individual Psychology. The responses to this crisis have been varied, with some proposing to disband the association, surrender to other therapies, and to become a 'hyphen', i.e. to fuse with other systems and become a solution focused-Adlerian, a narrative-Adlerian, etc. in order to guarantee the survival of Adlerian ideas (Carlson 2000). Other voices (Watts 2000) proclaim their faith in the survival capacity of Individual Psychology and affirm that it is still relevant in the new millennium, because it can successfully address the multicultural and social equality issues of a postmodern society.

The authors of this book do not believe that the only alternatives are either to 'surrender' to the tide of newer therapies or to cling desperately to orthodox Adlerian Psychology. We maintain that Adlerian Psychology has enough force of its own to survive without hanging on to other therapies that seem to have garnered, at the moment, a greater level of interest or attention in the changeable market of psychological interventions. On the other hand, we think that Individual Psychology cannot close its eyes to the recent challenges that all therapeutic approaches have to face: integrationism, constructivism, and postmodernism. In view of these tendencies we believe that Individual Psychology would benefit by examining the commonalities that it shares with other systems with respect to epistemology, personality theory and various types and modalities of intervention. This is what we have tried to do throughout the chapters of this book. We have pointed out the similarities of Individual Psychology with other theories and have proposed the incorporation of new techniques derived from other orientations. In the discussion below we will continue from the former chapter and examine the relationship of Individual Psychology with constructivism, and discuss its integrative potential, and the propositions that Individual Psychology can elaborate to answer the challenging questions of a postmodern society.

Challenges to Individual Psychology

Integration in psychotherapy

In their review of various psychotherapy systems, Feixas and Miró (1993) argue that the historical evolution of psychotherapy can be seen as a succession of proposals that imply different points of view of how psychological problems can be conceived and resolved. Karasu (1986) had already mentioned the proliferation of hundreds of different therapies, many of which have a different conceptualisation of the human being, and possess their own terminology. This makes a dialogue among different perspectives somewhat difficult. And though it is commonly accepted that 'therapy is good for people', Eysenck (1952) had already argued that no psychotherapeutic intervention is superior to spontaneous remission; actually, up until now no psychotherapeutic school has empirically proven to be more effective than another. There is an increasing consensus among investigators and practitioners that no treatments of choice exist for most disorders, but instead there are common factors in most therapies that are important for the effectiveness of the intervention, especially the therapeutic alliance (Ahn and Wampold 2001, Feixas and Miró 1993, Norcross 1986).

On the other hand, for a therapist trained in a specific method, usually by spending a considerable amount of money and time, belonging to a particular school may become an important sign of identity that allows him or her not only a specific conceptualisation of the patients' problems and the application of strategies he or she has been trained in, but also the access to a scientific and professional support system.

Both tendencies, the proliferation of therapy systems and the increasing awareness of the equivalence of at least the most important systems, lead to a certain confusion among practitioners and their clients. On one hand, there are therapists who opt for clinging to the approach they were trained in, but on the other, many prefer to maintain a neutral and eclectic perspective and resist identifying with or adhering to a particular orientation. Again according to Norcross (1986), the therapeutic community has shifted from an absolutist and simplicist dogmatism to a relativism that affirms that any intervention can be valid in certain circumstances. And although 'eclecticism' means choosing 'the best' from the different options, the selection many clinicians make is often spurious, arbitrary and uncritical. Without specific criteria of how to choose and combine intervention strategies and techniques, eclectic interventions risk being ineffective and, at their worst, harmful for the client.

Adlerian Psychology is no exception to this phenomenon. As in other therapies, we may find academic Adlerians and Adlerian practitioners who only accept the classical Adlerian ideas. Others who are probably more relativist combine Adlerian ideas with more or less related interventions, or tacitly shift from Individual Psychology to other systems. Between the Scylla of dogmatism and the Charybdis of defeatism, Adlerians have to find an answer to this problem.

Academic psychologists have elaborated several models of integration in psychotherapy, ranging from simple technical eclecticism to highly sophisticated models for the integration of two or more complete systems (e.g. Psychoanalysis and behaviour modification). For a review of the different models we refer the interested reader to Arkowitz's (1991) basic paper.

We would like to mention one particular integration model – Neimeyer's (1988) Theoretically Progressive Integration (TPI). This TPI model holds that therapies that share a common metatheoretical roof can cross-fertilise and mutually enrich each other with respect to their theoretical concepts and technical interventions. The author proposes constructivism as a suitable metatheoretical framework. We consider this approach particularly interesting for Adlerians. Both authors of this book have worked implicitly and explicitly with this model and have proposed techniques that represent the integration of Adlerian and constructivist techniques (Neimeyer and Stewart 1999, Oberst 1998b, 2002, Oberst et al. 2001). We think that constructivism can provide a suitable framework for Adlerians to work with and can point to new pathways out of the surrender-or-resist dilemma. Instead of fusing with other approaches, Individual Psychology can enter into a free, but theoretically supported exchange with certain other therapies (e.g. personal construct psychology). Adlerian Psychology has not only to receive from other therapies, it has also to give. And, as Adlerian Psychology *is* constructivist, there is no need for a hyphenated constructivist-Adlerian to exist.

Constructivism in psychotherapy

As we have outlined earlier, constructivism is an epistemic position that holds that it is the observer who actively construes meanings about the world and that reality can thus be interpreted in different ways. Perception is not an act that *represents* reality and, therefore, our subjective constructed reality does not necessarily correspond with the reality that is supposed to be 'out there'. We construe what we believe to detect, and we are thus unable to obtain an objective image of reality and hence can claim no true knowledge about it.

During the last decades, constructivism has penetrated not only into the human sciences, but into all disciplines, even into physics – the 'exact science' par excellence – and the emergence of the probabilistic conception of matter, indeterminism, and the unpredictability principle of quantum mechanics undermines the fundamental principle of the sciences; namely causality (see Capra 1982a, b, Riedl 1984).

The paradigm opposed to constructivism is usually called objectivism, although not all authors maintain this nomenclature and talk instead of 'realism' (Scott, Kelly and Tolbert 1995) or 'positivist epistemology' (Ibáñez

1992). Objectivism holds that reality can be known objectively and correctly, if our instruments and procedures are good enough. In the realm of psychotherapy, Mahoney and Gabriel (1987) make a distinction between 'rationalist' (read: objectivist) cognitive and 'constructivist' cognitive therapies. According to these authors, in rationalist therapies the existence of a correct interpretation of reality is assumed. In Beck's Cognitive Behavioural therapy, for example, the patient is thought to have distorted cognitions of himself or herself and his or her environment, and the goal of therapy is, by means of specific cognitive-behavioural techniques, to help the patient to develop a more correct or 'realistic' view (Beck 1976). This corresponds to the psychoeducational-cognitive approach of Adlerian therapy, as understood by Shulman (1985), who considers Individual Psychology to be a cognitive approach: the patient's 'mistakes' or 'faulty beliefs' have to be detected and changed into 'correct' (adaptive, useful) beliefs. This would also mean that the client has to be taught and educated, just like a child in school. Constructivist therapies, on the contrary, do not pretend to possess a correct interpretation of the patient's problems or of the solutions. For instance, in personal construct psychology (Kelly 1955/1991) the patient is simply invited to question his or her system of constructs and to generate new hypotheses and to test them in an experience outside the therapeutic setting, as if it were a scientific investigation. The patient's new hypothesis is considered confirmed if the new construct proves to be more useful in terms of interacting better with other people. This would mean the incorporation of the new construct in the patient's system. If the hypothesis is not confirmed, the elaboration process starts again.

So, in objectivism there is a criterion of truth as an epistemic value. Truth exists and can be discovered by accumulatively improving our instruments of perception. Translated into psychological terms, this postulate means that there is (at least theoretically) a criterion which tells us which behaviour, which thought, which cognition, which feeling or which construct is the right one (or the adaptive one or the healthy one). Constructivism does not accept the criterion of truth as a justification of knowledge. Botella (1995) emphasises as epistemic principles of constructivism the *pragmatic* value of knowledge claims, especially their predictive validity and their internal coherence (internal and external consistency and unifying power.) This concept of pragmatism or usefulness instead of an absolute and observer/knower-independent truth is broadly shared by constructivist psychologists.

As we showed in Chapter 6, Individual Psychology and constructivist therapies have many aspects in common. We have said that many contemporary Adlerian authors consider Individual Psychology to be a constructivist theory. But would constructivist authors also agree on this point? With very few exceptions, constructivist authors do not mention Adlerian Psychology, although there is a growing awareness of the common heritage of Adlerian and constructivist thought (Neimeyer and Stewart 1999, Oberst 1998a). We would like to resume one aspect of this discussion here and particularly mention one important point: the concept of Social Interest, the very essence of Adlerian Psychology.

Social Interest: constructivist or objectivist?

Whereas in the realm of personality, the notions of fictions and fictionate goals, holism, proactivity, social embeddedness, etc., may sound acceptable to constructivists, the concept of Social Interest versus striving for superiority as a criterion for mental health clearly does not. Even more, Stepansky (1983) accuses Adler of promoting a conservative morality because, in his view, Individual Psychology puts mental health on a par with social conformism.

The orthodox application of Adlerian therapy as a psychoeducational approach would mean, in fact, that Individual Psychology falls into what Mahoney and Gabriel (1987) called rationalist cognitive therapies, as opposed to constructivist therapies. Indeed, some of Adler's writings seem very rationalist (objectivist) and Adler himself often seems quite convinced of being in possession of the 'truth'. Not only does he qualify some cognitions as 'erroneous' (which, as we have seen, implies the assumption of a correct point of view), but also as 'antisocial' (which implies even a value-laden standpoint). A criterion for truth and rational thinking and behaviour appears throughout Adler's work: common sense and Social Interest. As we have said before, the more Social Interest we find in an individual, the healthier he or she is, while the neurotic individual is characterised by Adler as lacking in Social Interest.

Some Adlerian authors inspired by constructivism have already discussed the issues of truth and fiction in Adlerian Psychology. The German Gfäller (1996) comments that a superficial lecture on Adler can provoke the impression that Adler distinguishes between 'fiction' and 'truth', with fiction being something that clients possess and truth something the therapist has. Gfäller warns against a clinical practice that considers the therapist as possessing the knowledge of what the client has and how he or she should behave, feel and think, and the client as being possessed by erroneous fictions to be eradicated. According to this author, Adler precisely wanted to avoid this attitude in the therapist, although some of his expressions and explanations may have given rise to misinterpretations, for example the expression 'the patient's private logic', as if there were a public, and therefore better and more correct logic. But we cannot avoid stating that Adler often uses the term 'fiction' in a pejorative sense, as if the patient's problems consisted precisely in having fictions.

Another German author, Bruder (1996) also asserts that the Adlerian idea of 'error' (the patient's erroneous beliefs) seems not to be constructivist. But we must also state that for Adler the neurotic individual is not different from the healthy one because of *having* fictions, but for *clinging to* them. The neurotic individual is 'under the hypnotic influence of a ficticious life plan' (Adler 1912/1977: 75), he or she 'arbitrarily ascribes reality to it' and is 'nailed to the cross of his fictions' (Adler 1912/1977: 74).

We agree with Bruder (1996) that 'correcting the error' in Adlerian therapy should not be a pedagogical attempt at educating or instructing the client, telling him or her what to think, to feel, or to do. As practitioners we should keep in mind that clients are not pupils who make mistakes; they are 'mistaken' in the way they make use of their fictions. Bruder proposes to conceive Adlerian therapy as deconstructionist. Deconstruction, according to White (1992) aims at shaking our suppositions about reality and our habits we have received and now take as truths. Bruder argues that Adlerian therapy can be interpreted as being deconstructionist because it does not intend to dissolve the fiction but to recontextualise it. Fictions may have had a certain usefulness in the context of their production in childhood, but in adulthood, life circumstances have changed and their usefulness is doubtful. It was probably useful not to contradict an irascible father in order to avoid being battered, but doing the same in an adulthood context (with a calm and composed spouse) may be counter-productive and create problems.

The difference between the pedagogical and the deconstructionist attitude lies in the therapist's 'not-knowing-attitude' (Anderson and Goolishian 1992). Adler himself insisted on the therapist using Socratic questions in order to come to an understanding of what both therapist and client do not (yet) know about the client's problems. Similar to what Kelly (1955) maintained about the client being the expert, Adler was convinced that the client unconsciously knows what is the matter with him or her: 'Man knows more than he understands' (Adler 1933/1980: 22). The client is the expert and the therapist, in his or her condition of not-knowing, accompanies the clients in their process of construing and deconstruing their personal narratives by staying close to their personal meanings without imposing on them a preconceived opinion. Bruner (1990) called this the narrative position as opposed to the paradigmatic position. In this way, a dialogical understanding and subsequent construction of not-yet-told and not-yet-explained narratives emerges. The therapist does not discover a clinical picture but explores what has not been said before.

Although Adler showed a clear constructivist attitude in his publications, he did not always maintain this not-knowing position. And though the authors of this book, as contemporary constructivist-influenced Adlerians, would consider this not-knowing position to be preferable, maybe not all Adlerian practitioners maintain the same stance, and prefer the psychoeducational viewpoint of the Dreikursian influence. In his last publications, which have a more popular-science character, as well as in his clinical practice, Adler seems to have abandoned his formerly more constructivist theoretical positions in favour of a more pedagogic and therefore more objectivist viewpoint. Adler was very clear in maintaining that all patients ultimately have the same problem, independently of their individual symptoms and their individual personal narrative: the triad of lack of Social Interest, inferiority feelings, and striving for personal superiority. This bears similarity to the ways that an orthodox psychoanalyst would always find a sexual aetiology or a conflict among psychic instances, a cognitive-behavioural therapist cognitive distortions and a Rogerian a gap between real self and ideal self. Therefore we cannot completely absolve Adler from the constructivist accusation of applying an a priori narrative (Gergen and Kaye 1992) to the client. According to Gergen and Kaye, substituting the client's complex and refined story with the therapist's view of things can have fatal consequences, because in this way, the therapist knows what is the matter with the client before the beginning of the therapeutic process and so deprives the client of all control over it. These authors criticise this procedure severely and argue that it only gives the patients a lecture on inferiority by informing them, directly or indirectly, that they are ignorant, not sensible, or incapable of understanding reality. If we accept that the patient has to eradicate all the erroneous cognitions and change them for more correct ones, we also accept that the therapist, just because he or she is the therapist, is in the possession of the truth. The therapist shows the patient which vision is right and which cognitions he or she has to adopt. Orthodox Psychoanalysis has been criticised for its view of 'client resistance': if the client agrees with the therapist's interpretation, the therapist is right. But if the client disagrees with it, the client's attitude is interpreted as resistance, because he or she does not want to become aware of an uncomfortable issue, and this would mean that the therapist is even more right. So whatever the client says, the therapist cannot be wrong.

Constructivist therapists, of course, refuse to be in possession of the truth – first, because the existence of an absolute Truth is denied (as outlined above) and second, because the patient can be manipulated and put under the control of the therapist (Neimeyer 1994).

In our opinion, these critics have to be taken seriously, but in clinical practice the differences we discussed do not contrast so dramatically. Probably even an orthodox psychoanalyst would not insist that his interpretations contain the absolute truth despite the patient's denial. And Adlerian Life Style analysis does not reveal to us simply an 'inferiority complex' and nothing else, but an individual drama with multiple facets, idiosyncratic fictions and personal meanings, sublime goals and ordinary excuses, abominable suffering and stupid vanity. And when we 'discover' the client's mistakes, we have not discovered any truth, as Master (1991) argues. We have simply construed a form of understanding of the client's problems in a social context, which allows us to create together with him or her different fictions that allow him or her to interact better with his or her surroundings. All these new fictions have to be tested out in the patient's real life with respect to their viability and usefulness.

Yet, when client and therapist agree on the client's definition of his or her problem, there is usually no problem in being 'constructivist' and accepting the client's story ('I want to lose my fear of grasshoppers', 'I feel socially isolated and I need to interact better with my neighbours', 'I feel depressed because of my academic failure'), and the therapist can happily use any skill and strategy to help the client to achieve the desired goal (desensitisation techniques, social skill training, techniques to improve academic perform-ance, or counsel him or her for a more suitable career, etc.). Gergen and Kaye (1992) call this the 'advisory option'.

But what happens if client and therapist disagree on what should be the issue to be treated in therapy? What happens when the client is chronically and deeply distressed or suicidal ('I feel so bad, I just don't know what to do'), when he or she is psychotic ('I must get rid of those aliens who pursue me') or denies the existence of a personality disorder? Or when the goal expressed by the client is antisocial or differs greatly from the therapist's own values ('I want you to help me to outsmart my competitors'). This dilemma is nicely illustrated in the movie *Analyze this!* with Robert de Niro playing the part of a neurotic mafia boss who has developed a kind of 'killing phobia': he is not yet able to perform the skills (killing, hitting, extorting, cheating) required of an effective 'godfather', and now wants his 'shrink' (played by Billy Crystal) to 'cure' him. Of course, the psychoanalyst disagrees and makes considerable efforts to convert the criminal into a respectable member of society who has learned to resolve his conflicts in a non-violent way. The movie makes a slight 'constructivist turn': in the final showdown, the therap-ist finds himself in a dangerous situation, where 'socially adaptive behaviour' consists in the demonstration of power and violence in order to save his bacon, while the mafia boss quits his 'job' in order to prevent his son from suffering the same childhood trauma he had gone through: watching his father being killed.

As a way out of the dilemma, Gergen and Kaye (1992) propose the use of narrative reconstruction: instead of accepting uncritically the client's story or imposing the therapist's version, both therapist and client together should search for alternative narratives that are more functional within the client's personal and social circumstances.

In some of Adler's publications, the concept of Social Interest sounds like an absolute, eternal, and universal truth. But according to Ansbacher and Ansbacher's (1956) interpretation, Adler, when speaking of 'absolute truth', only expresses his conviction that human beings need a reference point for their orientation. Because we need orientation in the absence of absolute responses to guide our behaviour, the 'best' fiction or 'working hypothesis' (Ansbacher and Ansbacher 1956: 129) consists in considering the iron logic of social life 'as if' it was absolute truth:

> One of the basic facts for the advancement of our understanding of human nature is that we must regard the inherent rules of the game of a

group as these emerge within the limited organization of the human body and its achievements, as if they were an absolute truth.

Ansbacher and Ansbacher 1956: 128.

Thus the concept of Social Interest is only a fiction. For Adlerians it is the most pragmatic fiction, the most expedient error when dealing with human interaction. Even common sense, the logical task-oriented and non-egocentric reasoning related to Social Interest, is nothing absolutely given:

Incidentally the common sense is not unalterable. We shall observe in it continuously new turns. . . . The common sense is nothing fixed. It is rather the sum of all psychological movements which are reasonable, generally approved, and connected with the continuance of culture.

Ansbacher and Ansbacher 1956: 149

In other words, Social Interest and common sense can be seen as social constructions subject to constant changes. It is society that negotiates what is to be considered as 'common sense' and normality, and it is the individual who, in interaction with society, construes and reconstrues his or her fictions, which are more or less congruent with this social consensus. Without these permanent revisions, the individual is unable to develop more adaptive fictions, which would reduce the gap between himself or herself and what is commonly held in society. Interpreting Social Interest in this sense, it can be affirmed that although Adler emphasises the ever-present necessity of construing ways to meaningfully relate to others, he does not postulate an absolute criterion of truth but a social consent with pragmatic value for the orientation of the single individual. Thus putting on a par mental health and common sense or Social Interest is not as arbitrary and objectivist as it may seem: if the individual's behaviour, reasoning and feeling are in line with what the majority of society does, thinks or feels, he or she will, of course, be considered as mentally healthy by this community!

It is precisely Gergen (1994) with his idea of social constructionism who emphasises, just like Adler, the influence of community for the construction of the individual's self and the important role of social processes for the construction of meanings. According to social constructionism, knowledge emerges neither inside the individual nor outside, but among interacting individuals who share and negotiate constantly their meanings.

Social constructionism can also absolve Individual Psychology of Stepansky's (1983) accusation (see above) for being conservative and conformist. The Spanish social constructionist Serrano maintains precisely the opposite: Adlerian Psychology is a model which underlines the social criticism and individual nonconformism with respect to the ruling system, because the individual is an active creator of the social structures and mechanisms, not their passive product (Serrano 1988, 1991).

Postmodernism

An important aspect yet to elucidate is the relationship between Adlerian Psychology and postmodernism. Several authors (e.g. Gergen 1991, Polkinghorne 1992, Botella 1995, among others) have argued that constructivism is the epistemological paradigm most linked to postmodernism, while modernity is characterised by objectivism. There is a great amount of literature on these topics, and entering into a detailed discussion would be beyond the scope of this book. We would just like to pinpoint a few aspects of postmodernism and discuss its relevance for Adlerian Psychology.

Postmodernism (or postmodernity) is considered to be the contemporary cultural condition of the developed post-industrial societies. It is thought that this postmodern turn is a consequence of increasing dissatisfaction with the project of modernity with its rationalist concepts and its belief in the values of Enlightenment, such as Reason, Truth, Progress, Science, etc. In postmodernism, these beliefs in universal values have been lost in favour of a more relativist attitude: incredulity, ambivalence, and disbelief (Botella 1995). Postmodern thought has even been associated with a mentality of 'anything goes': any artistic, philosophical, political, etc. expression or standpoint is as valid as any other, none is better or preferable. As basic themes of postmodern thought, Polkinghorne (1992) identifies four aspects: foundationlessness (as we have no direct access to reality, we have no sure epistemological foundation on which knowledge can be built), fragmentariness (the real is a disunited, fragmented accumulation of disparate elements and events, so knowledge claims should be concerned not with the search for context-free laws, but with these local and specific occurrences), constructivism (knowledge is not a mirrored reflection of reality, but a construction built from cognitive processes), and neopragmatism: given the three other aspects, the only valid criterion for accepting a knowledge claim is not its correspondence with the inaccessible reality, but its predictive usefulness for guiding human action to fulfil intended purposes.

From his postmodern and social constructionist standpoint, Gergen (1991) suggests an interesting classification for therapy systems by considering their underlying philosophical, literary and cultural context (this context is usually called *zeitgeist*). Gergen distinguishes psychotherapy approaches that reflect a romantic, modern, or postmodern view of the individual and of human existence. A romantic vision of the human being is reflected in Psychoanalysis but also in the humanistic approaches with their concepts of transcendence, self-actualisation and personal growth. The paradigm of modern *zeitgeist* in therapy would be the behavioural and cognitive therapies, which focus on observable behaviour and empirically tested treatment techniques. On the other hand, Gergen considers the constructivist/constructionist and systemic approaches to be representative for the postmodern view of the self. As investigators and clinicians, we find particularly challenging the positioning of Individual Psychology among these three dimensions. As we have seen, Individual Psychology has objectivist and constructivist elements, it has romantic (humanistic), modern (cognitive) and postmodern aspects, and this is what makes Individual Psychology particularly interesting with respect to psychotherapy integration.

Nonetheless, we have to keep in mind that although there were already beginnings of postmodern tendencies in art and architecture (e.g. the dadaist movement) in the last stage of Adler's life (he died in 1937), it is only since the last decades that we talk of constructivism and the postmodern condition. The predominant *zeitgeist* in Adler's time was still modern. But apparently, there is a dissatisfaction in Adler's works with modern thought and he went in search of alternatives. The alternatives he traces out are of a clear constructivist nature. Adler's view of the human being and human conditions, his refusal of determinism and of physicalist viewpoints in psychology, his agreement with Vaihinger's ideas, make Individual Psychology a first project of constructivism in psychology and psychotherapy (Neimeyer and Stewart 1999). But all these interpretations notwithstanding, we have to keep in mind that Adler was not only a man 'ahead of his time', as his son Kurt Adler said (Dinkmeyer, Jr and Sperry 2000), but also a man *of* his time. He was certainly a *precursor* of psychological constructivism. By means of a thorough review of his bibliography we can appreciate the evolution of his personal epistemological standpoint (Oberst 1998a). It is interesting to learn how the young Adler (before World War I) struggled to free himself from Psychoanalysis and the medical model, and how the adult Adler elaborated an innovative and early constructivist theory. In contrast, the mature Adler (approximately from 1925 on) seems to turn his back on some of his theoretical constructivist standpoints for the sake of his humanist and sometimes even missionary desire to improve the psychological conditions of mankind and the living together of people. At the threshold of postmodernism, Adler decides to take a step backwards towards a predominantly humanist world-view.

Thus Adler took a clear stance in his personal and professional life: that of humanist ethics. Perhaps the experience of World War I, the beginning of the persecution of the Jews by the Nazi regime and the menace of an even more horrible cataclysm ('Auschwitz' is precisely the metaphor used by postmodern philosophers to designate the failure of the project of modernity) made him feel the need for an ethical foundation of society against an idea of 'anything goes' with its unforeseeable consequences.

Adlerian Psychology and ethics

Adler's humanist view of the human being sees individuals as endowed with free will and thus responsible for their acts. We have already pointed out the innocent–guilty aspect of neurotic safeguarding behaviour (see Chapter 2). The concept of Social Interest has a marked utopian and ethical accent. In

Adler's last and most mature publications, directed to the wider public and not (only) to the academic reader or the clinical practitioner, the issue of the sense of life (the title also of one of his books, published in 1933) is predominant. For Adler, the sense or meaning of life is expressed in Social Interest, and the life of an individual is meaningful when it is guided by 'the goal of pursuing the welfare of all mankind' (Adler 1933/1980: 168), if he or she aspires to a state of 'major capacity for cooperation' (ibid.) and if 'everybody is presented, more than before, as part of a totality' (ibid.). In other words: life makes sense if people do not seek to overcome the difficulties, uncertainties, and inclemency of their lives by moving against or over other people, but work together with them and for the sake of (theoretically) the whole of mankind. If people do not seek their own perfection, but the perfection of their acts and products, then this is moving in the direction of emotional health. This ideal and utopian – and therefore unattainable – community, impregnated with the Social Interest of the people who constitute it, should, in Adler's view, guide people's acts. Humanity approaches this utopia when more and more people have a greater degree of Social Interest. The maximum expression of this utopia of perfection is the idea of God.

Of course, Adler was perfectly aware that this utopian community is a fictionate goal that can never be achieved. On the contrary, wanting to be perfect, to be godlike, is precisely considered to be a neurotic striving for superiority, and thus a neurotic tendency. That is why Adler also used to encourage his patients to accept their imperfections. As we have said above, Social Interest and ideal community are a fiction, a 'working hypothesis' with pragmatic value. It has to be submitted to constant revision and established by social consensus. It is nothing eternal and invariable.

The ethical component of Social Interest and community also has its counterpart in religious issues. A Christian principle is precisely: 'Love your neighbour as yourself' (*The Bible*, Matthew 22: 39) and this is what is implicit in the concept of Social Interest. Adler, who was a Jew converted into Protestantism (although apparently an atheist, see Sperber 1983) published a discussion held with a Protestant theologian (Adler and Jahn 1933/1983) on how to counsel people and how and to what degree Individual Psychology could be conceived as a form of spiritual assistance or profane care of souls. Although Adler argues that Individual Psychology could serve as 'protector of the sacred good of humanity where religion has lost its influence' (Adler and Jahn 1933/1980: 75), Adler made clear that the spiritual care of souls corresponds to religion and clergymen and not to psychology and psychotherapists. Nevertheless, he proposes that Individual Psychology can put its knowledge and techniques at the disposal of clergymen and other spiritual leaders in order to provide them with the skills to orient their parish members with respect to problems that are not exclusively spiritual, such as child guidance and marital counselling. With this idea, Adler has established the basis for psychological counselling done by non-psychologist professionals, such as trained clergymen and others.

Adler's humanist drive, the somewhat religious tone of some of his statements, and the identification of mental health with Social Interest and, therefore, with ethics, may deter many psychologists from Individual Psychology. Even if we accept that caring for other people contributes to our personal well-being, Adler's therapeutic recommendation to a patient to do something good for somebody else every day (as referred to by Sperber 1983) may sound like a boy scout philosophy to many people. And it may not be very popular in a highly individualist and competitive society.

Nonetheless, we can find in this same ethical position a possibility for the return to a constructivist stance: to some authors (e.g. Botella and Figueras 1995), the pragmatism of postmodernism has produced a legitimating void; pragmatism is not enough to justify our acts, particularly the 'anything goes' attitude: if anything goes for pragmatic or heuristic reasons and there is no instance that tells us what is right or wrong, how can we justify what we do? If anything goes, it may be acceptable and highly 'useful' (pragmatic) to kill your hated mother-in-law and get away with her money. Constructivism has no answer to this dilemma, because it is epistemologically neutral to moral values. If any option has the same epistemological value as another, there must be a criterion that comes from outside epistemology. A criterion that allows us to legitimise our acts must come from philosophy or religion, or from inside the individual. Botella and Figueras argue that the loss of the general legitimisation systems, the great meta-narratives (such as Christianity, Marxism, etc.), which had given us prescriptions or proscriptions to guide our behaviour (it is bad to kill, bad to exploit the working population, it is good to help an old woman cross the street, it is bad to be a racist but good to be a feminist, it is good to greet your neighbour but bad to desire his wife and to throw rocks at his dog) has largely precipitated this dilemma. Contemporary life is full of pressing moral issues, where taking a clear-cut universal moral stance is nearly impossible: abortion, cloning, manipulation of the human genome, ecology, etc. are new problems to mankind and where no satisfying yes-or-no answer can be given. It seems that every individual has to find his or her own standpoint.

According to Botella and Figueras, this void of legitimisation gives us back hope for the recuperation of the subject, which modernity has forgotten for the sake of Reason and Progress and Universal Truth. The individual becomes again a subject, although postmodernism has deprived him or her of the commodity and security that supposed a universal good or bad. 'Paradoxically, postmodern relativism leads directly to putting in first line the ethics of action and discourse' (Botella and Figueras 1995: 20). The existence of an immense quantity of options and the freedom to choose among them on one hand, and the lack of absolute and universal truths on the other, makes it difficult for people to adopt a definitive moral standpoint. Never before in history have individuals had such a great amount of freedom and possibilities to live their lives; but the individual's responsibility has also increased. Instead of clinging to traditional moral values (or deliberately violating them!), the individual must now take responsibility for his or her own acts.

From this point of view, the Adlerian opportunity for an ethical stance – Social Interest – may be a valid option for individuals, if we understand Social Interest in the sense we have interpreted it in this chapter: a socially shared fiction and not an absolute truth somebody possesses by virtue of being an Adlerian psychologist. In this sense, Social Interest can represent a commitment, as defined by Perry (1970): a conscious and responsible act in the face of relativism. Adlerian Psychology also offers a different notion of 'usefulness': while (neo-)pragmatic usefulness refers to the predictive value of knowledge and the practical value of successfully helping individuals to fulfil their intended purposes (Polkinghorne 1992), Adler's view of usefulness, as we saw in Chapter 2, refers to Social Interest. Thus it may be pragmatically useful to enrich oneself by robbing a bank (but only if you are not caught by the police!), but not useful in the Adlerian sense. 'Usefulness' in the neo-pragmatic sense could suggest you should not throw rocks at the neighbour's dog because you have seen that the neighbour gets mad at you and your interaction will be difficult, so if you want to avoid conflicts, you had better refrain from hurting the dog; in the Adlerian sense, it is not useful – not morally good – to throw rocks at the neighbour's dog because you will hurt your neighbour's feelings.

Thus here is precisely a new opportunity for Adlerian Psychology within a constructivist and postmodern framework: to explore to what degree Social Interest can become an acceptable answer to the ethical questions that emerge from the postmodern condition.

With these reflections, we have abandoned Adlerian Psychology as being only a counselling and therapy system. Individual Psychology, in spite of its name, is a social psychology too. It is psychosocial because it does not describe the human being as possessing specific characteristics, but also because it maintains that the healthy and neurotic individual can only be understood in his or her social context. The capability to construe one's own narrative underlies the capability to improve society and the self. It has been said (Sperber 1983), that Freud considered neurosis as being the tribute people have to pay for civilisation, but Adler defined neurosis as a lack of civilisation. The potential of Individual Psychology as a social psychology with respect to politics, violence, and armed conflicts has been described by Serrano (1991) and by Wiegand (1990). The Adlerian notion of Social Interest as related to mental health (and the lack of it to psychopathology) can be applied not only to individuals but also to groups and nations. Hanna (1998) argues that the desire for status is an unacknowledged source of prejudice and racism, a craving to be superior to people that are seen as 'different' by means of degrading them and their worthiness or intelligence. Not only individuals, but groups and nations can be obsessed with inferiority feelings and striving for superiority (Brachfeld 1970). The Nazis' mass slaughter of Jewish people is certainly the most dramatic expression of this attitude, but we dare say that other and more recent armed conflicts can also be explained by an attempt of certain groups or nations to attain status or to get even for a real or imaginary offence or injustice. A thorough analysis of the terrorist attacks of 11 September 2001 on the World Trade Center in New York from an Adlerian viewpoint would certainly be interesting.

In the last decades, Adlerian authors have also begun to emphasise communitarian and cultural issues. A monographic edition of the *Journal of Individual Psychology* (volume 54, 1998) is dedicated to the Life Style and counselling of people from different cultures. Stasio (1998) analyses to what degree Social Interest or community feeling (the more literal translation from the original German *Gemeinschaftsgefühl*) serves to connect an individual to his or her cultural life and how it can be helpful in the acculturation process. But the author also warns against idealising altruistic behaviour such as volunteerism, co-operation, and generosity. Helpfulness, such as donating money, can be an expression of true Social Interest, but it can also disguise an intrinsically selfish behaviour (donating money can provide social approval as well as tax reduction). As an example, Stasio mentions the United States' willingness to participate in the Gulf War: one can interpret this action as an intervention to protect the Kuwaiti people from the invading Iraqi troops, but one can also argue that the USA was probably more motivated to protect their strategic and natural resource interests in Kuwait. Drawing on Cushman's notion of the Empty Self and Fromm's 'ambiguity of freedom', Richardson and Manaster (1997) brilliantly analyse the apparent dilemma of the individual between freedom and commitment, the contrast between the modern idea of an individual who is supposed to be self-actualising, autonomous, and self-sufficient and the fact that there is a growing isolation and a growing feeling of insignificance in the individual. The authors argue that western psychologies place greater importance on autonomy and self-development than on interpersonal relatedness, co-operation and community. Also that psychotherapies do stress the importance of parental support and caring in the shaping of children's personality, but that they usually ignore the influence of social factors and discuss how the lack of stable moral values or an atmosphere of disillusionment and cynicism, so common in our competitive society, can negatively influence the child's development. Richardson and Manaster emphasise the importance of prevention in the mental health field and lament the difficulty of talking about community, commitment, common good, and shared purposes. Psychologists should speak of

> our need for a greater sense of belonging to traditions or communities, or
> for a sense of healthy limits that welcomes larger loyalties and enjoys

relief from endless striving against the intractable boundaries and confinement of the human situation.

Richardson and Manaster 1997: 304

The authors invite Adlerians to do more than only criticise egoistic and pampered behaviour; they should also make attempts 'to clarify how socially interested living represents a distinct third alternative to *both* fearful conformity *and* insensitivity to moral norms and tasks in living' (Richardson and Manaster 1997: 305, italics in the original).

Conclusions and anticipations for the future

The possibilities for extending and integrating Individual Psychology are far from exhausted. Future research could explore the cross-fertilisation between Adlerian Psychology and other systems – especially those with a constructivist epistemology – with respect to theoretical concepts but also to technical skills. As Shulman and Watts (1997) stated, the constructivist terminology is clearer and easier to use, while Adlerian language is less technical and more colloquial. Kelly's (1955/1991) terms are much more precise, and could enrich Individual Psychology and make it less prone to misunderstandings and translation problems. On the other hand, Kellian language is more academic, while Adlerian language is more accessible to both the layperson and client.

With respect to technical integration, Individual Psychology can provide strategies and techniques for the elicitation of explicit and tacit constructs (the analysis of early recollections and Life Style assessment). Psychological Birth Order analysis (Campbell, White and Stewart 1991, Stewart and Campbell 1998) and dream interpretation (Oberst 1998b, 2002) are Adlerian assessment and therapeutic techniques that can be useful in personal construct psychology (PCP). On the other hand, we also use PCP techniques such as the repertory grid in our Adlerian therapies.

Individual Psychology also has to meet what for Botella (1998) is the future dilemma of clinical psychology and psychotherapy: the author anticipates a rebirth of the discourse of the objectivist viewpoint, although not as in orthodox behaviourism (everything is learned) but as a kind of 'neural Darwinianism': the attempt to reduce psychological processes to their biological (especially neurophysiological) components. This approach, increasingly popular in the neurosciences, is called the medico-biological model and affirms that mental disorders, like other bodily disturbances, have an organic aetiology that has to be diagnosed adequately and treated causally. In contrast, authors like Gergen (1994) propose a view of psychological disturbances as a socially shared form of discourse to refer to a highly subjective experience (the social construction of mental disorders), narrative approaches to psychotherapy, etc. As an Adlerian reply to this dilemma, we have already mentioned Sperry's biopsychosocial approach (see Chapter 2).

Individual Psychology may successfully interpret this newly emerging iteration of the subjectivist–objectivist dialectic through the traditional lens of the psychology of use. Individual Psychology acknowledges that physical/biological influences (regardless of how these are described currently) and familial, societal, and cultural contexts (regardless of how these evolve with time) influence people's behaviour and experience. Individual Psychology goes beyond merely listing the repertoire of conditions or situations that people possess and poses the ever relevant question of how people use what they have in this regard to make their way through life. Despite the myriad different values each life-influencing variable may assume, all people must find a way to meet the inescapable requirements of life (whether construed from a modern or postmodern perspective) to develop a career or vocational path, to relate intimately with a spouse or partner, and to interface meaningfully and productively with others in a variety of social contexts. Although Individual Psychology may provide guidance to clinicians about the ways to meet these tasks, as they are socially construed by psychologists and wider society at any given time, the real and timeless value of Individual Psychology stems from its identification of these existentially given tasks of life and its examination of how people use their real or perceived resources (or lack thereof) to address these tasks. In this regard, the crisis in Individual Psychology that we discussed at the beginning of this chapter may be more apparent than real.

Appendix 1: Measures for research and practice in Individual Psychology

Details are given here of the White–Campbell Psychological Birth Order Inventory (PBOI), the Birth Role Repertory Grid (BRRG), and the Sulliman Scale of Social Interest (SSSI).

White–Campbell Psychological Birth Order Inventory (PBOI)

History

Campbell, White and Stewart (1991) developed the PBOI over ten years ago to assess the extent to which siblings' experiences of themselves in their families of origin corresponded with one of the four prototypical psychological birth order roles that Adler described (Adler 1927, Ansbacher and Ansbacher 1956). The PBOI's items were developed on the basis of Adler's descriptions of the feelings, experiences, thoughts, and behaviours of persons within each position. The items were constructed so that they were highly descriptive of only one of the four positions.

The thematic content of items for the first-born or oldest position includes descriptions of feeling powerful and important, emphasis on following rules and protocol, and an achieving and pleasing orientation. The middle child scale contains items that assess having to compete with siblings for attention, feeling 'squeezed' out of the family, and feeling less loved or important than others in the family. Items for the youngest child scale assess experiences of being the boss of the family at times, having other family members do things or provide things, and being perceived as a charming, initiating, and sociable person. Finally, the items for the only child scale assess perceptions of being scrutinised, protected, and intruded on by other family members. Before conducting an empirical examination of the items, four experienced Adlerian counsellors surveyed the items for their ability to discriminate one psychological position from another. Items were retained for the initial version of the PBOI if all four counsellors agreed on the worthiness and uniqueness of the item. The initial item pool consisted of forty items, with ten corresponding to each of the four psychological positions.

Studies using the PBOI

Two factor analytic studies on the PBOI have examined the construct validity of the forty initial items (Campbell, White and Stewart 1991, Stewart 1994, Stewart and Campbell 1998). The first of these factor analyses resulted in several items being realigned to different birth order scales than originally intended, largely due to the way study participants interpreted the items and, consequently, on the basis of the items' factor loadings. Subsequent investigations involved performing a cluster analysis to select items for each scale followed by traditional confirmatory factor analyses on the resulting items (Stewart 1994). Because the PBOI's factor structure differed for men and women, separate PBOI scales were developed for each gender. The factor structure of the PBOI items for each gender appears stable across two samples (Stewart and Campbell 1998). In addition the four PBOI scales for each gender exhibited very good temporal stability over an 8-week test–retest interval, with reliability coefficients ranging from 0.84 to 0.95 for the female scales and from 0.81 to 0.90 for the male scales (Stewart and Campbell 1998).

We have continued to refine and develop the PBOI to enhance its psychometric properties. In this regard, our latest efforts involved the development of additional items that focally contribute to the existing content assessed by the four scales. Our reasons for increasing the 'depth' of the scales stem primarily from the acceptable, although not optimal, internal consistency estimates (α) that we observed. These estimates ranged from 0.51 to 0.94 for women and from 0.55 to 0.77 for men (Stewart and Campbell 1998). That is, the factor analyses pared the scales down to between four and nine items per scale, with the shorter scales exhibiting lower internal consistencies, as would be expected.

The version of the PBOI that we offer in this appendix contains forty-six items that also include nineteen new items constructed for the four scales. Our efforts to increase the internal consistency of the scales appear to have been successful. From a pilot study involving ninety-four women we observed the following coefficient alphas (α): first (0.77), middle (0.87), youngest (0.78), only (0.82). As we gather additional data using the new items we will again conduct factor analyses to assess item contributions.

We have used the PBOI in several studies to examine various aspects of Adlerian theory and to explore the relationship between psychological birth order and other constructs. In this regard, the PBOI scales were predictably and significantly related to actual birth order, gender, and spacing variables (Campbell, White and Stewart 1991). The PBOI exhibited meaningful and predicted relationships with Kern's Lifestyle Inventory (LSI) in that the

PBOI first scale was correlated with pleasing and perfectionistic scales of the LSI. The PBOI middle scale was related to the LSI's victim and martyr scales (White, Campbell and Stewart 1995). Another study observed generally no meaningful relationships between the PBOI and career interests as assessed by the UNIACT Interest Inventory (White et al. 1997).

More recently, Stewart, Stewart and Campbell (2001) examined the contributions of the family atmosphere (i.e. its thematic emphases, values, emotional climate, and social support dimensions) to psychological position and observed significant and theoretically expected relationships. For example, the psychological first-born position scores were predicted by being an actual first-born child and by a family atmosphere emphasising achievement. Further, the psychological only position scores were predicted by level of overall family dysfunction, family control, and a lack of independence. A second study in this article also explored the contributions of personality characteristics and actual birth order to PBOI scores. For instance, the Personality Research Form scales assessing needs for achievement, dominance, social recognition, and a lack of impulsivity predicted the psychological first-born scores for men. An interesting result of this study was that, consistent with other research, actual birth order exhibited a small and largely non-significant relationship to personality, while psychological birth order demonstrated moderate and very statistically significant relationships. The second author is currently using structural equation modelling techniques to examine the nature of psychological birth order's mediation of the relationship between actual position and personality.

Administration, scoring, and interpretation

The PBOI can be administered individually or in a group setting along with other measures. Participants are asked to read each item and to reflect on how they felt when they lived in their families of origin (or the family in which they grew up or lived for most of their lives). Then they respond yes or no according to whether the item describes their experiences. Only children are asked to think of their extended family (i.e. cousins) or same-aged peers when responding to items that pertain to sibling relationships.

The PBOI is scored by summing the items that are aligned with each scale. Because the scales contain different numbers of items, we recommend calculating standard (z) scores so that the relative elevations on the four scales can be compared; from this format, it is easy to calculate other formats such as T scores. If the full complement of PBOI items listed below is used, then researchers should rely on the descriptive statistics from their samples to calculate the standard scores. If the original item set (Stewart and Campbell 1998) is used, researchers can either use descriptive statistics we have reported or rely on their own. Raw scores should not be used in between-scale comparisons. Consult Stewart and Campbell (1998) for descriptions of the scales and for information on the concordance rates between actual birth order and respondents' predominant psychological position.

Interpretation of the PBOI can take two forms, the first of which is to examine respondents' scores on all four scales (i.e. the profile method). This method has the advantage of revealing and incorporating respondents' experiences in all four of the roles. This is especially important in cases where children occupied two actual positions in the family. For instance, all first-born children initially entered their families of origin as only children but became ordinally first-borns when the second and subsequent siblings were born. In this regard, the PBOI's first-born and only child scales may be especially revealing of a person's experiences. Similarly, all middle children were at one time youngest children. Consideration of this pair of PBOI scores, consequently, can provide valuable information. We recommend that all empirical studies using the PBOI include at least the profile approach to the statistical analyses that may be undertaken.

The second interpretation method involves categorising people according to their predominant (high point) psychological position (i.e. the nominal method). Such an approach may be useful when comparing the PBOI to other nominally or ordinally based variables, such as actual position in a cross tabulation analysis. A caveat of this approach is that by using only the high-point birth order, data from the other scales are ignored or discarded. Methods for determining the predominant psychological position are described in Stewart and Campbell (1998).

White–Campbell Psychological Birth Order Inventory (PBOI) © 1991 Joanna White, Linda Campbell and Alan E. Stewart (reprinted with permission)

Instructions:
Please read each item and then circle **YES** or **NO** according to how you felt when you lived in the family in which you grew up. If you lived in several families, please think of the one that you spent the most time in as you respond to these items. If you had no brothers or sisters please think of your extended family (e.g. cousins) or your same-aged friends to complete the items that refer to brothers and sisters.

1. YES NO I believed my parents had high expectations of me. F/f
2. YES NO I was babied by my family members. Y/fm-n
3. YES NO My family was more involved in my life than I wanted. O/fm-n
4. YES NO It seemed like I was in a race trying to catch up. M/f
5. YES NO It was important to me to please adults. F/fm
6. YES NO My family did not respect my privacy. O/fm-n

7.	YES	NO	I felt isolated from others. M/f
8.	YES	NO	It was easy to talk my brothers and sisters into giving me things. Y/fm-n
9.	YES	NO	My parents worried a lot about me. O/m
10.	YES	NO	I was taken less seriously than anyone in the family. M/fm
11.	YES	NO	It was important to me to advise my brothers and sisters about right and wrong. F/f
12.	YES	NO	I was seen as being the most charming in the family. Y/fm
13.	YES	NO	It seemed like I never had my parents' full attention. M/fm
14.	YES	NO	My parents tried to control me. O/fm
15.	YES	NO	I am more organized and structured than others in my family. F/f
16.	YES	NO	I was pampered by my family members. Y/fm
17.	YES	NO	Other family members saw me as the least capable. M/f
18.	YES	NO	It was important to me that others do things right. F/fm
19.	YES	NO	My parents tried to manage my life. O/fm-n
20.	YES	NO	I was good at getting others to do things for me. Y/fm
21.	YES	NO	It seemed like I was less important than other members of my family. M/fm
22.	YES	NO	I wanted to satisfy my parents. F/fm-n
23.	YES	NO	My parents wanted to know about everything that was going on in my life. O/fm-n
24.	YES	NO	It was easy to talk my parents into giving me things. Y/fm
25.	YES	NO	I often felt less loved than others in my family. M/fm
26.	YES	NO	I felt smothered by my parents. O/fm
27.	YES	NO	It was important to me to do things right. F/fm
28.	YES	NO	When I wanted to I could be the ruler of the family. Y/fm-n
29.	YES	NO	I often felt that I was treated more unfairly than others in the family. M/fm
30.	YES	NO	I was good at getting what I wanted from my family. Y/fm-n
31.	YES	NO	I felt like I lived in a fishbowl. O/fm
32.	YES	NO	It was important to me to make good grades in school. F/fm
33.	YES	NO	I felt disconnected from others in my family. M/fm-n
34.	YES	NO	My parents considered everything that was my business, their business. O/fm
35.	YES	NO	It was important to me to be the best. F/m
36.	YES	NO	I could be the boss in the family when I wanted to. Y/m
37.	YES	NO	I felt squeezed out by my brothers and sisters. M/fm
38.	YES	NO	My parents were busybodies. O/fm-n
39.	YES	NO	I liked order more than other people in my family. F/fm-n
40.	YES	NO	I was seen as the most adorable in the family. Y/fm-n

41. YES NO It was important to me that my brothers and sisters do things right. F/fm-n
42. YES NO I was treated less justly than others in my family. M/fm-n
43. YES NO I wanted others in my family to do things properly. F/fm-n
44. YES NO I felt like I was less valuable than other members of my family. M/fm-n
45. YES NO I liked doing things the correct way. F/fm-n
46. YES NO I felt left out by my brothers and sisters. M/fm-n

Scale Alignment Key: F=First, M=Middle, Y=Youngest, O=Only. For gender, f=female, m=male. New items are indicated by -n. The new items can be scored for both men and women. For example, M/fm-n, indicates an item for the middle scale that is new and scored for both genders.

Birth Role Repertory Grid (BRRG)

History

The Birth Role Repertory Grid (BRRG) represents a synthesis of the White–Campbell Psychological Birth Order Inventory (Campbell, White and Stewart 1991) and Kelly's (1955) role construct repertory grid technique from personal construct psychology (Stewart 1994). Although this is a new technique for which psychometric properties remain to be established, its heuristic and therapeutic value warrants its inclusion here. The BRRG allows for a more in-depth examination of the participant's birth role-related perceptions by requiring an evaluation of the extent to which the supplied birth order constructs apply to all members of the family of origin (parents included) and not just to the self. This is a particularly appealing feature of the grid because family or sibling roles represent situated identities within the family, not merely one person's perceptions of the position he or she may occupy.

The repertory grid is a general method (rather than a specific test instrument) for assessing the variety of personal constructs that people have developed for a range of people and personalities that they have known in their lives. The grid also allows an assessment of the relationships these constructs exhibit with each other. Constructs, or dimensions of meaning that may operate implicitly or somewhat automatically, represent ways people have of understanding the world – their uniquely developed meanings for how their lives and the world works. Constructs may be elicited anew from the people completing the grid provided in this appendix by asking them to consider how two of three people that they know are alike in some way, yet different from the third person they are asked to consider. This triad method, as it is known, allows for the construct to be dimensioned and its extremes (or endpoints) to be identified. Once elicited, a checklist or rating scale can be used to indicate the extent to which the construct and its two poles apply to the other people included in the grid exercise (see Kelly 1955, Fransella and Bannister 1977). Alternatively, constructs can be supplied to people rather than elicited. Here, some pre-existing sets of meanings or dimensions are given to the people so they can evaluate the individuals (or things) that they know according to the supplied constructs.

The BRRG uses both elicited and supplied constructs to explore the sibling and family role-related constructs that people may use. The first five rows of the BRRG require the participant to articulate constructs via the triad method using various combinations of three family members. The remaining rows of the grid contain supplied constructs that were adapted from the PBOI. These supplied sibling role constructs were identified by latent trait analyses as being the most salient and discriminating contributors to the four PBOI scales (Stewart 1994). That is, each scale of the PBOI (first, middle, youngest, or only child role) is represented in abbreviated form in the supplied constructs. The mix of elicited and supplied constructs was thought optimal for assessing psychological position because such role perceptions may consist of common features for many people (i.e. the supplied constructs) along with idiopathic and unique constructions indigenous to a particular family (i.e. elicited constructs).

The BRRG represents a newer approach to the assessment of family and sibling role-related perceptions. Consequently, only one study thus far has examined the performance of this grid (Cavalleri 2001). This study involved approximately sixty people from three racial groups (African American, Caucasian, and Hispanic American) who completed the BRRG individually with the investigator. The purpose of this study was to assess the extent to which the participants' race differences may relate to differences in the features and characteristics that comprise each psychological position. That is, do people of different races have different or dissimilar ways of fitting in and belonging with their families? The results of this small-scale analysis suggested that gender differences in family and sibling role-related perceptions existed, but that racial differences generally were non-significant.

The BRRG would be a very appropriate and an informationally rich method for use in assessing families. In this scenario, each family member would complete the BRRG individually and then a discussion would ensue about the extent to which family members' application of the supplied constructs for each person converge or diverge. An analysis of the level of disagreement in relation to other pertinent family atmosphere dimensions such as communication, cohesion, emotional expressiveness, and overall health or dysfunction also could be pursued.

Administration, scoring, and interpretation

The BRRG provided in this appendix requires approximately one hour to complete and is individually administered. The technique begins by soliciting the names of the siblings and writing these on the grid columns. On the accompanying grid, it will be noted that there are columns for two parents and five siblings. The grid can be expanded or slightly contracted from this arrangement depending on the family's size. If the respondent is from a primarily single-parent family, then it may be permissible to write the name of that parent along with another person, outside the family, who was most like a parent (e.g. parent's friend, aunt, uncle, grandparent, etc.); this is a judgement call to be made by the grid administrator. If the respondent is an only child and has no siblings, then he or she is asked to indicate both a male and a female who were most like a brother and sister, respectively, when he or she lived in the family of origin. Other extra-familial figures who functioned as siblings may be added if the respondent desires. Once these persons have been identified, their names are written on the grid columns, including the name of the respondent. The genders of the family figures can be indicated on the columns, including the respondent (self). The placement of individuals in particular rows is not important as long as the grid administrator remembers the order of figures on the columns. In research applications, however, the positions of the parents and respondent in the columns should be consistent to make analyses meaningful.

After identifying the people who will be included in the analysis, their names are written on index cards (one name per card). The administrator should also use separate index cards or a piece of poster board to create a seven-point Likert scale (the second author prefers a seven-point scale as a matter of convention when completing the grid). As the grid is completed, the index cards with family members' names will be placed along the seven-point scale in different places.

The process begins by eliciting constructs for the first five rows. If using index cards, the names of the three people who have circles in their columns are laid in front of the respondent who is then asked to consider the three people and to decide which two are alike in some way, yet different from the third. Any two of the three may be paired. For instance, in the first row the two cards for the parents along with the card for sibling number 4 are laid down.

The two that are chosen as alike are arbitrarily moved to the 'seven' position on the rating scale and the person who is different is moved to the 'one' position; this in effect sets the dimensions for the construct that is about to be elicited. The way in which the two people are alike is written at the far right of the grid form (explicit pole), while the way in which the third person differs is written towards the left of the centre column of numbers. Care must be taken to help the respondent elicit one dimension that applies to all three people rather than two dimensions that apply separately. For instance, if the two people were described as 'easy going and calming' and the third was depicted as 'likes to play cards', then the administrator may respond with something like, 'try to describe a single way in which the two groups differ'. The

Names

1. *Parent* m f
2. *Parent* m f
3. *Sib*   m f s
4. *Sib*   m f s   m = male
5. *Sib*   m f s   f = female
6. *Sib*   m f s   s = self
7. *Sib*   m f s

Implicit pole

1.	
2.	
3.	
4.	
5.	
6.	Never had parent's full attention
7.	Important to them that others do things right
8.	They could easily talk parents into giving them things
9.	Parents considered everything that was going on their business
10.	Were seen as the most charming in the family
11.	It was important to make good grades in school
12.	Felt smothered by parents
13.	Were taken less seriously than anyone in the family
14.	Were pampered by family memers
15.	Felt less important than other members of the family
16.	Parent(s) tried to control
17.	It was important to them that they do things right
18.	Felt squeezed out by brothers and sisters
19.	Were good at getting others to do things for them
20.	Seemed to feel less loved than others in the family
21.	Believed their parents had high expectations of them
22.	Felt they were treated more unfairly than others in the family
23.	Felt they were in a race trying to catch up
24.	Felt it was important to please adults
25.	Are more organized and structured than others in their family
26.	Felt isolated from others
27.	Felt it was important to advise their sibling(s) about right and wrong
28.	Other family members saw them as the least capable

Rows for Firstborn constructs: 7 11 17 21 24 25 27
Rows for Middle child constructs: 6 13 15 18 20 22 23 26
Rows for Youngest child constructs: 8 10 14 19 28
Rows for Only child constructs: 9 12 16

Birth Role Repertory Grid

(c) 1994 Alan E. Stewart

Name:_____

Constucts	Explicit pole

_____
_____
_____
_____
_____

1 2 3 4 5 6 7	Had parent's full attention
1 2 3 4 5 6 7	It was less important to them that others do things right
1 2 3 4 5 6 7	Had a difficult time talking parents into giving them things
1 2 3 4 5 6 7	Parents did not consider everything that was going on their business
1 2 3 4 5 6 7	Were seen as the least charming in the family
1 2 3 4 5 6 7	It was less important to make good grades in school
1 2 3 4 5 6 7	Did not feel smothered by parents
1 2 3 4 5 6 7	Were taken more seriously than anyone in the family
1 2 3 4 5 6 7	Were not pampered by family members
1 2 3 4 5 6 7	Felt more important than other members of the family
1 2 3 4 5 6 7	Parent(s) did not try to control
1 2 3 4 5 6 7	Not as important to them that they do things right
1 2 3 4 5 6 7	Did not feel squeezed out by brothers and sisters
1 2 3 4 5 6 7	Were not good at getting others to do things for them
1 2 3 4 5 6 7	Seemed to feel more loved than others in the family
1 2 3 4 5 6 7	Believed parents did not have high expectations of them
1 2 3 4 5 6 7	Felt they were treated more fairly than others in the family
1 2 3 4 5 6 7	Did not feel like they were in a race trying to catch up
1 2 3 4 5 6 7	Did not feel it was important to please adults
1 2 3 4 5 6 7	Are less organized and structured than others in their family
1 2 3 4 5 6 7	Did not feel isolated from others
1 2 3 4 5 6 7	Did not feel it was important to advise their sibling(s) about right and wrong
1 2 3 4 5 6 7	Other family members saw them as the most capable

respondent may then indicate, 'Oh, OK. The third person is a bit more strict and is uptight more often.' Once the constructs are understood, they can be written on the grid form. The respondent next is asked to consider the remaining members of the family and to apply the construct to them using the one to seven scale. This whole process is completed four more times until the supplied constructs are encountered. Care should be taken to introduce respondents to the task and to show them how it is done in such a way as to avoid injecting content or constructs that would cloud the grid results; the grid is supposed to reveal something about the person who completes it, not the person who administers it.

When the respondent is ready to complete the supplied constructs, no new constructs need to be elicited. Instead, he or she is told to look at the implicit and explicit poles. For example in row 6, these would be: 'Never had parent's full attention' as against 'Had parent's full attention'. The respondent is asked to apply the construct to each person in the family and to fill in the rating that corresponds to how each family member is perceived with respect to the construct. This process is continued until the last row of the grid has been completed. For both the elicited and supplied constructs, as respondents review their work, they should be allowed to change and revise the ratings that they have given. Sometimes the process of completing the grid necessitates these kinds of evaluative adjustments.

As an intervention assessment method, respondents will probably derive the most benefit from the grid exercise simply by completing it. The second author's (AES) previous experience in administering numerous grids is that it requires people to think explicitly, perhaps revealing for the first time the implicit ways that others were understood or assumed to be. Consequently, it should not be surprising to hear respondents make new connections, express relationship attributes in new ways, or express a sense of puzzlement as they articulate constructs. These reactions all represent the respondent or client seeing existing relationships in a new light. These experiences along with additional discussions about the grid process as it concludes effectively seem to represent 'the take' or primary benefits of the grid exercise.

A wide variety of methods exist for analysing grid data depending on the clinician's or researcher's needs. The prototypical analysis consists of performing a principal components factor analysis on both the rows (birth-order constructs) and columns (family figures). As a data reduction technique, factor analyses will reveal the underlying primary dimensions (psychological roles or positions in the case of an analysis on construct rows) that are responsible for the observed relationships. A factor analysis of constructs that allows for the plotting of family figures in the construct space is particularly revealing of the extent to which the respondent construes the family members in terms of one or more of the prototypical psychological positions. Cluster analyses also can be performed to assess the groupings of the constructs. Finally, a simple correlational analysis of the constructs can reveal which ones are used together and appear to be related to each other. The second author (AES) uses this method occasionally for giving 'technical' feedback to grid respondents by reviewing how ensembles of constructs are used together. Readers interested in a more technical approach to grid analysis should consult resources that describe the analysis of repertory grid data (Fransella and Bannister 1977).

Sulliman Scale of Social Interest (SSSI)

History

The Sulliman Scale of Social Interest (SSSI; Sulliman 1973) was an instrument ahead of its time when its author, Dr James R. Sulliman, developed it nearly thirty years ago. Although the SSSI was one of the first instruments that emerged specifically for the assessment of social interest, this measure received scant attention until the mid-1980s – stemming perhaps from the qualitative and case-study emphasis that has been a hallmark of research in Individual Psychology. Currently, this instrument enjoys increasing use in Adlerian research and therapy.

The SSSI consists of fifty items that are answered as either True or False. Sulliman developed the instrument by rationally deriving 100 items that exemplified levels and facets of social interest. Sulliman then administered the initial item pool to 173 high school students and identified the fifty items that best discriminated students' levels of social interest as rated by their teachers. A second sample of 452 high school students responded to the fifty items. The Kuder-Richardson reliability coefficient for the SSSI in this sample was 0.91 and the test–retest reliability was 0.93 (Sulliman 1973). The validity of the SSSI was estimated, in part, by correlating students' scores on the instrument with teachers' subject social interest ratings of the student; the observed validity coefficient was 0.71. Sulliman (1973) factor analysed the fifty items and observed two sub-scales: (1) concern for and trust in others, and (2) confidence in oneself and optimism in one's view of the world.

Studies using the SSSI

Most of the existing studies utilising the SSSI have investigated the instrument's psychometric properties for demographically different samples of respondents. To begin, Mozdzierz, Greenblat and Murphy (1986) observed that the SSSI possessed a greater degree of validity for assessing the presence of pathology in a sample of hospitalised alcoholics than the Social Interest Scale (SIS; Crandall 1975). These same authors reported that the SSSI correlated negatively with most of the MMPI Supplementary Scales (e.g. maladjustment, prejudice, dependency) and correlated positively with scales such as ego strength, dominance, and sociability; none of the variables related significantly with the SIS (Mozdzierz, Greenblatt and Murphy 1988). Groups possessing high as against low levels of Social Interest (as measured by the SSSI) differed in the hypothesised ways regarding therapist ratings of psychopathology, self-report of depressive symptoms, anxiety, and hostility (Fish and Mozdzierz 1988). Watkins and St John (1994) observed that the SSSI scores for Social Interest were positively and significantly correlated with empathy, interpersonal contact, and happiness, and negatively related to narcissism. Finally, Watkins and Blazina (1994) reported that the instrument possessed moderate to good test–retest reliabilities over 3- and 5-week intervals.

Daugherty, Murphy and Paugh (2001) conducted an interesting study with ninety-one adult male offenders that supported the SSSI's predictive validity. Specifically, the SSSI predicted recidivism two years after the offenders were released and contributed unique variance to an existing set of demographic predictors of recidivism. These researchers observed that low levels of Social Interest as measured by the SSSI were associated with negative outcomes that included a greater likelihood of unemployment, additional felony arrests, and an increased likelihood of being reincarcerated.

Administration, scoring, and interpretation

The authors would like to express their sincere thanks to Dr James R. Sulliman for giving us his permission to include the SSSI in this book. Although we have provided the items of the SSSI so that psychologists and counsellors may examine them and use them for research or clinical purposes, people who intend to score the instrument should contact Dr Sulliman directly to obtain instructions on how to calculate the full and sub-scale scores. Dr Sulliman may be reached at:

Pastoral Care and Counseling
1317 North 8th Street, Suite 200
Abilene, Texas 79601, USA.
Telephone: 915.672.5683

The interpretation of the SSSI is straightforward with scores on the full scale and the sub-scales indicating a greater level of social interest.

Sulliman Scale of Social Interest (SSSI)
© 1973 James R. Sulliman (reprinted with permission)

Instructions:

This scale is comprised of fifty statements. Read each statement carefully and decide whether the statement is true or mostly true as applied to you. If it is true or mostly true then circle the 'T'. If it is false or mostly false, then circle 'F'. Respond to all statements. There are no right or wrong answers on this scale. Your answers are confidential. Please be honest in your responses.

T F   1. People are all of equal worth, regardless of what country they live in.
T F   2. If it were not for all the bad breaks which I have had, I could really have amounted to something.
T F   3. I often feel like I am completely alone in the world.
T F   4. I think that most people are friendly.
T F   5. I get angry when people do not do what I want them to do.
T F   6. Members of my family have great concern for me.
T F   7. I wish that everyone would leave me alone.
T F   8. I like to watch movies where the bad guy wins.
T F   9. If people make things difficult for me, then I will try to make things even more difficult for them.
T F   10. It seems like nothing ever changes for me.
T F   11. A person must watch out for himself because no one else will help him.
T F   12. Most people only appear to be honest but do many dishonest things.
T F   13. I don't let anyone tell me what to do.
T F   14. I would like to make the world a perfect place in which to live because then I would be seen by others as the most important person alive.
T F   15. The world is a great place in which to live.
T F   16. I like animals more than I like people.
T F   17. I like to make new friends.
T F   18. Some people do not deserve to live.
T F   19. It seems like people are always doing bad things to me.
T F   20. Most people have little respect for others.
T F   21. It seems like everything I do turns out wrong.
T F   22. There are some individuals whom I hate.
T F   23. No one really cares about me.
T F   24. Things usually work out for the best.
T F   25. I would rather complete a 'perfect crime' and not be caught than complete a work of art such as a painting.
T F   26. Most people are concerned only with themselves.
T F   27. Sometimes I like to hurt people.
T F   28. I wish that I could run away and leave everyone in the world behind me.
T F   29. I am an important person in the lives of some other people.
T F   30. I would like to help every person in the world.
T F   31. Most people treat me more like a little kid than an adult.
T F   32. Most people would take advantage of me if they could.

T   F   33.   I am a happy person.
T   F   34.   I care about people that I know but not about total strangers.
T   F   35.   I sometimes like to hurt animals for no reason at all.
T   F   36.   No one tries to understand me and my feelings.
T   F   37.   I wish that I could destroy the world and build it back up the way that I would like it to be.
T   F   38.   People cooperate with me most of the time.
T   F   39.   If something goes wrong for me, I become extremely angry.
T   F   40.   There aren't very many things that I care about.
T   F   41.   I hope that I get the chance to get back at some people for the bad way they have treated me.
T   F   42.   People can't be trusted.
T   F   43.   This is a great time to be alive.
T   F   44.   People are not very friendly.
T   F   45.   I have confidence in other people.
T   F   46.   To get ahead in this world, you have to step on people along the way.
T   F   47.   I hate to listen to other people's problems.
T   F   48.   People are basically good.
T   F   49.   There are several people whom I hate.
T   F   50.   If I had control over people, I would make them do what I wanted them to do.

Appendix 2: A case study

Barbara, 20 years old, university student

Barbara was referred to me (UO) by a psychiatrist with the diagnosis of anorexia nervosa. The referring psychiatrist thought it would be better for her to continue her treatment with a female therapist, because she had developed 'resistance' against him as a male doctor. Her mother had been hospitalised several times for schizophrenia. My first impression of Barbara was that of an attractive, intelligent and lively young woman. She was rather slim, though not underweight, but she hid what she called her 'excessive weight' under wide and flowing clothes. Her weight was, from the beginning to the end of our therapy, 108 lbs, with only slight variations. The sessions were conducted once a week.

Session I

Barbara stated that she was too fat and that she wanted to lose weight. Sometimes she experienced aversions to males, but when she did become involved in an intimate relationship, her romantic feelings disappeared quite quickly. On the other hand, she wanted to fall in love and have a serious relationship. She also stated that she had problems with her studies; her performance and evaluations were average, and she thought they could be better, if not excellent, if she devoted more time and persistence to her studies. On many occasions she felt inadequate and self-conscious, constantly fearing that her conversation might not be interesting enough for other people. She shared a flat with other female university students.

Although it was evident that she experienced low self-esteem, her 'weight problems' were what had brought her in, so they were addressed from the beginning of the therapy. She stated, not aware of the contradiction, that she had objectively an ideal weight, but that she also was too fat. If she were slimmer, she would have fewer problems with men. When she saw somebody slimmer, she felt fat. And 'when I'm slim, then I'm attractive'. She had tried several times to lose weight with the help of strict diet plans, but while she was on diet she used to have binge eating attacks, during which she stuffed herself uncontrollably and then vomited to avoid putting on weight. As usual in these cases, she was ashamed of not being able to control her behaviour and hid her binge eating and vomiting from other people, even from her family and room mates. Interestingly, she construed people who have no control over their eating as individuals who try to hide their psychological problems, as superficial, and as 'petty' (and as she would never like to be). Somebody slim and being able to control his or her eating was, in her view, an open-minded, sensitive, and intellectual person. When she had eaten her fill, she sometimes felt 'great' because of satiation, sometimes terrible.

Sessions 2 to 5

These sessions were dedicated to performing a Life Style analysis. Barbara described herself as a child as being lively, bright, curious, precocious, sweet, and pretty. As a young girl she was pampered by her mother and by her grandmother (she was her mother's first child and her grandma's first grandchild). She was also her father's darling and got his attention and acknowledgement by being good (in terms of both behaviour and academic achievements).

She had a younger sister (Laura, 18 years old) and a younger brother (Peter, 17 years) and was apparently the brightest, but also the most ambitious and rebellious child of the three. She had many friends. Her father was an engineer, and she described him as achievement-oriented, sporty, intellectual, but also inhibited and prudish. He took care of his children, but also used moral pressure and tried to make them feel guilty when they had done something wrong. Her mother was described as being unpredictable and often absent-minded, sometimes also childish and of a 'pleasant naiveté'. Many of these characteristics may have stemmed from her mental illness which broke out shortly after the youngest child had been born.

Barbara indicated that her parents' marriage was bad, with Barbara's mother sometimes trying to hit her husband. Her parents had many arguments and there was a 'chaotic sleep situation': at times, husband and wife slept apart and for lack of space Barbara then slept with her father in the double bed. She was 10 or 12 by then. I immediately thought of a possible situation of sexual abuse, but Barbara answered negatively to my question. When her mother's mental health situation worsened, the children were brought to stay with an aunt, and when Barbara was 15, her father left the family and went to live with his female friend and later wife. Barbara and her father's second wife did not get on well with each other, so Barbara was sent to a boarding school. She had always been a good student in her earlier years, but at the university she lacked motivation, and her grades were not so good when she started therapy.

Her sexual development was normal and she had her first intercourse at the age of 16. Her eating problems started 2 years later. Her answer to the Question was:

> If I had no eating problems, I would have more energy for my studies and have higher grades, I would have more self-esteem and have less problems with men.

Barbara's early recollections

1   Mom is coming home from the hospital, with new-born Peter. He is an enormous baby, sleeping peacefully in her arms, while mother is crying helplessly. Dad stands beside her, not knowing what to do. My sister Laura and I should be happy, but we are confused. Our aunt, who had been taking care of us while Mom was in the hospital tries to get hold of the situation, but there is a speechless confusion overall. (age: 3 years)

2   We (a couple of children from our neighbourhood) are playing 'doctor' in the bushes of our garden. The elder brother of a friend of mine pulls down our pants (mine and my friend's). Nothing more happens, but a neighbour discovers us and tells my parents. Mom makes me come into the house and as a punishment, I must stay in my brother's playpen, although I'm already 4.

3   We are playing with a dog-do (i.e., faeces) and smear it under the handles of the house doors, to make the neighbours mad. My parents learn about it and my Dad takes me to task for it, but I deny having taken part in it. He knows I'm lying and gets very sad, not angry, and this makes me feel very guilty and ashamed. There are so few moments that I can be with him, and when I'm with him, he always tries to make me feel bad. (5 years)

4   One night, stepping out of the house, I see a bald man all dressed in black looking around the corner and grinning at me with scorn. Scared to death I run back into the house. Nobody believes what I have seen. And now I do not know whether I had seen a real man or if it was just my imagination. But he was the incarnation of all evil, of temptation. (5 years)

5   I'm about 10 or 11. I happen to see my parents making love. I start to cry recklessly and run back to my room. They follow me and ask me, acting the innocent, what is the matter, and I know they are lying to me. I feel so deceived that I can't stomach it. Feeling of being left alone, loneliness, maybe jealousy, no it's not jealousy, it is their secretiveness, their hypocrisy, that makes everything so dirty. A few days later, my father asks me, again acting the innocent, if I don't like my parents 'giving each other a hug'. Then I feel guilty and ashamed about my being so bad, angry about his lies, confusion, especially because I know that my parents' good understanding never lasts very long.

On the basis of these recollections, the other information given by the patient, and her associations to her recollections, we now could start to understand her Life Style. We co-construed a few important aspects:

- her mother's psychological problems (unstable, pampering on one hand, punishing on the other)
- her father's punishing and repressing style that made her feel guilty and ashamed
- her parents' marriage: on one hand, they have a sexual life, on the other, the marriage is extremely unhappy, her father is helpless with respect to his wife's problems; both parents demonstrate little understanding with Barbara, they lie to her and are hypocritical
- there are no other people to relieve the situation (e.g. aunt, neighbour); other people may even be dangerous (the man at night)
- Barbara's (natural) interest in the sexual aspects of life, a tendency towards transgression (playing with excrement)
- an ambivalent situation at home without stable attachment patterns
- her father tried to impose strict moral standards on her, but he himself did not live up to them.

Barbara's Life Style

- I am small and I'm bad, I do bad things. But I'm bright and a good observer.
- The others cannot be trusted, they tell me lies. I cannot rely on them. People can do me harm.
- Life can be interesting and worth being discovered, but there is also something ominous and evil about it.
- I'm a good observer and I'm bright and I don't let people make a fool out of me. I know the truth and I want to be acknowledged for knowing it.
- Therefore I must always watch out and avoid being fooled. I can use my intellectual superiority to avoid being fooled.

I handed out a summary of her Life Style to take it home and re-read it whenever she wanted. It was meant to be the basis for discussion that related what happened in her childhood to her problems as an adult. She immediately pointed out the relationship between her father's hypocrisy and her problems with men. She said she would find it difficult to trust someone, for fear of being betrayed and lied to.

Session 6

We resumed our conversation about her problems with men. Barbara had had seven boyfriends; the relationships had lasted between 2 months and 1 year, all of them were broken off by her, because 'our interests were so different' or because she stopped feeling in love. She admitted that she often was only interested in a one-night stand or in sporadic sexual encounters. On the other hand, she had experienced feelings of disgust and revulsion in these situations. She stated that, actually, she would like to fall in love and stay in love with one boyfriend, but she was afraid of becoming dependent on him. She would be waiting for 'the big emotion'. I pointed out to her that she also used to speak disdainfully about her lovers; while waiting for 'Mr Right', nobody seemed good enough for her.

Sessions 7 and 8

She came in reporting that she had been binge eating the night before, and therefore her day had been 'like shit'. She had not been attending her classes. We analysed the situation that might have provoked the bingeing (the eating problems had shown spontaneous remission during the last few weeks). She stated that she had stayed at home with a girlfriend who had a similar problem, taking care of her emotional distress. Therefore she had not been able to see her occasional lover, C., with whom she maintained sporadic sexual encounters. We spoke about her feelings toward her girlfriend and toward C. She liked the other girl and really wanted to help her, but in that situation she would have preferred to go with C. She should have been more assertive, but she is afraid to disappoint other people because she might need their help one day and then they would withhold support for her friend. We examined this aspect more deeply and identified some of her inferiority feelings. She often felt inadequate and boring; according to her, all her positive aspects were only a façade, and behind there were only negative points. 'All that is good in me, is only a façade, a mask, and all that is bad, that is really me.' With respect to a possible boyfriend, she was also afraid of not being good enough; after some time of dating, the man would become aware of how bad and worthless she really was. We discussed the possibility that the decrease of her feelings after a short time of dating was a kind of preventive measure to avoid having her boyfriends discover her real (bad) self. I also commented that her feelings did not decrease just by themselves, but that she took an active part in generating negative emotions against the man by giving selective attention (selective apperception) to his (real or presumed) shortcomings (not intelligent enough, not interesting enough, etc.).

Sessions 9 and 10

Two binge attacks occurred in the past week, but she had followed my suggestion to attend her classes even when her day was 'shit' and when she had problems in paying attention to the lectures. We worked intensively on her self-esteem and on her general social skills with respect to other people.

At the end of session 10 she started to talk about her father, who kept writing her letters full of 'fatherly love', as she expressed it with scorn, and she insisted that all his words were 'damned lies and hypocrisy'. Barbara believed that her father pretended to have feelings for her, but in reality he did not love her. He should write in a more neutral tone to reflect his true feelings. Later, Barbara admitted that she would not be satisfied with this either; she wanted revenge. She wanted to tell him the truth about his failure as a father. Carefully, I kindled her feelings of anger, and at that point she started to cry. Now we had the possibility of exploring deeper what had happened between father and daughter when she was a young girl, and she admitted, blushing and avoiding eye-contact with me, that her father had 'fumbled' her on several occasions when sharing the bed (probably followed by his masturbating in the bathroom). Apparently, there was not much more than touching her breasts, but she remembered that she had been aware that this was not a normal fatherly hug. She had disliked it, but did not dare say no. She had felt ashamed and still felt like that. She was confused about who was the guilty one in that situation. Her feelings told her that it was her fault, but her intellect told her it had been her father who submitted her to that situation of abuse. We talked about the possibility of confronting her father with what we called the 'the truth' from that moment on, but she argued that her father would deny everything and never admit having done something wrong. He would again try to make her feel guilty and ashamed, he would certainly try to make her believe that this was a product of her imagination.

Session 11

Barbara came in and started to cry. She bitterly accused her father of being the cause of her problems and unhappiness, now putting the blame for all her problems on to the abusive childhood situation. This was somewhat difficult for me; on one hand, I did not want to minimise the potential effects of the abuse, but on the other hand I wanted to avoid her taking these experiences as a permanent excuse for her present situation. So, in the first 20 minutes of the session, I allowed her to express her feelings of anger and hatred against her father, as a kind of cathartic experience. Then I tried to help her to realise how, as a consequence of her childhood situation, her broader personality processes became organised around men who were unavailable and untrustworthy; but I also challenged her and asked her if she really believed that if these things had not happened she would not have problems now (and she said no). I also insisted on the point that, of course, her father was responsible to an extent for her feelings of guilt, shame, and being unworthy, but this did not mean that she actually was guilty and unworthy. We elaborated how she managed to provoke these feelings again and again in her relationships with men (having intercourse without really wanting it or getting involved with men who treated her inadequately, etc.).

Session 12

Barbara felt better and had not been bingeing during the last week. She had been very active and busy and, therefore, had had less time for brooding. She reported that she had become more spontaneous and natural with respect to other people. Barbara commented that, on one hand, she could be very critical and harsh with other people (and her friends actually would consider her quite assertive), but on the other hand, she was afraid of expressing her needs and desires, for fear of losing her friends; she was afraid that they would 'tear down the mask I wear and see my real self behind the façade'. I asked her to provide some examples, and we worked through them cognitively and emotionally. We found out that in social situations she tended to react in a very apprehensive way and to overestimate others' criticism of her. Because of her own inferiority feelings on many occasions, she often interpreted the behaviour of others in a negative way and then, in overcompensation for these feelings, she tended to put them down (verbally or for herself). I tried to use humour and cited Groucho Marx's famous statement: 'I would not like to be part of an association that accepts members like me.' She understood that this statement reflects the individual with inferiority feelings who compensates for them by despising those whom he or she feels inferior to.

Session 13

Barbara had a binge attack during the week before our session, and according to her it was due to an attempt at losing weight. The result was a weight gain of two pounds, and she was horrified. We talked about the uselessness of restrictive diets and their rebound effect. I asked her to draw the figure of her body shape with respect to a standard figure and then the shape of her female friend who sometimes accompanied her to my practice and was now waiting for her outside. I estimated that Barbara's friend wore about the same size of clothes or one size larger than Barbara. Barbara drew her own body slightly fatter than it was and also slightly fatter than her friend's. These perceptual distortions are not unusual in patients with eating disorders. I asked her if her friend was slim, and she said yes. On an impulse, I decided to challenge her and put forward the hypothesis that, if she was really fatter than her friend, she would not fit into her friend's blue jeans. She said no, she would certainly not fit into them. Considering that we had already achieved a good therapeutic alliance and a friendly relationship I asked her permission to invite her friend in; I invited both girls to exchange their trousers. This is, of course, not a standard Adlerian procedure, nor would I recommend it necessarily in those cases, but it allowed us to complete Kelly's Cycle of Experience (anticipation, implication, encounter, validation or invalidation, and constructive revision) during the therapeutic setting. Of course, I was completely sure that Barbara would fit in her friend's jeans, so I was certain about the invalidation of her construing herself as fatter than her friend. Barbara had predicted that she would not fit into her friend's jeans and was tremendously astonished about fitting perfectly into them. So her initial anticipation was disconfirmed in the encounter stage of the cycle, and we could go on to constructive revision of her construing herself as being 'fat' and of the contradiction of seeing herself as 'normal weight' and 'fat' at the same time.

Sessions 14–16

Barbara was now prepared to accept the possibility that her problem (fighting against imaginary fatness) was an excuse for not facing her real problems: her studies and her relationships. With respect to her studies, she immediately admitted this interpretation:

> When I fight against fatness, I feel busy without really doing anything. When I feel bad because of bingeing, I have an excuse for not working, because I have an emotional problem to be addressed. My fight against fatness is a good excuse when I flunk exams: it's not because I'm not good enough, it's because I have this disorder.

At high school, it had been easy for her to be a brilliant student, but at the university, it turned out to be more difficult and she had to dedicate more time to her studies. We could also elaborate how she actually programmed her own failure: she was lazy for weeks, and then tried to master a whole subject the day before the exam. I suggested a paradoxical technique to her: she had to work at least 1 hour every day, and then, as a 'reward', she had to indulge, for the same amount of time, in self-pitying behaviour, imagining how useless, worthless and fat she was.

Session 17

Barbara brought a letter from her father to the session and again criticised bitterly his hypocrisy. Without discarding the possibility of hypocrisy, I considered that her tendentious apperception, certainly related to her negative experiences with him, made her interpret his every statement as negative, so I invited her to analyse the letter sentence for sentence, and for each of her father's statements I asked her to come up with alternative explanations to her usual 'he feigns having fatherly feelings'. She found out that the letter could also be interpreted as the lines of a loving and caring parent who would like to know how she was doing. She even admitted the possibility that her father, in a somewhat helpless way, was trying to make up with her. I pointed out to her that maybe he was also ashamed and sorry for what he had done to her during a time of personal and marital crisis (apparently, he was happily remarried now), although he was not able to admit it directly and ask her forgiveness. Barbara finally decided to interpret her father's letter in a more commonsensical and literal way ('Daughter, I like you and I hope you are okay') and reply in the same sense ('Thanks for your concern, I'm doing fine. I hope you are well too'). She also reinterpreted the money cheque that came with the letter (as every month!) not as an attempt to 'buy her love' but as something that normal and caring parents send as a support for their student children.

Sessions 18–22

From this session on, I sometimes made Barbara switch roles with me, so that she became more and more her own therapist who replied to herself – for example, when she presented a social situation that was difficult for her. With time and experience, she became quite good at giving herself advice, and she also learned to put her own advice into practice. For instance, she reported that one day she had refused a date with C., because she had planned to work that day. As a consequence she neither worked nor passed a nice day with C., but had stuffed herself (by that time, her bingeing had almost completely disappeared). She realised by herself that going out with C. had become a regular activity. She felt good with him and enjoyed sex with him greatly, so she was 'at risk' of engaging in a deeper emotional relationship, which implied that C. could probably know her better, and know her real ('bad') self. Going out with C. that day would have confronted her with her inferiority feelings, as studying would also have done. Thus eating was again the best possibility of doing something without really doing something.

Session 23

Another incident made Barbara doubt the efficacy of her therapy, i.e. her possibility of changing. She felt that she had disappointed me (that she was not a good patient). I asked her about the positive aspects of the therapy, and she replied that here, she was allowed to talk only about herself and to feel important, which was not always the case outside the therapy setting. I also pointed out to her that an improvement in her condition would mean the end of her therapy, which threatened her feelings of being important to someone else. We talked about other possibilities she had of feeling important (without falling into the opposite: feeling superior) and how she could not only encourage herself, but encourage others (making others feel important means that I am important for them).

Later in the session she commented that her latest binge attack probably happened because a few days before she had had a one-night stand with a new man, which made her feel bad, dirty and abused. She criticised that man's abusive and 'macho' behaviour, but I showed her that it was she who had engaged voluntarily in this kind of relationship. Sleeping with a stranger could be one of her 'tricks' to reassure herself in her attitude towards men, who are all abusive and 'male chauvinist pigs' and that she should better not fall in love with them.

Sessions 24–30

In these sessions, we went back again to Barbara's childhood situation of early discouragement, her mother's failure because of her mental illness, her father's secretiveness and demanding attitude ('You should be the best of your class'), and her feelings of shame, guilt, and worthlessness. Although there had been signs of rebellion (her recollections where she was 'misbehaving'), the feelings of shame had remained. She also remembered her parents' reproachful attitude to their children, as if the children were to blame for their mother's illness.

But Barbara could now see that it was not she who had disappointed her father, it was he who had disappointed her. Her father, although representing a strict morality, was 'the sinner'. He had predicated decency and was indecent with her. Barbara also realised the relationship between being thin and not being womanly. She said that when she was more 'plump', she would look more womanly and seductive. Being thin meant being more like a boy, and therefore, no temptation for her father 'to sin'. But being thin also meant being intellectual and sophisticated to her, and therefore superior to people who indulge in sensual and animal behaviours. I asked her if all men were like her father and if sex was always a 'sin' or 'animal', and she definitively denied it. She considered C. to be very different from her father, more straightforward, natural and respectful of what she liked. She laughed and said she and C. would 'sin a lot', but she enjoyed it.

I also asked her if there was something positive about her parents and her upbringing that could help her now and in the future, and she identified their intellectual attitude, interest for aesthetics, and the capacity for coping with difficult situations.

Sessions 31–34

The following sessions were devoted to deepening the insights Barbara had gained in the sessions before. At my request, she brought forth a new (newly remembered) childhood recollection. She saw herself sitting on her father's knees, and her mother was with them. She experienced feelings of harmony, warmth and security. She started weeping. Then we talked about her longing for harmony and security, her early loss of it, and the possibility of finding it again in a partnership and with children of her own.

Session 35

Barbara kept improving. She was making plans for the summer holidays that involved travel to South America with a slightly older female friend. She admired the other woman very much (especially her ways of dealing with social situations and other people) and looked forward to learning from her.

Her studies were improving as well, though she still had some problems. For example, one problem arose when she had to interpret a poem. She thought that it was not enough for her to interpret the poem once, so she sought desperately for another hidden and more profound meaning. When she felt unable to find it, she considered herself stupid and simple-minded. But when the teacher confirmed her first (more simple) interpretation, then she considered the poem to be trivial. This was her way of avoiding positive feedback. And she also realised that this kind of over-interpretation was what she also used to do when interacting with other people: instead of taking people's statements at face value, she often tried to look for a hidden meaning. We agreed that she should work more with fellow students and work towards common interpretations.

Sessions 36–38

As we were approaching the end of the term and the beginning of Barbara's holidays, we planned the end of her therapy (unless she felt it necessary to come back after the summer break). Her binge eating had completely stopped, her weight was stable (as before), and she had stopped compulsive weighing (we had agreed that she should weigh herself only once a week and not twice a day, as before), just to make sure that she would maintain her weight, which she thought was normal now. She said she was 'not thin, but slim enough'. She dated C. regularly and enjoyed being with him, although she had not yet decided whether to engage in a formal relationship with him. She thought she had still plenty of time for this kind of decision.

She managed to pass all her exams and looked forward to the next term. She kept receiving her father's monthly letter and cheque, to which she always replied politely. At that moment, she did not feel the need to talk with him about what had happened in her childhood, and was willing to attribute her father's 'sin' to an emotional disturbance, due to his complicated and unhappy marital situation at that time. She considered that she would like to talk with him 'maybe later', when she felt more mature and more stable with respect to her present concerns (e.g. partnership, etc.).

Comment on Barbara's case

We can interpret Barbara's problems as a mild form of a non-specific eating disorder, though no formal DSM-IV classification was made, nor was it assessed by the administration of a specific diagnostic measure, such as the EDI-2 (Eating Disorder Inventory). At the beginning of the therapy, she showed restrictive eating behaviours. The binge eating took place about twice a week, and was usually, but not always, followed by provoked vomiting. Her eating pattern normalised quickly, except for occasional binge eating attacks. In the foreground was her obsessive preoccupation with being too fat, related to slight perceptual distortions with respect to her silhouette.

It was important to establish the relationship with her childhood experiences. Several authors have found a correlation between eating disorders (especially bulimia) and sexual abuse in childhood (e.g. Vanderlinden et al. 1993; Oberst et al. 2001), but in Barbara's case, her family situation, her parent's secretiveness, hypocrisy, lies, and excessive demands certainly contributed to Barbara's inferiority feelings too. In her Life Style we could see an early discouragement and, therefore, a distrust of other people's expression of feelings. She tried to cope with the help of her observation skills and her intellectual capacity, but this was not enough to distinguish between 'good and evil'; she was confused about who was to blame and was not able to ward off feelings of shame and guilt for what other people (her father) had done to her.

She compensated for these feelings with what she called 'the mask', expressed as intellectual superiority. When the demands of life, the beginning of her university studies and the beginning of her dating with men, became stronger, her intellectual compensation was not enough to cope with her feelings of worthlessness. She found out that concerns about her weight were a good means to fight with on the 'sideline battlefield', in order to avoid facing her real problems. Controlling and restricting her eating meant control over herself and feeling superior to those people who succumb to more animal instincts (enjoy meals and sex). Thus it can be seen as a safeguarding behaviour against inferiority feelings (feeling worthless and 'bad'), a trick to feel superior, and an excuse for not facing the life tasks of work (studies) and partnership. At the end of therapy, Barbara was emotionally stable, with improved self-esteem and an increased level of Social Interest (instead of being constantly concerned about how she was seen by others, she had developed a more genuine interest in other people). Her eating problems had disappeared (though I still considered her at a risk of an occasional relapse). We could have worked more on her relationship with her father, her feelings of shame and guilt and her need for revenge. Although she considered the possibility of having a talk with him about what had happened and telling him how much he had harmed her, she did not think it was necessary at that time in her life. For the moment, it was her desire to 'let the past be the past' and to consolidate her social skills and enjoy the present.

Appendix 3: Glossary of selected Adlerian terms

Antithetical apperception A highly dichotomised (all-or-nothing) method of incorporating a new perception into the existing corpus of meanings one has developed. For example, the rigid classification of men into the categories of 'like my father' versus 'not like my father' without consideration of intermedite positions or without having other ways to understand men exemplifies antithetical apperception. A related set of terms, antithetical thought, refers not so much to new people or situations encountered, but to a generalised tendency to think in a dichotomous, either–or style. Antithetical apperception underlies, in part, basic mistakes and faulty life goals.

Biased apperception The process of recognising or attributing value to a perception through the filter of a person's life goal. That is, things, people, and events in the world are not perceived so much as they are or as they exist, but in terms of their significance for people's life goals and guiding lines. Such perception is largely indistinguishable from the process of the assimilation of percepts into an existing schema within the person. This term is synonymous with **tendentious apperception**.

Birth order (actual or ordinal position) The numerical rank order in which siblings are born into or enter the family of origin. Adler believed that because each person seeks a unique way to belong, the order in which a person enters the family to some extent affects the available routes by which significance will be sought. Adler described the prototypical characteristics of five birth orders: first-born, second-born, middle-born, youngest child, and only child. Adler believed, however, that the child's perceived position or role in the family (i.e. **psychological birth order**) was more influential in affecting the Life Style. Recent research has suggested that actual position may affect one's psychological position, which in turn may affect personality (Stewart, Stewart and Campbell 2001).

Degree of activity The assiduousness or verve with which a particular line of movement within the **Life Style** is pursued. The degree of activity is assumed to be relatively constant throughout the life span and is affected by both environmental and hereditary influences. Courage in meeting life tasks stems from a relatively high degree of activity coupled with concern and care for others (i.e. **Social Interest**).

Depreciation tendency   Attitudes and behaviours that are used to preserve or enhance a person's tenuous sense of self-esteem or superiority by finding faults, problems, or shortcomings with other people or situations. This tendency frequently takes the form of relative comparisons between self and others and involves highly **biased** or **antithetical apperception** that results in the self being evaluated as superior to someone or something else. This tendency typically is pursued by discouraged, neurotic people as a last-ditch effort to thwart feelings of inferiority and to restore some sense of self-esteem. As a type of **safeguarding** manoeuvre, depreciation invariably involves a distortion in the perception of self and the world.

Early recollections   The content of memories reported by people – typically clients undergoing a Life Style or other Adlerian assessment – of the earliest events that they can remember in their lives. This content is valuable because it reveals the clients' contemporary concerns and perhaps some of the content of their **fictional** life **goals** as these are projected on to material reconstructed from the past. In other words, early recollections do not provide actual accounts of individuals' earlier life experiences as much as they reflect ongoing concerns and challenges.

Family atmosphere   The predominant feeling quality within a family that is created by the family members and their interactions (i.e. what does it feel like to live or spend time in the family?) Similar to the **Life Style**, family atmospheres can be healthy to the extent that they help members to meet the tasks of love, work and community. Alternatively, family atmospheres may be negative such that family members are precluded from regularly meeting the tasks of life because they have adopted a defensive or survival-based posture within the family.

Family constellation   The structure of the family (i.e. what people are members of the family) and the qualities of their relationships. This includes information on the **birth order** of siblings and the entry and exit of extended family members. The family constellation is analogous to the descriptions of players provided at the beginning of a dramatic production in that each person is described and his or her relationships to other significant members are characterised. Family constellations will change over time as new children are born into the sibship and as children leave or parents divorce and remarry.

Fictional finalism (also, fictional goal and guiding fiction)   This term conveys Adler's fundamental epistemological position that people contact the world through their subjective perceptions and constructions of it. That is, similar to the sentiments conveyed by Epictetus, people are more affected by their views of the world than by the world itself. Adler acknowledged that the German analytic philosopher Hans Vaihinger and his *Philosophy of 'As-if'* significantly affected his theory in this regard. From this perspective, behaviours, feelings, cognitions and other psychological events do not stem from objective, physical causes but from synthetic and subjective causes. The significance of the term 'fiction' stems from the idea that, in assembling bits and pieces of perceptions to construct a manageable and workable representation of events, the final product inevitably represents a compromise between external reality and the person's wants, needs, and goals for the future. Adler maintained that the creation and use of fictions largely occurs outside of consciousness, and also that ensembles of guiding fictions used together in particular situations or contexts comprise the private logic.

Genogram   A graphical method of depicting the **family constellation** and **family atmosphere** for at least two or more generations, beginning with the client's current generation and working backwards in time. The process of completing a genogram may reveal recurrent maladaptive ways that family members have of relating to each other that are transmitted across generations. Like other methods of assessment that individual psychologists use, the genogram is a process-oriented technique in that the act of genogram completion may also help some clients to create a narrative that describes their roles or experiences within their families of origin.

Hesitating attitude   A symptomatic orientation in emotionally distressed people that is designed to safeguard their self-esteem through the avoidance of responsibility, hesitancy to make commitments to self or others, difficulty in reaching a conclusion or taking a stand on some issue or decision, etc. The hesitating attitude typically appears in client statements that take the form of 'Yes, but . . .' Given Adler's statement that 'All [life] is movement' (Ansbacher and Ansbacher 1956: 195), he found this attitude particularly self-defeating and problematic in his patients in that it minimised their participation in the ongoing discourse of life. Although this orientation may represent people's fledging efforts to re-establish some sense of agency or control in their lives, paradoxically, it may actually broaden their difficulties in life. See Clark (1999, 2000) for further discussion.

Life Style (style of life)   A broad term that encompasses what is typically meant by the term 'personality'. The style of life can be observed from how people attempt to attain a sense of completion and belongingness while also meeting the life tasks of relationship, work, and community. Beyond these influences, the Life Style is reflected in the way people experience and respond to their family atmospheres, their role(s) in the family of origin, their genetic endowments and special abilities, early developmental experiences, long-term health status, and so forth.

Masculine protest   An attitude or emotional orientation, originally thought to characterise the striving of women and some men, in which people seek to overcome feelings of inertness and powerlessness by obtaining the privileges, prerogatives, and rights enjoyed by men. Although this term was used earlier in the history of Adlerian theory when larger disparities in opportunities existed between the genders, it is relatively dated now. The term has since taken on newer meanings that convey a general striving to overcome not just bodily based limitations but general constraints imposed by family, community and societal contexts. In this regard the meaning conveyed is quite consistent with the general tendency to strive from a felt-minus to a felt-plus situation.

Organ inferiority An idea Adler developed earlier in his theorising that psychological distress emanated from a weak or malfunctioning bodily organ. This idea later was transformed into an awareness or emotional experience of inferiority about the self in some respect that comprised the basis of people's attempts to overcompensate and overcome. Adler maintained that failed attempts at compensation or overcompensation resulted in the development of neurosis.

Private logic The often unconscious reasons for feeling, thinking, and behaving as one does. Knowledge of the private logic may render meaningful the otherwise apparently meaningless behaviour that people display in a given situation; it may also reveal the contours of people's fictional guiding lines in life. The goals of Adlerian counselling and therapy are to build the client's awareness of the private logic and to help him or her translate this into modes of thought and action that are healthy and that more effectively meet the life tasks. That is, the act of sharing or otherwise symbolising one's private constructions renders them more meaningful and allows for the constructions to be tested, validated, or revised given the existing social constructions.

Psychological birth order (perceived position) The family or sibling role that an individual develops in part through his or her efforts to find a way to belong in the family, depending on the available or ascribed roles that exist in the family. The psychological birth order may be affected by the **family atmosphere** and the individual's **actual birth position**, although neither of these influences strongly determine the perceived position. Research has suggested that psychological and actual birth position may be concordant for 12–15 per cent of people (depending on gender), with the remainder having psychological and actual positions that differ (Stewart and Campbell 1998). Psychological position is important in that it reflects people's initial efforts to find a way to belong and contribute to the family group. The White–Campbell Psychological Birth Order Inventory (PBOI) is a measure designed to assess people's perceived roles within their families of origin (Campbell, White and Stewart 1991, Stewart and Campbell 1998). The PBOI is provided in Appendix 1 of this book.

Safeguarding tendencies Behaviours and attitudes that are designed to protect an individual's sense of self-worth and self-esteem from a perceived threat and the ensuing experience of inferiority feelings. Anticipations of failure in some domain or endeavour typically trigger the need to safeguard oneself. Safeguarding tendencies are often accompanied by heightened striving for success to overcome perceived shortcomings or failures. Safeguarding may appear in at least four ways which include (1) distancing oneself from or avoiding life challenges or obstacles that pose a threat, (2) **hesitating** or ambivalent **attitudes** towards life activities, (3) detouring or circumventing an encounter with important life challenges by busying oneself with trivial, peripheral details of the challenges, and (4) the narrowed path of approach in which the person applies himself or herself to only a partial solution to a problem or challenge, leaving other significant parts largely ignored. Clark (1999, 2000) provides an informative discussion of Adler's conceptualisation of safeguarding tendencies.

Social Interest This is an approximate translation of the German, *Gemeinschaftsgefühl* or community feeling. Social Interest reflects both the attitudes and behaviours of caring, concern, and compassion for fellow humans. Adler described Social Interest as, 'to see with the eyes of another, to hear with the ears of another and to feel with the heart of another' (Ansbacher and Ansbacher 1956: 135). Social Interest embodies efforts to meet the tasks of the community and it is also enhanced by contributing to others' welfare. Social Interest functions both as a cause of meaningful and healthy engagement with others and as a cumulative effect of such involvement. Consequently, Social Interest embodied in people's attitudes and behaviours is one indicator of emotional health in Adlerian theory. The Social Interest construct has been operationalised through several measures that Watkins (1994) has reviewed. One of these measures, the Sulliman Scale of Social Interest (SSSI), is provided in Appendix 1 of this book.

Striving for perfection (completion) An innate and ceaseless striving from a position of relative inertness, dependency, helplessness, or inferiority to a position of agency, activity, mastery, or superiority. Such striving pervades the life space of people and can assume different forms at different times. Psychological health results from such striving coupled with **Social Interest**; that is, being all one can be while also forging a meaningful way to belong with others. Ansbacher and Ansbacher (1956) noted a remarkable similarity between striving for perfection and the term 'self-actualisation' (the implementing of one's innate talents and potentialities), as articulated by Goldstein (1939) and later adopted by Maslow (1954).

Striving for superiority A goal orientation that involves attempts to achieve mastery in a given domain of interest or activity. This represents an intermediate construct in the evolution of Adler's thinking about the fundamental motives to achieve completeness and belonging. Consistent with one of its conceptual predecessors, **masculine protest**, the notion of striving for superiority conveys movement from a felt-minus to a felt-plus position. Individual psychologists also differentiate between two levels of superiority striving, one of which involves competition with oneself to achieve personal bests in some area of endeavour. The more unhealthy orientation involves striving for personal superiority over others. Here, one achieves a sense of mastery and power over others by defeating them or relishing their losses or shortcomings. Superiority striving in this sense precludes the kind of co-operation and caring for others that underlies emotional health and **Social Interest**.

Tasks of life   Adler initially described three tasks or responsibilities that all people had to find a way to approach: work (i.e. vocation, profession or occupation), love (i.e. long-term and emotionally intimate relationship with a partner), and community (i.e. caring for and contributing to the welfare of other persons in one's family, community or wider society). Adler maintained that people face the dual challenge in life of approaching and fulfilling these tasks while also seeking completion. A key element here is in developing a **style of life** that fulfils both purposes. Dreikurs and Mosak (1977a, b) proposed additional life tasks that involved (1) developing the sense of self and getting along with self, and (2) spiritual and existential efforts to developing life meanings. No theoretical or empirical research, however, has been conducted to explore the viability of adding these extra tasks (Mansager and Gold 2000).

Teleological position   Part of Adler's theory concerning psychological causation, whereby people's present beliefs, emotions, and behaviours are guided by their goals and expectations for the future. That is, it is not the future itself that affects a person's present mental events, but the anticipated future as it is constructed in the present. This position is consistent with Adler's epistemological assumptions that the world in both its present and future forms is subjectively constructed, forming the 'fictional reality' to which the person responds.

Tendentious apperception   The tendency, according to Adler, that all people have to understand new perceptions or novel experiences in terms of their pre-existing network of meanings. With regard to **fictional** life **goals**, an object, event, or person may be perceived in terms of its implications or relevance to the life goal. This term is synonymous with **biased apperception**.

Unconscious   The state of being unaware of some aspect of one's **Life Style**, **fictional** life **goals**, or life plan. For individual psychologists unconscious functions as an adjective (i.e. a state of awareness) rather than as a noun (i.e. a place where unacceptable wishes or impulses originate). One goal of Adlerian counselling and psychotherapy is to help the client become aware of how his or her life plan (i.e. ways of dealing with responsibilities or challenges in life) has resulted in a characteristically unhealthy or maladaptive Life Style. Another goal may to be help the client become aware of how a mistaken life goal has contributed to his or her distress.

Useless side of life/wasting orientation   A self-defeating **Life Style** in which people fail to engage themselves in meeting the tasks of life (i.e. work, relational intimacy, and social interest). Instead of belonging usefully and productively with others, people who have gravitated to the useless side of life are known for failing to co-operate and to contribute. These people possess guiding lines that preclude them from assuming the usual responsibilities of life and at the same time supply them with myriad reasons for occupying their inert positions. In the movement that comprises the experience of life, people with this orientation do not apply their talents and abilities and may remain generally untested by the challenges of life.

References

Ackerman, N. W. (1958) *The psychodynamics of family life: Diagnosis and treatment of family relationships*, New York: Basic Books.

Adler, A. (1907/1977) *Studie über die Minderwertigkeit von Organen*, Frankfurt: Fischer. (English translation: *A study of organ inferiority and its psychical compensation: A contribution to clinical medicine*, New York: Nervous Mental Diseases Publishing Company.)

Adler, A. (1908a/1914/1973) 'Der Aggressionstrieb im Leben und in der Neurose', in W. Metzger (ed.) *Heilen und Bilden*, Frankfurt: Fischer. (Title of the article in English: 'The aggression drive in life and in neuroses'. Title of the book: *Healing and education*.)

Adler, A. (1908b/1914/1973) 'Das Zärtlichkeitsbedürfnis des Kindes', in W. Metzger (ed.) *Heilen und Bilden*, Frankfurt: Fischer. (Title of the article in English: 'The child's need for affection'. Title of the book: *Healing and education*.)

Adler, A. (1910/1914/1973) 'Der psychische Hermaphroditismus im Leben und in der Neurose', in W. Metzger (ed.) *Heilen und Bilden*, Frankfurt: Fischer. (Title of the article in English: 'Psychic hermaphroditism in life and in neuroses'. Title of the book: *Healing and education*.)

Adler, A. (1911/1914/1973) 'Zur Kritik der Freudschen Sexualtheorie des Seelenlebens', in W. Metzger (ed.) *Heilen und Bilden*, Frankfurt: Fischer. (Title of the article in English: 'Criticism of Freud's sexual theory'. Title of the book: *Healing and education*.)

Adler, A. (1912/1977) *Über den nervösen Charakter*, Frankfurt: Fischer. (English translation: *The neurotic constitution*, New York: Moffat, Yard, 1917.)

Adler, A. (1927/1981) *Menschenkenntnis*, Frankfurt: Fischer. (English translation: *Understanding human nature*, New York: Garden City Publishing, 1927.)

Adler, A. (1929) *The science of living*, New York: Garden City Publishing.

Adler, A. (1931/1981) *Wozu leben wir?*, Frankfurt: Fischer. (English translation: *What life should mean to you*, New York: Grosset and Dunlap, 1931.)

Adler, A. (1933/1980) *Der Sinn des Lebens*, Frankfurt: Fischer. (English translation: *Social interest: A challenge to mankind*, London: Faber & Faber Ltd, 1938.)

Adler, A. (1968) *The practice and theory of Individual Psychology*, Totowa, NJ: Littlefield Adams. (Original work published 1925.)

Adler, A. (1998) *Social interest: Adler's key to the meaning of life*, Oxford: Oneworld. (Original work published 1938 as *Social interest: A challenge to mankind*.)

Adler, A. and Jahn, E. (1933/1983) *Religion und Individualpsychologie*, Frankfurt: Fischer. (Title in English: *Religion and Individual Psychology*.)

Adler, K. A. (1959) 'Life style in schizophrenia', in K. A. Adler and D. Deutsch (eds) *Essays in Individual Psychology: Contemporary application of Alfred Adler's theories*, New York: Grove Press.

Ahn, H. and Wampold, B. E. (2001) 'Where oh where are the specific ingredients? A meta-analysis of component studies in counseling and psychotherapy', *Journal of Counseling Psychology* 48: 251–257.

Albee, G. W. (1982) 'Preventing psychopathology and promoting human potential', *American Psychologist* 37: 1043–1050.

American Psychiatric Association (ed.) (1994) *Diagnostic and statistical manual of mental disorders DSM-IV*, Washington, DC: American Psychiatric Association.

Anderson, H. and Goolishian, H. (1992) 'The client is the expert: A not-knowing approach to psychotherapy', in S. McNamee and K. Gergen (eds) *Therapy as social construction*, London: Sage.

Anderson, W. T. (1990) *Reality isn't what it used to be*, San Francisco: HarperSanFrancisco.

Ansbacher, H. L. (1992) 'Alfred Adler, pioneer in prevention of mental disorders', *Individual Psychology* 48: 3–34.

Ansbacher, H. L. and Ansbacher, R. R. (eds) (1956) *The Individual Psychology of Alfred Adler: A systematic presentation in selections from his writings*, New York: Basic Books.

Arkowitz, H. (1991) 'Introductory statement: Psychotherapy integration comes of age', *Journal of Psychotherapy Integration* 1: 1–3.

Balint, M. (1968) *The basic fault: Therapeutic aspects of regression*, London: Tavistock.

Baumeister, R. F. and Leary, M. R. (1995) 'The need to belong: Desire for inter-personal attachments as a fundamental human motive', *Psychological Bulletin* 117: 497–529.

Beck, A. T. (1976) *Cognitive therapy and emotional disorders*, New York: International Universities Press.

Beck, A. T. (1995) 'Cognitive therapy: Past, present, and future', in M. J. Mahoney (ed.) *Cognitive and constructive psychotherapies: Theory, research, and practice*, New York: Springer.

Belove, P. L. (1980) 'First encounters of the close kind (FECK): The use of the story of the first interaction as an early recollection of a marriage', *Journal of Individual Psychology* 36: 191–208.

Benjamin, L. S. (1974) 'Structural analysis of social behavior', *Psychological Review* 81: 392–425.

Benjamin, L. S. (1993) *Interpersonal diagnosis and treatment of personality disorders*, New York: Guilford Press.

Bitter, J. R. (1987) 'Communication and meaning: Satir in Adlerian context', in R. Sherman and D. Dinkmeyer (eds) *Systems of family therapy: An Adlerian integration*, New York: Brunner-Mazel.

Bitter, J. R. and Nicoll, W. G. (2000) 'Adlerian brief therapy with individuals: Process and practice', *Journal of Individual Psychology* 56: 31–44.

Botella, L. (1995) 'Personal construct theory, constructivism, and postmodern thought', in R. A. Neimeyer and G. J. Neimeyer (eds) *Advances in personal construct theory*, Greenwich, CT: JAI Press.

Botella, L. (1998) 'Clinical psychology, psychotherapy and mental health: Contemporary issues and future dilemmas', *International Journal of Psychotherapy* 3(3): 255–263.

Botella, L. and Figueras, S. (1995) 'Cien años de psicoterapia:¿El porvenir de una ilusión o un porvenir ilusorio?', *Revista de Psicoterapia* IV(24): 12–28. (Title in English: 'One hundred years of psychotherapy: The future of an illusion or an illusive future?'.)

Brachfeld, O. (1970) *Los sentimientos de inferioridad*, Barcelona: Luis Miracle. (Title in English: *The inferiority feelings.*)

Bruder, K.-J. (1996) 'Die Erfindung der Biographie im therapeutischen Gespräch', *Zeitschrift für Individualpsychologie* 21: 313–324. (Title in English: 'The invention of biography in the therapeutic conversation'.)

Bruner, J. (1990) *Acts of meaning*, Cambridge, MA: Harvard University Press.

Burns, D. (1989) *The feeling good handbook: Using the new mood therapy in everyday life*, New York: William Morrow Co.

Campbell, L. F., White, J. and Stewart, A. E. (1991) 'The relationship of psychological birth order to actual birth order', *Individual Psychology* 47: 380–391.

Capps, S. C., Searight, H. R., Russo, J. R., Temple, L. E. and Rogers, B. J. (1993) 'The family of origin scale: Discriminant validity with adult children of alcoholics', *The American Journal of Family Therapy* 21: 274–277.

Capra, F. (1982a) *The Tao of Physics*, Berkeley, CA: Shambala.

Capra, F. (1982b) *The turning point: Science, society, and the rising culture*, New York: Bantam Books.

Carich, M. S. (1989) 'Variations of the "as-if" technique', *Individual Psychology* 45: 538–545.

Carlson, J. (2000) 'Individual Psychology in the year 2000 and beyond: Astronaut or dinosaur? Headline or footnote?', *Journal of Individual Psychology* 56(1): 3–13.

Carlson, J. and Sperry, L. (1998) 'Adlerian psychotherapy as a constructivist psychotherapy', in M. F. Hoyt (ed.) *The handbook of constructive therapy*, San Francisco: Jossey-Bass.

Cavalleri, D. I. (2001) 'Are we similar? A cross-cultural examination of psychological birth order', unpublished MPhil thesis, University of Florida, Gainesville, Florida.

Clark, A. J. (1994) 'Conflict resolution and Individual Psychology in the schools', *Individual Psychology* 50(3): 329–340.

Clark, A. J. (1999) 'Safeguarding tendencies: A clarifying perspective', *Journal of Individual Psychology* 55: 72–81.

Clark, A. J. (2000) 'Safeguarding tendencies: Implications for the counseling process', *Journal of Individual Psychology* 56: 192–204.

Corsini, R. J. (1979) 'Individual Education: A system based on Individual Psychology', in E. Ignas and R. J. Corsini (eds) *Alternative Educational Systems*, Itasca, IL: Peacock.

Corsini, R. J. (1982) 'The relapse technique in counseling and psychotherapy', *Individual Psychology* 38: 380–386.

Crandall, J. E. (1991) 'A scale for social interest', *Individual Psychology* 47: 106–114. (Original paper published 1975.)

Crandall, J. E. and Harris, M. D. (1991) 'Social interest, cooperation, and altruism', *Individual Psychology* 47: 115–119.

Csikszentmihalyi, M. (1990) *Flow: The psychology of optimal experience*, New York: HarperCollins.

Csikszentmihalyi, M. (1993) *The evolving self*, New York: HarperCollins.

Curlette, W. L., Kern, R. M., Gfroerer, K. P. and Whitaker, I. Y. (1999) 'A comparison of two social interest assessment instruments with implications for managed care', *Journal of Individual Psychology* 55: 62–71.

Cushman, P. (1991) 'Psychotherapy to 1992: A historically situated interpretation', in D. K. Freedheim (ed.) *History of psychotherapy: A century of change* (pp. 21–64), Washington, DC: American Psychological Association.

Cyrulnik, B. (2002) *Los patitos feos. La resiliencia: una infancia infeliz no determina la vida*. Barcelona: Gedisa. (Title in English: *The ugly ducklings. Resilience: An unhappy childhood does not determine life.*)

Dagley, J. C. (2000) 'Adlerian family therapy', in A. M. Horne (ed.) *Family counseling and therapy* (3rd edn), Itasca, IL: Peacock.

Dagley, J. C., Campbell, L. F., Kulic, K. R. and Dagley, P. L. (1999) 'Identification of subscales and analyses of reliability of an encouragement scale for children', *Journal of Individual Psychology* 55: 355–364.

Daigneault, S. D. (1999) 'Narrative means to Adlerian ends: An illustrated comparison of narrative therapy and Adlerian play therapy', *Journal of Individual Psychology* 55: 298–315.

Daugherty, D. A., Murphy, M. J. and Paugh, J. (2001) 'An examination of the Adlerian construct of social interest with criminal offenders', *Journal of Counseling and Development* 79: 465–471.

Davanloo, H. D. (1996) 'Unlocking the unconscious', in J. Groves (ed.) *Essential papers on short-term dynamic therapy*, New York: New York University Press.

Dinkmeyer, D. and Dinkmeyer, J. (1982) 'Adlerian marriage therapy', *Individual Psychology* 38: 115–122.

Dinkmeyer, D. C., Dinkmeyer, D. C. Jr and Sperry, L. (1987) *Adlerian counseling and psychotherapy* (2nd edn), Columbus, OH: Merrill Publishing.

Dinkmeyer, D. C. and McKay, D. (1976) *Systematic training for effective parenting*, Circle Pines, MN: American Guidance Service.

Dinkmeyer, D., McKay, G. and Dinkmeyer, D. Jr (1997) *The parent's handbook from systematic training for effective parenting (STEP)*, Circle Pines, MN: American Guidance Service.

Dinkmeyer, D. Jr and Sperry, L. (2000) *Counseling and psychotherapy: An integrated Individual Psychology approach*, Upper Saddle River, NJ: Prentice Hall.

Disque, J. G. and Bitter, J. R. (1998) 'Integrating narrative therapy with Adlerian Lifestyle assessment: A case study', *Journal of Individual Psychology* 54: 431–450.

Dobson, K. S. (ed.) (1988) *Handbook of cognitive-behavioral therapies*, New York: Guilford.

Dreikurs, R. (1946) *The challenge of marriage*, New York: Hawthorn Books.

Dreikurs, R. (1967) *Psychodynamics, psychotherapy, and counseling*, Chicago: Alfred Adler Institute.

Dreikurs, R. (1968) *Psychology in the classroom*, New York: Harper and Row.

Dreikurs, R. (1972) 'Family counseling: A demonstration', *Journal of Individual Psychology* 28: 207–222.

Dreikurs, R. (1989) *Fundamentals of Adlerian psychology*, Chicago: Alfred Adler Institute.

Dreikurs, R. (1997) 'Holistic medicine', *Journal of Individual Psychology* 53(2): 127–205.

Dreikurs, R., Grunwald, B. B. and Pepper, F. C. (1971) *Maintaining sanity in the classroom: Illustrated teaching techniques*, New York: Harper and Row.

Dreikurs, R. and Mosak, H. H. (1977a) 'The tasks of life I: Adler's three tasks', in H. H. Mosak (ed.) *On purpose*, Chicago: Alfred Adler Institute. (Original publication 1966.)

Dreikurs, R. and Mosak, H. H. (1977b) 'The tasks of life II: The fourth life task', in H. H. Mosak (ed.) *On purpose*, Chicago: Alfred Adler Institute. (Original publication 1966.)

Dreikurs, R. and Soltz, V. (1964) *Children: The challenge*, New York: Duell, Sloan and Pearce.

Dreikurs Ferguson, E. (2000) 'Individual Psychology is ahead of its time', *Journal of Individual Psychology* 56(1): 14–20.

D'Zurilla, T. J. and Nezu, A. M. (1999) *Problem-solving therapy: A social competence approach to clinical intervention*, New York: Springer.

Eckstein, D. (1999) 'An early recollections skill-building workshop', *Journal of Individual Psychology* 55: 435–448.

Edwards, D. L. and Gfroerer, K. P. (2001) 'Adlerian school-based interventions for children with attention-deficit/hyperactivity disorder', *Journal of Individual Psychology* 57: 210–223.

Ellis, A. (1995) 'Reflections on rational-emotive therapy', in M. J. Mahoney (ed.) *Cognitive and constructive psychotherapies: Theory, research, and practice*, New York: Springer.

Ellis, A. and Dryden, W. (1987) *The practice of rational-emotive therapy*, New York: Springer.

Epstein, N. B., Baldwin, L. M. and Bishop, D. S. (1983) 'The McMaster family assessment device', *Journal of Marital and Family Therapy* 9: 171–180.

Erikson, E. H. (1951) *Childhood and society*, New York: Norton.

Erikson, E. H. and Erikson, J. M. (1997) *The life cycle completed*, New York: Norton.

Ernst, C. and Angst, J. (1983) *Birth order: Its influence on personality*, Berlin: Springer-Verlag.

Eysenck, H. J. (1952) 'The effects of psychotherapy: An evaluation', *Journal of Consulting Psychology* 16: 319–324.

Feixas, G. and Miró, M. (1993) *Aproximaciones a la psicoterapia*, Barcelona: Paidós. (Title in English: *Approaches to psychotherapy*.)

Fish, R. C. and Mozdzierz, G. J. (1988) 'Validation of the Sulliman Scale of Social Interest with psychotherapy outpatients', *Journal of Individual Psychology* 44: 307–315.

Framo, J. L. (1982) *Explorations in marital and family therapy*, New York: Springer.

Fransella, F. and Bannister, D. (1977) *A manual for repertory grid technique*, London/New York: Academic Press.

Freedheim, D. K. (ed.) (1992) *History of psychotherapy: A century of change*, Washington, DC: American Psychological Association.

Freeman, A. and Urschel, J. (1997) 'Individual Psychology and cognitive behavior therapy: A cognitive therapy perspective', *Journal of Cognitive Psychotherapy: An International Quarterly* 11(3): 165–179.

Gergen, K. J. (1991) *The saturated self*, New York: Basic Books.

Gergen, K. J. (1994) *Realities and relationships: Sounds in social construction*, Boston: Harvard University Press.

Gergen, K. J. and Kaye, J. (1992) 'Beyond narrative in negotiation of meaning', in S. McNamee and K. J. Gergen (eds) *Therapy as social construction*, London: Sage.

Gfäller, G. R. (1996) 'Kritische Überlegungen zu Fiktion und Wahrheit', *Zeitschrift für Individualpsychologie* 21(4): 292–300. (Title in English: 'Critical reflexions on fiction and truth'.)

Goldfried, M. R. and Robins, C. J. (1983) 'Self-schema, cognitive bias, and the processing of therapeutic experiences', in P. C. Kendall (ed.) *Advances in cognitive-behavioral research and therapy*, San Diego, CA: Academic Press.

Goldstein, K. (1939) *The organism: A holistic approach to biology derived from pathological data on man*, New York: American Book Company.

Greenberg, L. S. and Safran, J. D. (1987) *Emotion in psychotherapy: Affect, cognition, and the process of change*, New York: Guilford.

Greenson, R. R. (1967) *The technique and practice of psychoanalysis* (Vol. 1), Madison, WI: International Universities Press.

Griffith, J. and Powers, R. L. (1987) *An Adlerian lexicon*, Chicago, IL: America's Institute of Adlerian Studies.

Halberstadt, A. G. (1983) 'Family expressiveness styles and nonverbal communication skills', *Journal of Nonverbal Behavior* 8: 14–26.

Halberstadt, A. G. (1986) 'Family socialization of emotional expression and nonverbal communication styles and skills', *Journal of Personality and Social Psychology* 51: 827–836.

Halberstadt, A. G., Cassidy, J., Stifter, C. A., Parke, R. D. and Fox N. A. (1995) 'Self-expressiveness within the family context: Psychometric support for a new measure', *Psychological Assessment* 7: 93–103.

Haley, J. (1976) *Problem-solving therapy: New strategies for effective family therapy*, San Francisco: Jossey-Bass.

Hanna, F. J. (1998) 'A transcultural view of prejudice, racism, and community feeling: The desire and striving for status', *Journal of Individual Psychology* 54: 336–345.

Hartmann, H. (1958) *Ego psychology and the problem of adaptation*, New York: International Universities Press.

Herron, W. G. and Welt, S. R. (1992) *Money matters: The fee in psychotherapy and psychoanalysis*, New York: Guilford.

Hoffman, E. (1994) *The drive for self: Alfred Adler and the founding of Individual Psychology*, Reading, MA: Addison-Wesley.

Horney, K. (1937) *The neurotic personality of our time*, New York: Norton.

Hovestadt, A. J., Anderson, W. T., Piercy, F. P., Cochran, S. W. and Fine, M. (1985) 'A family of origin scale', *Journal of Marital and Family Therapy* 11: 287–297.

Howard, G. S. (1991) 'Culture tales: A narrative approach to thinking, cross-cultural psychology, and psychotherapy', *American Psychologist* 46: 187–197.

Ibáñez, T. (1992) '¿Cómo se puede no ser constructivista hoy en día?' *Revista de psicoterapia* III(12): 17–27. (Title in English: 'How can one not be a constructivist today?')

Jefferson, T., Herbst, J. H. and McCrae, R. R. (1998) 'Associations between birth order and personality traits: Evidence from self-reports and observer ratings', *Journal of Research in Personality* 32: 498–509.

Jones, J. V. Jr (1995) 'Constructivism and Individual Psychology: Common ground for dialogue', *Individual Psychology* 51: 231–243.

Jones, J. V. Jr and Lyddon, W. J. (1997) 'Adlerian and constructivist psychotherapies: A constructivist perspective', *Journal of Cognitive Psychotherapy* 11: 195–210.

Jordan, E. W., Whiteside, M. M. and Manaster, G. J. (1982) 'A practical and effective research measure of birth order', *Individual Psychology* 38: 253–260.

Kaplan, H. I. and Saddock, B. J. (1995) *Comprehensive textbook of psychiatry*, Baltimore: Williams and Wilkins.

Karasu, T. B. (1986) 'The specificity versus nonspecificity dilemma: Toward identifying therapeutic change agents', *American Journal of Psychiatry* 143: 678–695.

Kefir, N. (1971) 'Priorities: A different approach to life style and neurosis', paper presented at the ICASSI Conference, Tel-Aviv (Israel).

Kelly, G. (1955/1991) *The psychology of personal constructs*, London: Routledge.

Kern, R., Gfroerer, K., Summers, Y., Curlette, W. and Matheny, K. (1996) 'Life-style, personality and stress coping', *Individual Psychology* 52: 42–53.

Kiesler, D. J. (1996) *Contemporary interpersonal theory and research*, New York: Wiley.

Kohlberg, L. and DeVries, R. (1987) *Child psychology and childhood education: A cognitive-developmental view*, New York: Longman.

Klerman, G. L., Weissman, M. M., Rounsaville, B. J. and Chevron, E. S. (1984) *Interpersonal psychotherapy of depression*, New York: Basic Books.

Kohut, H. (1971) *The analysis of the self*, New York: International Universities Press.

Kohut, H. (1977) *The restoration of the self*, New York: International Universities Press.

Kopp, R. R. and Lasky, A. (1999) 'Brief therapy using Kopp's typology: A case example', *Journal of Individual Psychology* 55: 51–61.

Korzybski, A. (1933) *Science and sanity*, Lakeville, CT: Institute of General Semantics.

Krysan, M., Moore, K. A. and Zill, N. (1990) *Identifying successful families: An overview of constructs and selected measures*, Washington, DC: Child Trends.

Kutchins, C. B., Curlette, W. L. and Kern, R. M. (1997) 'To what extent is there a relationship between personality priorities and lifestyle themes?', *Journal of Individual Psychology* 53: 373–387.

Kvale, S. (ed.) (1992) *Psychology and postmodernism*, London: Sage.

Langenfeld, S. D. and Main, F. (1983) 'Personality priorities: A factor analytic study', *Individual Psychology* 39(1): 40–51.

Langs, R. (1992) *A clinical workbook for psychotherapists*, London: Karnac Books.

Leary, T. (1957) *Interpersonal diagnosis of personality: A functional theory and methodology for personality evaluation*, New York: Ronald Press.

Leman, K. (1985) *The birth order book: Why you are the way you are*, Grand Rapids, MI: Spire Books.

León, R. (2000) 'Los psicólogos hispanohablantes y la teoría de Alfred Adler en la revista *Internationale Zeitschrift fuer Individualpsychologie*', *Revista Latinoamericana de Psicología* 32: 107–126. (Title in English: 'The Spanish-speaking psychologist and Alfred Adler's theory in the journal *Internationale Zeitschrift fuer Individualpsychologie*'.)

Lingg, M. and Kottman, T. (1991) 'Changing mistaken beliefs through visualization of early recollections', *Individual Psychology* 47: 255–260.

Loevinger, J. (1987) *Paradigms of personality*, New York: Freeman.

Lohman, J. F., Lohman, T. G. and Christensen, O. (1985) 'Psychological position and perceived sibling differences', *Individual Psychology* 41: 313–327.

Lynn, S. J. and Garske, J. P. (eds) (1985) *Contemporary psychotherapies: Models and methods*, Columbus, OH: Merrill.

McCall, G. and Simmons, J. L. (1978) *Identities and interactions* (2nd edn), New York: Free Press.

McGoldrick, M. and Gerson, R. (1985) *Genograms in family assessment*, New York: Norton.

Maddi, S. R. (2001) *Personality theories: A comparative analysis*, Prospect Heights, IL: Waveland Press.

Mahoney, M. J. and Gabriel, T. (1987) 'Psychotherapy and the cognitive sciences: An evolving alliance', *Journal of Cognitive Psychotherapy* 1: 39–59.

Mandler, G. (1984) *Mind and body: Psychology of emotion and stress*, New York: Norton.

Mansager, E. and Gold, L. (2000) 'Three life tasks or five?', *Journal of Individual Psychology* 5: 155–171.

Maslow, A. H. (1943) 'A theory of human motivation', *Psychological Review* 50: 370–396.

Maslow, A. H. (1954) *Motivation and personality*, New York: Harper and Row.

Maslow, A. H. (1962) *Toward a psychology of being*, New York: Van Nostrand.

Maslow, A. H. (1979) 'Holistic emphasis', *Journal of Individual Psychology* 26: 39.

Maslow, A. H. (1987) *Motivation and personality* (3rd edn), New York: Harper and Row.

Master, S. B. (1991) 'Constructivism and the creative power of self', *Individual Psychology* 47: 447–455.

Maturana, H. and Varela, F. (1980) *Autopoiesis and cognition*, Boston: Riedel.

Mazer, G. E., Mangrum, O. L., Hovestadt, A. J. and Brashear, R. L. (1990) 'Further validation of the family of origin scale: A factor analysis', *Journal of Marital and Family Therapy* 16: 423–426.

Meichenbaum, D. (1990) 'Evolution of cognitive behavior therapy: Origins, tenets and clinical examples', in J. Zeig (ed.) *The evolution of psychotherapy: II*, New York: Brunner Mazel.

Mestre, M. V. and Carpintero, H. (1988) 'Unas notas sobre la entrada de Adler en España', *Revista de Historia de Psicologia* 9: 47–62. (Title in English: 'Some comments on Adler's theory in Spain'.)

Meunier, G. F. (1990) 'The pampered child grows older', *Individual Psychology: Journal of Adlerian theory, research, and practice* 46: 133–138.

Minuchin, S. and Fishman, H. C. (1981) *Family therapy techniques*, Cambridge, MA: Harvard University Press.

Moos, R. H. and Moos, B. S. (1986) *Family Environment Scale manual* (2nd edn), Palo Alto, CA: Consulting Psychologists Press.

Mosak, H. H. (1958) 'Early recollections as a projective technique', *Journal of Projective Technique* 22: 302–311.

Mosak, H. H. (1971a) 'Lifestyle', in A. Nikelly (ed.) *Techniques for behavior change*, Springfield, IL: Charles C. Thomas.

Mosak, H. H. (1971b) 'Strategies for behavior change in schools: Consultation Strategies', *Counseling Psychologist* 3: 58–62.

Mosak, H. H. (1972) 'Life style assessment: A demonstration focused on family constellation', *Journal of Individual Psychology* 28: 232–247.

Mosak, H. H. (1985) 'Interrupting a depression: The pushbutton technique', *Individual psychology* 4: 210–214.

Mosak, H. H. (1989) 'Adlerian Psychology', in R. J. Corsini and D. Wedding (eds) *Current psychotherapies*, Itasca, IL: Peacock.

Mozdzierz, G. J., Greenblatt, R. L. and Murphy, T. J. (1986) 'Social interest: The validity of two scales', *Individual Psychology* 42: 35–43.

Mozdzierz, G. J., Greenblatt, R. L. and Murphy, T. J. (1988) 'Further validation of the Sulliman Scale of Social Interest and the Social Interest Scale', *Individual Psychology* 44: 30–34.

Mozdzierz, G. J., Macchitelli, F. J. and Lisiecki, J. (1976) 'The paradox in psychotherapy: An Adlerian perspective', *Journal of Individual Psychology* 32: 169–184.

Murphy, T. J. (1984) 'Encouraging client responsibility', *Individual Psychology* 40: 122–132.

Neimeyer, R. A. (1988) 'Integrative directions in Personal Construct Therapy', *International Journal of Personal Construct Psychology* 1: 283–297.

Neimeyer, R. A. (1993) 'Constructivist approaches to the measurement of meaning', in G. J. Neimeyer (ed.) *Constructivist assessment: A casebook*, Newbury Park, CA: Sage.

Neimeyer, R.A. (1994) 'Problemas y posibilidades de la Psicoterapia Constructivista', *Revista Argentina de Clínica Psicológica* 3(2): 125–145. (Title in English: 'Problems and possibilities of constructivist psychotherapy'.)

Neimeyer, R. A. and Mahoney, M. J. (eds) (1995) *Constructivism in psychotherapy*, Washington, DC: American Psychological Association.

Neimeyer, R. A. and Stewart, A. E. (1996) 'Trauma, healing, and the narrative emplotment of loss', *Families in Society* 77: 360–375.

Neimeyer, R. A. and Stewart, A. E. (1999) 'Constructivist and narrative psychotherapies', in C. R. Snyder and R. E. Ingram (eds) *Handbook of Psychotherapy: The processes and practices of psychological change*, New York: Wiley.

Newbauer, J. F. and Blanks, J. W. (2001) 'Group work with adolescent sexual offenders', *Journal of Individual Psychology* 57: 37–50.

Nichols, W. C. (2000) 'Integrative family therapy', in A. M. Horne (ed.) *Family counseling and therapy* (3rd edn), Itasca, IL: Peacock.

Nichols, W. C. and Everett, C. A. (1986) *Systemic family therapy: An integrative approach*, New York: Guilford Press.

Nicoll, W. G. and Hawes, E. C. (1985) 'Family lifestyle assessment: The role of family myths and values in the client's presenting issues', *Individual Psychology* 41: 147–160.

Norcross, J. C. (1986) *Handbook of eclectic psychotherapy*, New York: Brunner Mazel.

Oberst, U. E. (1998a) 'Alfred Adler's Individual Psychology in the context of constructivism' *Constructivism in the Human Sciences* 3: 153–176.

Oberst, U. (1998b) 'El trabajo terapéutico con sueños: Una aproximación adleriana-constructivista', *Revista de Psicoterapia* 34/35: 137–150. (Title in English: 'Working with dreams in psychotherapy: An Adlerian-constructivist approach'.)

Oberst, U. (2002, in press) 'An Adlerian/constructivist approach to dreams', *Journal of Individual Psychology* 58(2).

Oberst, U., Baltà, M., Sánchez-Planell, L. and Rangil, T. (2001) 'Trastornos disociativos en mujeres con trastornos alimentarios', *Revista de Psiquiatría de la Facultad de Medicina de Barcelona* 28: 284–290. (Title in English: 'Dissociative disorders in women with eating disorders'.)

Oddy, M. and Humphrey, M. (1980) 'Social recovery during the year following severe head injury', *Journal of Neurology, Neurosurgery, and Psychiatry* 43: 798–802.

Pepper, F. C. and Roberson, M. (1982) 'Consequences: An alternative to punishment', *Individual Psychology* 38: 387–397.

Perry, W. G. (1970) *Forms of intellectual and ethical development in college years: A scheme*, New York: Rinehart and Winston.

Polkinghorne, D. E. (1992) 'Postmodern epistemology of practice', in S. Kvale (ed.) *Psychology and postmodernism*, London: Sage.

Popkin, M. H. (2000) 'Youth violence in our community – and what we can do', *Journal of Individual Psychology* 56: 395–410.

Pulakos, J. (1987) 'The effects of birth order on perceived family roles', *Individual Psychology* 43: 319–328.

Rattner, J. (1972) *Alfred Adler*, Reinbek: Rowohlt.

Reik, T. (1948) *Listening with the third ear: The inner experience of a psychoanalyst*, New York: Farrar, Straus.

Richardson, F. C. and Manaster, G. J. (1997) 'Back to the future: Alfred Adler on freedom and commitment', *Journal of Individual Psychology* 53: 286–309.

Riedl, R. (1984) 'The consequences of causal thinking', in P. Watzlawick (ed.) *The invented reality*, New York: Norton and Company.

Robins, C. J. and Hayes, A. M. (1993) 'An appraisal of cognitive therapy', *Journal of Consulting and Clinical Psychology* 61: 205–214.

Rogers, C. R. (1959) 'A theory of therapy, personality, and interpersonal relationships, as developed in the client-centered framework', in S. Koch (ed.) *Psychology: A study of science*, New York: McGraw-Hill.

Rogers, C. R. (1961) *On becoming a person*, Boston: Houghton Mifflin.

Rogers, C. R. (1972) *Becoming partners: Marriage and its alternatives*, New York: Delacorte Press.

Rogers, C. R. (1977) *Carl Rogers on personal power*, New York: Delacorte Press.

Rogers, C. R. and Sanford, R. C. (1984) 'Client-centered psychotherapy', in H. I. Kaplan and B. J. Sadcock (eds) *Comprehensive textbook of psychiatry*, Baltimore: Williams and Wilkins.

Rosenthal, H. (1959) 'The final dream: A criterion for the termination of therapy', in K. A. Adler and D. Deutsch (eds) *Essays in Individual Psychology: Contemporary application of Alfred Adler's theories*, New York: Grove Press.

Saarni, C. (1999) *The development of emotional competence*, New York: Guilford.

Sarbin, T. R. (ed.) (1986) *Narrative psychology: The storied nature of human existence*, New York: Praeger.

Satir, V. (1983) *Conjoint family therapy* (3rd edn), Palo Alto, CA: Science and Behavior.

Sayger, T. V. and Horne, A. M. (2000) 'Common elements in family therapy theory and strategies', in A. M. Horne (ed.) *Family counseling and therapy* (3rd edn), Itasca, IL: Peacock.

Schaumberg, A. (1959) 'A case of remission after short-term Adlerian therapy', in K. A. Adler and D. Deutsch (eds) *Essays in Individual Psychology: Contemporary application of Alfred Adler's theories*, New York: Grove Press.

Scott, C., Kelly, F. D. and Tolbert, B. L. (1995) 'Realism, constructivism, and the individual psychology of Alfred Adler', *Individual Psychology* 51: 4–20.

Selman, R. L. (1980) *The growth of interpersonal understanding: Developmental and clinical analyses*, New York: Academic Press.

Serrano, J. (1988) 'Individuo y sociedad en la obra de Alfred Adler: Hacia una perspectiva ética en psicología', *Revista de Historia de la Psicología* 9: 89–101. (Title in English: 'Individual and society in Alfred Adler's writings: Towards an ethical perspective in psychology'.)

Serrano, J. (1991) 'La visión psicosocial de Alfred Adler: Alcance y límites de la perspectiva adleriana en psicología social', unpublished doctoral dissertation, University of Barcelona. (Title in English: 'The psychosocial standpoint of Alfred Adler: Scope and limits of the Adlerian perspective in social psychology'.)

Sherman, R. and Dinkmeyer, D. (1987) *Systems of family therapy: An Adlerian Integration*, New York: Brunner/Mazel.

Sherman, R. (1993) 'Marital issues of intimacy and techniques for change: An Adlerian systems perspective', *Individual Psychology* 49: 318–329.

Shulman, B. H. (1962) 'The family constellation in personality diagnosis', *Journal of Individual Psychology* 18: 35–47.

Shulman, B. H. (1971) 'Confrontation techniques in Adlerian psychotherapy', *Journal of Individual Psychology* 27: 167–175.

Shulman, B. H. (1972) 'Confrontation techniques', *Journal of Individual Psychology* 28: 177–183.

Shulman, B. H. (1973) *Contributions to Individual Psychology*, Chicago: Alfred Adler Institute.

Shulman, B. H. (1980) *Essays in schizophrenia*, Chicago: Alfred Adler Institute.

Shulman, B. H. (1985) 'Cognitive therapy and the Individual Psychology of Alfred Adler', in M. J. Mahoney and A. Freeman (eds) *Cognition and psychotherapy*, New York: Plenum.

Shulmann, B. H. and Watts, R. E. (1997) 'Adlerian and constructivist psychotherapies: An Adlerian perspective', *Journal of Cognitive Psychotherapy: An International Quarterly* 11(3): 181–193.

Sifneos, P. E. (1987) *Short-term dynamic psychotherapy: Evaluation and technique*, New York: Plenum.

Snyder, C. R. and Ingram, R. E. (2000) *Handbook of psychological change: Psychotherapy processes and practices for the 21st century*, New York: John Wiley.

Sonstegard, M. A. and Bitter, J. R. (1998) 'Counseling children in groups', *Journal of Individual Psychology* 54: 252–267.

Sperber, M. (1983) *Alfred Adler oder das Elend der Psychologie*, Frankfurt: Klett-Cotta. (Title in English: *Alfred Adler or the misery of psychology*.)

Sperry, L. (1991) 'The psychotic disorders: An update', *N.A.S.A.P. Newsletter* 24(4): 5–6.

Sperry, L. (1992) 'The "rediscovery" of interventive interviewing', *N.A.S.A.P. Newsletter* 25: 3–4.

Sperry, L. (1999) 'Biopsychosocial therapy', *Journal of Individual Psychology* 55(2): 233–247.

Sperry, L. (2001) 'The biological dimension in biopsychosocial therapy: Theory and clinical applications with couples', *Journal of Individual Psychology* 57(3): 310–317.

Sperry, L. and Carlson, J. (1996) *Psychopathology and psychotherapy: From diagnosis to treatment of DSM-IV disorder*, Philadelphia: Taylor & Francis.

Stasio, M. J. (1998) 'Social interest and community feeling as cultural common thread: Key issues and research directions', *Journal of Individual Psychology* 54: 310–323.

Steinthal, H. (1881) *Einleitung in die Psychologie und Sprachwissenschaft*, Berlin: Harrwitz and Gossman. (Title in English: *Introduction to psychology and linguistics*.)

Stepansky, P. E. (1983) *In Freud's shadow: Adler in context*, Hillsdale, NJ: Analytic Press.

Stewart, A. E. (1994) 'Psychometric development of the White–Campbell Psychological Birth Order Inventory through exploratory factor analyses and latent trait analyses', unpublished doctoral dissertation, University of Georgia (Dissertation Abstracts International, 55–09B).

Stewart, A. E. (2001) 'Language and family of origin experiences', *Journal of Individual Psychology* 57: 141–157.

Stewart, A. E. and Campbell, L. F. (1998) 'Reliability and validity of the White–Campbell Psychological Birth Order Inventory', *Journal of Individual Psychology* 54: 41–60.

Stewart, A. E., Stewart, E. A. and Campbell, L. F. (2001) 'The relationship of psychological birth order to the family atmosphere and to personality', *Journal of Individual Psychology* 57.

Stryker, S. (1983) 'Toward a theory of family influence in the socialization of children', in A. C. Kerckhoff (ed.) *Research in the sociology of education and socialization. Volume 4. Personal change over the life course*, Greenwich, CT: JAI Press.

Stryker, S. and Stathan, A. (1985) 'Symbolic interaction and role theory', in M. Snyder and W. Ickes (eds) *Handbook of social psychology, Volume 2*, New York: Random House.

Sulliman, J. R. (1973) 'The development of a scale for the measurement of social interest', *Dissertation Abstracts International* 34.

Sullivan, H. S. (1953) *The interpersonal theory of psychiatry*, New York: Norton.

Teyber, E. (1997) *Interpersonal process in psychotherapy: A relational approach* (3rd edn), Pacific Grove, CA: Brooks/Cole Publishing.

Toman, W. (1993) *Family constellation: Its effects on personality and social behavior* (4th edn), New York: Springer.

Vaihinger, H. (1925) *The philosophy of 'As-if': A system of the theoretical, practical, and religious fictions of mankind*. New York: Harcourt, Brace and Company.

Vakoch, D. A. and Strupp, H. H. (2000) 'Psychodynamic approaches to psychotherapy: Philosophical and theoretical foundations of effective practice', in C. R. Snyder and R. E. Ingram (eds) *Handbook of psychological change* (pp. 200–216), New York: Wiley.

Vanderlinden, J., Vandereycken, W., van Dyck, R. and Vertommen, H. (1993) 'Dissociative experiences and trauma in eating disorders', *International Journal of Eating Disorders* 13: 187–193.

von Glasersfeld, E. (1984) 'An introduction to radical constructivism', in P. Watzlawick (ed.) *The invented reality: Contributions to constructivism*, New York: Norton.

Wallach, M. and Wallach, L. (1983) *Psychology's sanction for selfishness*, San Francisco: W. H. Freeman.

Watkins, C. E. (1994) 'Measuring social interest', *Individual Psychology* 50: 69–96.

Watkins, E. C. and Blazina, C. (1994) 'Reliability of the Sulliman Scale of Social Interest', *Journal of Individual Psychology* 50: 164–165.

Watkins, E. C. and St John, C. (1994) 'Validity of the Sulliman Scale of Social Interest', *Journal of Individual Psychology* 50: 166–169.

Watts, R. E. (1998) 'The remarkable parallel between Rogers's core conditions and Adler's social interest', *Journal of Individual Psychology* 54: 4–9.

Watts, R. E. (2000) 'Entering the new millennium: Is Individual Psychology still relevant?', *Individual Psychology* 56: 21–30.

Weiss, J. (1993) *How psychotherapy works*, New York: Guilford.

West, J. D., Main, F. O. and Zarski, J. J. (1986) 'Paradoxical prescription in Individual Psychology', *Individual Psychology* 42: 214–224.

Wheeler, M. S. (1996) 'Using the BASIS-A Inventory: Examples from a clinical setting', *Individual Psychology* 52: 104–118.

White, J., Campbell, L. and Stewart, A. E. (1995) 'Association of scores on the White–Campbell Psychological Birth Order Inventory and the Kern Lifestyle Scale', *Psychological Reports* 77: 1187–1196.

White, J., Campbell, L., Stewart, A., Davies, M. and Pilkington, L. (1997) 'The relationship of psychological birth order to career interests', *Individual Psychology* 53: 89–104.

White, M. (1992) *Therapie als Dekonstruktion*, Frankfurt: Suhrkamp. (Title in English: *Therapy as deconstruction.*)

White, M. and Epston, D. (1990) *Narrative means to therapeutic ends*, New York: Norton.

Wiegand, R. (1990) *Alfred Adler und danach: Individualpsychologie zwischen Weltanschauung und Wissenschaft*, Munich: Reinhardt. (Title in English: *Alfred Adler and afterwards: Individual Psychology between world view and science.*)

Winnicot, D. W. (1988) *Human nature*, New York: Schocken Books.

Yelsma, P., Hovestadt, A. J., Nilsson, J. E. and Paul, B. D. (1998) 'Clients' positive and negative expressiveness within their families and alexithymia', *Psychological Reports* 82: 563–569.

Young, J. E. (1994) *Cognitive therapy for personality disorders: A schema-focused approach*, Sarasota, FL: Professional Resource Press.

Young, J. E. and Lindemann, M. D. (1992) 'An integrative schema-focused model for personality disorders', *Journal of Cognitive Psychotherapy* 6: 11–23.

Index